Scuba Diver's
Travel
Companion

Help Us Keep This Guide Up to Date

Every effort has been made by the author and editors to make this guide as accurate and useful as possible. However, many things can change after a guide is published—regulations change, techniques evolve, and so on.

We would love to hear from you concerning your experiences with this guide and how you feel it could be improved and kept up to date. While we may not be able to respond to all comments and suggestions, we'll take them to heart and we'll also make certain to share them with the author. Please send your comments and suggestions to the following address:

The Globe Pequot Press
Reader Response/Editorial Department
P.O. Box 480
Guilford, CT 06437

Or you may e-mail us at:

editorial@GlobePequot.com

Thanks for your input, and happy travels!

Scuba Diver's Travel Companion

JEREMY AGNEW

FALCON®

GUILFORD, CONNECTICUT
HELENA, MONTANA
AN IMPRINT OF THE GLOBE PEQUOT PRESS

To my scuba-diving girls:
Sylvia, Tracy, and Christine

Text design by Deborah Nicolais
Illustrations by Diane Blasius
Maps by Rusty Nelson © The Globe Pequot Press

Library of Congress Cataloging-in-Publication Data
Agnew, Jeremy (Jeremy A.)
    Scuba diver's travel companion / Jeremy Agnew.-- 1st ed.
        p. cm. -- (A Falcon guide)
    Includes index.
    ISBN 0-7627-2668-7
        1. Scuba diving--Guidebooks. I. Title. II. Series.

GV838.672.A46 2003
797.2'3--dc21   2003043416

Manufactured in the United States of America
First Edition/First Printing

CONTENTS

INTRODUCTION

If you're a newly certified diver, you've studied and worked hard to earn your C-card and are ready and anxious to start your real diving experience. Or perhaps you earned your C-card a number of years ago but haven't had the opportunity to do as much diving as you'd like. Maybe you're a seasoned diver but you haven't been diving in several years. If any of these situations applies to you, then this book is for you!

Though your classroom instruction will have taught you the basics of scuba diving, there are many practical tips that can make dive trips easier and safer. Divers typically learn these helpful hints over a period of time, through experience and from instructors, mentors, divemasters, and fellow divers. This book condenses years of hands-on experience to help you select the right dive vacations, to feel more relaxed in the water and comfortable with diving skills, and to become a more competent and skilled diver.

On the following pages you'll find the mechanics of planning and traveling on a diving vacation, including travel tips, options for different types of dive vacations, and a comprehensive list of the most popular dive destinations around the world with information about each one, including not-to-be-missed dive sites. Also discussed are tips for airline travel, since that's the most common method of travel to a dive destination.

In some sections the text emphasizes international travel by airplane and boat diving at the dive destination, using the Caribbean as an example. This is deliberate, because this is how a majority of modern recreational scuba divers experience a dive vacation: It's been estimated that almost 80 percent of all scuba diving is devoted to coral reefs. Where appropriate, however, the discussions also cover topics of nonboat diving and dive locations, such as lakes and wells.

Additionally, you'll find a number of underwater topics that you can use as a refresher once you get to your dive destination, as well as tips for purchasing your own gear and the maintenance and minor repair of dive equipment to help you get the most out of your investment in your scuba equipment.

This book is based on established dive knowledge, combined with my own experience and opinions about what makes sense on a dive trip. In the past eighteen years, I've had the opportunity to experience thousands of hours of travel and dive time and experiment with different aspects of both. But these opinions are not intended to be handed down like established edicts of law. Rationale for all the discussion is included, and you can, and should, make up your mind on whether or not to follow my advice and preferences.

As well as telling you what this book *is*, it's just as important to tell you what it *isn't*. This book is not intended to teach the technical aspects of diving. These skills must be learned through formal classroom training from an accredited dive organization under the supervision of a competent instructor. Instead, this book is intended to be a next step in helping you amplify and add to your skills.

For similar reasons, topics such as Boyle's Law of Gases, the use of dive tables, diving physiology, and technical aspects of regulator operation are omitted from this book. You will have learned these aspects of diving during scuba training classes, and they may be reviewed in your training manual. While it's important to learn and understand topics such as these, they are also not commonly used after training or during dive trips. This book concentrates, rather, on practical information that you can use during a recreational dive trip.

As you read, you may think that many of the subjects I discuss are common sense. In a way, they are! As a good friend of mine once said, however, common sense is not necessarily intuitive. For example, the natives of a forested jungle region may know that it's common sense not to step close to a certain type of green snake because it's poisonous and can lunge at its intended victim. To these people, avoiding these snakes is common sense. To city dwellers who've never seen one, though, it isn't necessarily intuitive to stay far away from them. This isn't necessarily a lack of common sense. The city dwellers simply haven't had the learned experience of the jungle tribe and could find themselves in trouble as a result. The same holds true for much of what's in this book. Even though some of the topics may seem like common sense after reading about them, many people without similar experiences wouldn't even think to ask the right question.

Remember: A novice diver is not only someone who's recently completed a certification course, but anyone on a planned dive who has no recent experience in similar waters under similar conditions. For example, experience gained from boat diving in the Caribbean doesn't prepare you for shore diving in California or high-altitude diving in an inland lake. To gain further experience and explore different dive situations, take additional training in your area of interest, dive with folks experienced in the same conditions and water, or seek the advice of a local dive shop with instructors who know the area and dive conditions.

As you read this book, you'll recognize that some of the topics have been repeated from diving classes. This is deliberate. I wanted to emphasize some of the most important aspects of diving. Hopefully, I'll present from a slightly different viewpoint than you gained in classroom study, which may help reinforce the crucial information.

Many of the items discussed here do not have absolute answers. I've tried to make unbiased suggestions and recommendations, but these must be weighed individually and either accepted or rejected, depending on your particular preferences and circumstances.

What's Your Divability?

This categorization of ability is somewhat arbitrary, but here's one way to group divers. Always consider which category you fit into when planning a dive.

- **Novice diver.** *Just certified, with less than twenty open-water dives to depths of less than 60 feet in calm conditions. Has not dived in conditions similar to those of the current dive.*
- **Intermediate diver.** *Holds advanced certification or has experienced deep and night dives, has good navigation skills, and has completed between twenty and a hundred dives. Has experienced different water conditions. Has dived in conditions similar to those of the current dive.*
- **Advanced diver.** *Seasoned diver with several hundred dives—including deep dives, drift dives, night dives, and wreck dives—in many different water conditions and dive situations, including strong currents.*

Diving is a highly technical and equipment-intensive sport. Modern dive equipment is very reliable and is designed to fail in a safe manner. Modern regulators, for example, are designed to free-flow in case of equipment failure, instead of shutting off the supply of air. But the potential for death or injury is present in any sport, and scuba diving is no exception. Though diving is an extremely safe sport, dive equipment must be maintained in topnotch condition, and diving skills must be regularly practiced.

Be aware that most diving accidents are due to human error rather than equipment failure. This point emphasizes the need for good dive training, adherence to safe diving procedures, and selecting the proper dive site for your skill level. If there is one overall take-home message for you to gain from this book, it is that *each diver is ultimately responsible for his or her own life and safety—nobody else is!* If you don't feel comfortable with a dive or dive situation, or if you don't feel comfortable with your equipment, your dive partner, the weather conditions, the water conditions, or any other aspect of the dive, *either don't dive or abort the dive.* There will always be other dives, but you only have one life. You alone are responsible for protecting it!

Having said all that, scuba diving is an incredible experience and sport, so enjoy yourself, and remember to always to practice good sense and safety.

Happy diving!

1

TIPS FOR
DIVE TRAVEL

B

ack in the "old days" of diving—which were only thirty or forty years ago—
dive travel was very different from what we experience today. Travel to exotic locations was restricted to hardy individuals who were willing to endure
erratic transportation, relatively primitive accommodations, and dive boats
that were often fishing boats commandeered for transportation to the site.
Diving was pretty much considered to be a male-oriented macho sport.

In the last twenty years, there has been a radical shift from the "old days"
to modern expectations of easy and convenient airplane travel, luxury leisure
hotels, and well-equipped dive boats that transport divers quickly and comfortably to superb dive sites. Divers entering the sport in the 1980s and
1990s wanted to travel in comfort and had the money to pay for it. In
response, resorts became luxurious and dive travel catered to a destination
business, with upgraded hotels, resorts, restaurants, dive shops, and dive
boats. Live-aboard boats became popular. Families started diving together.

At the same time, advances in dive equipment made diving safer and easier.
The 1980s and 1990s saw improvements in dive equipment, educational programs, and diver training. Formalized training programs, from entry level to
instructor, were standardized and upgraded, and the quality of instructors and
instruction improved. As a result of all this, the past decade has seen an unprece-
dented boom in recreational dive travel to the Caribbean, the Pacific, and other
exotic destinations. This chapter provides general information on how to travel
to dive destinations. Chapter 2 will discuss specific dive destinations.

Dive Opportunities

The diving world is basically divided into two environments: fresh water and salt water.

Freshwater diving is performed in an inland setting and includes lakes, rivers, quarries, and underground sinkholes, springs, and caverns. Diving may be at sea level or may include high-altitude environments. *High-altitude* in terms of scuba diving refers to bodies of water, such as lakes, occurring more than 1,000 feet above sea level.

Saltwater diving is performed in the ocean. Saltwater diving is commonly one of four types, depending on the water temperature: tropical, temperate, cold, and arctic environments.

Choosing a Destination

Some lucky people have unlimited time and aren't bound by the constraints of a week's vacation from the office or other job. Very few of us have this luxury. Also, very few people have unlimited money. So in general, most divers live within some sort of constraints of cost and time when planning a dive vacation.

These and other factors should be considered when choosing a dive destination. Among them are the amount of money you have to spend, the time that you have available, the type of diving you wish to do, the type of diving with which you are comfortable, the method of travel to the dive destination, and the type of accommodation, if you wish to stay at your destination. Because there are very few warm-water dive destinations within the United States, you may also have to consider your level of comfort with international travel.

*O*ut of Your Depth?

Most dive operations and resorts have dive sites that accommodate differing levels of skill and experience, thus allowing novice, intermediate, and advanced divers to enjoy their own preferences.

- *Tell the divemaster about your level of skill and comfort.*
- *Ask for specific information about a dive site and dive plan before the boat leaves.*
- *If you feel uncomfortable with the dive plan, don't hesitate to say that you prefer to dive something more closely matched to your skill and experience level.*

There is no "best" dive destination. There are magnificent places to dive all over the world, and part of your decision will consider the range of destinations from local diving to a distant area of the globe.

There are several ways to research the different destination options available. Among them are talking to fellow divers or travelers, asking travel

Dive accommodations can range from grass huts to luxury hotels.

agents, checking with local dive shops, reading dive magazines, searching travel books in your local library, and exploring the Internet. Chapter 2 outlines the most popular dive sites around the world, and may be used as a starting point for reference when deciding on a dive destination.

Not all dive trips are necessarily expensive. Relatively inexpensive dive trips can be day or weekend jaunts to local lakes, springs, reservoirs, or quarries. If you live within easy driving distance of an ocean, you can enjoy local diving at minimal cost. These trips can be good ways to extend your diving time, experience, and budget. Local dive shops can tell you where such dives are available close to home.

Even if you can and do dive local areas, most people eventually want to venture farther afield and go to a warm-water destination, if only to experience new dive areas and experiences. It's been estimated that a million or so divers every year go to warm-water dive destinations. Because of the length of time necessary for travel to these destinations, these trips are typically undertaken for a week or more. Trips can range from staying in inexpensive motels and buying food at the local grocery store to staying at luxurious five-star resorts that cater to your every whim. You will have to decide where your budget and preferences fit within the spectrum of choices.

For those whose dive budget is smaller than their tastes (which probably includes most of us!), there are several ways to reduce costs while enjoying a luxurious vacation. Think about shopping the airlines for the cheapest flights (which may involve changing from your desired departure times or dates), asking for economy hotel rooms, eating at less expensive restaurants or cooking your own food, using local buses instead of hiring a rental car, cutting down on expensive evenings on the town, and shore diving (which is possible at many places in the Caribbean) instead of boat diving.

*E*xtending Your Dive Dollar

- *Shop around for airline fares. Airlines to the same destination may offer different fares.*
- *Buy airplane tickets early. While they may be nonrefundable, such tickets are often cheaper.*
- *Ask if the hotel has lower-priced rooms or package deals. The first price quoted may not be the lowest price.*
- *Check into all-inclusive rates. Sometimes they're cheaper than separate hotel, diving, and airfare.*
- *Be flexible about travel dates. Different dates may save money.*
- *Travel in the low season. High season in the Caribbean is mid-December to May.*
- *Travel midweek, if possible. Airline tickets are often cheaper on Tuesday, Wednesday, or Thursday.*
- *Don't get a rental car unless you need it. Occasional travel by taxi may be cheaper.*
- *Use free or discount hotel shuttles at the destination, instead of a taxi.*
- *Do some shore diving, instead of all boat diving.*
- *Buy some food at a local grocery store, perhaps for breakfast or picnic lunches.*
- *Eat an occasional dinner at a cheaper restaurant. Save up for one or two good meals.*
- *Buy beer or a bottle of wine and drink it on the beach, instead of having cocktails in the bar.*

Where to Stay

Once you've decided where you want to go, where you stay at your destination will depend on the particular type of vacation you enjoy and how you want to spend your time. For most divers who travel to dive sites away from home, such as to the Florida Keys or to islands in the Caribbean, there are three basic choices: package vacations, land-based hotel/motel/condo/time shares, or live-aboard dive boats. For divers going to U.S. destinations, such as Florida, the choice is more likely to be the second one.

There are various ways to gather information on these options to help you make a decision. Try talking to folks at a travel agency or your local dive shop, looking at advertisements in dive magazines, exploring the travel guides in your local library, or asking fellow divers. The following are some of the features of the three different types.

Package Vacations

Various packages are available combining the features that divers typically want in a dive vacation into one hotel, motel, or resort vacation package, often with all the features at a single location. Typically these packages are available at a total cost less than if you were to pay for each part separately. There is also the element of convenience. The package may include a combination of lodging and dive services or, depending on the particular package, may combine room, food, drink, airport transportation, and diving into one fixed-price package. Air travel to your destination may be included and arranged by the packaging agent, either via major airlines or through charter airlines, special vacation carriers, or as part of an air travel consolidation package with discounted fares.

All-inclusive vacation packages offer the convenience of everything at one location, at one price. Depending on the size and scope of the hotel or resort, there are often other amenities available on-site, such as tennis, golf, fishing, shopping, horseback riding, local sight-seeing, sailboarding, sea kayaks, or paddleboats. It's possible to go to such a resort at the beginning of a trip and to stay there without leaving the hotel grounds for the entire vacation, unless you want to. Depending on your preferences, it isn't necessary to deal with taxis, rental cars, buses, or walking to get around or to find a restaurant at night. For those seeking simplicity and a hassle-free vacation, an all-inclusive package may be an appropriate option. The downside may be that if you have a sudden urge for a pizza, or become tired of dining at the same hotel restaurant every night and prefer more variety in food, then this option may not be for you.

All-inclusive vacation packages are commonly found on small islands. The reason for this, of course, is that there are often few (or no!) other available choices for restaurants and other services at a remote location.

Another consideration is the food itself. Eating overseas may be an undesired adventure for some travelers. Some resorts may serve food native to its country. U.S. travelers expecting a typical Western diet in the dining room may be disappointed, or may not even like the food at their hotel or local restaurants. It's wise to inquire about food types when making a booking to make sure the cuisine meets your expectations. Similar comments apply to those with special dietary requirements.

Dive Lodging: The Pros and Cons

Type of Lodging	Advantages	Disadvantages
Land-based all-inclusive package at a resort	• Everything is included • Everything is on-site • Total price is known before departure • No need for a rental car • No need to search for nearby restaurants	• Repetition of eating at the resort's restaurants • Limited flexibility of choices
Land-based nonpackage vacation	• Your choice of restaurants • May be less expensive than an all-inclusive package (but may not)	• Usually requires a rental car, taxi, other transportation, or walking to find local restaurants • May have to arrange local transportation to and from the dive boat • Total vacation price may be more than a package deal
Live-aboard boat	• Flexibility of dive locations • Maximizes diving opportunities • Visits offshore dive sites that may not be convenient or possible for shore-based operations • Maximum camaraderie and interaction among a small group of divers	• Stuck on one boat, typically for a week or so, before return to home port • Can't visit land-based tourist attractions • Can be a problem if you don't like the other people on the boat • May be a problem for those susceptible to motion sickness • Can be a problem if you're claustrophobic • Diving may be too intense for novices

Land-Based Hotel/Motel/Condo/Time Share

The second option on the list is more the traditional type of vacation, and usually gives you more variety and flexibility. This option involves booking a room at a hotel or motel, or renting a condominium or time-share unit at your destination. Meals, local transportation, and diving arrangements are made separately. This option may be the best choice for those who prefer to try different restaurants, either to enjoy a variety of foods and establishments or for economy. The condominium or time-share option is also appealing to those who wish to cook for themselves, either to maintain a special diet, for economy reasons, or for convenience with small children or large families. Condominiums or time shares are often associated with a larger resort, so you can use the restaurants and other facilities of the resort if you like.

When considering a hotel or condominium, be sure to check ahead for features that may be important to you. For example, some hotels in the Caribbean offer air-conditioning and some don't, relying instead on open windows and ocean breezes. Some hotels have air-conditioning in all rooms; others have it only in selected rooms that must be requested when booking. Thus, if air-conditioning is important to you, be sure to check whether it's available in your room at your destination hotel. Similarly, some hotels have television and a telephone in every room, some have only a television in the bar or recreation room, and some have no television at all. Some have satellite channels, others only local channels. If this is an important feature for you when traveling, be sure your lodging has what you want.

When choosing a hotel you may also wish to check the description, or with the hotel, to determine whether it's located on the beach or in a town. Also find out where the hotel is in relation to the dive shop or dive boat. If you're staying at a hotel on a beach, the dive shop is often adjacent, on the water, at the same location. Sometimes, however, the two are separate and may involve a walk down the beach. If the hotel is inland, away from the beach, you may have to commute to where the dive boat picks you up. This may mean taking a taxi or shuttle bus, or driving back and forth to and from the hotel in a wet swimsuit or other wet clothes, following the day's dive. Check also on the availability and location of nearby restaurants or grocery stores, if you plan to eat out or if you wish to purchase supplies and cook your own meals.

Live-Aboard Dive Boats

Live-aboard dive boats offer a third option. Dedicated dive boats, ranging up to 110 or 120 feet in length and 25 feet wide, operate as a floating hotel and

Live-aboard boats offer the maximum amount of diving but may be too intense for some novices.

restaurant and create mobile access to a variety of dive sites. The number of passengers varies with the size of the boat—typically six to twenty. The boats are typically well equipped for photo and video enthusiasts, and E-6 color slide processing is often available on board.

Some live-aboard boats anchor at a site and stay there for an extended period of time, allowing almost constant diving on the same site. Others cruise on a set schedule, stopping every few hours to allow diving at a fresh site. If you consider a live-aboard, inquire about the type of travel and diving the particular boat does, so that your vacation is in tune with your expectations.

Also, be sure you understand the facilities that the boat has to offer. Live-aboards offer a range of accommodations—from luxurious suites on the upper deck to belowdeck cabins that seem like the innards of an old slave vessel. Inquire closely before booking if comfort and luxury are more important to you than a basic budget dive vessel to get you to a dive site.

On some live-aboard boats, cabins are shared by single travelers and the occupants are assigned by the boat. Roommates of the same gender may not be guaranteed if there's a preponderance of one or the other. Some boats also have communal bathrooms. Private shower and toilet facilities may not be available. Some boats have a range of prices for different levels of accommodation, and private bathrooms may only be available to those in the expensive cabins. If these, and similar, features are important, be sure to check before finalizing a booking.

For those who are enthusiastic—even fanatic—about maximizing their dive time underwater, live-aboard boats offer the convenience of diving right off the stern as often as you (and the nitrogen loading in your tissues!) can tolerate. Live-aboards are typically sought by those who enjoy diving, diving, diving. Although most modern live-aboard boats are very luxurious, with gourmet cooking and often added amenities from hot tubs to video movies on demand, the primary focus and activity is diving. This is the ultimate way to dive as much as possible.

Live-aboards often travel to remote dive sites that either have no land-based hotels or are too far for land-based dive boats to visit in a day, thus offering diving on relatively untouched reefs and wrecks. A further advantage is that if the weather at a particular site is bad, the boat can weigh anchor and move to another area to avoid localized storms or high waves. And this can be a safer way to dive the waters of a country with an unstable political situation.

The convenience of live-aboards for the person who likes to do a lot of diving is that the boat is typically moored over a different site every day, and diving is available twenty-four hours a day. If sites are relatively shallow, the opportunity to do five dives a day isn't unusual. Obviously, safety rules and no-decompression depths and times have to be observed, but other than that the ocean is always available off the back of the boat.

Some divers enjoy diving with the same people for the whole trip, really getting to know the other divers on the boat. Others don't. Also, if you are mildly claustrophobic, don't like the thought of being cooped up on a boat for a week with the same people, or feel the need to walk and sleep on solid ground at night, then a live-aboard dive vacation may not be for you. Individuals prone to motion or seasickness may not enjoy the experience of a live-aboard boat. It's probably better to accumulate some dive experience at land-based operations before trying a live-aboard.

If you don't like the rocking of boats on the open water, you may wish to inquire about the construction of a live-aboard dive boat before making a booking. A catamaran design—with the living quarters basically built on a platform laid across two parallel hulls—theoretically offers better stability in the water than a single V-hulled boat. Some live-aboard boats also have built-in stabilizers to reduce the effects of sideways motion in the water on the passengers.

Money

Major credit cards, such as Visa and MasterCard, are widely accepted at tourist destinations around the world. Credit card users don't have to worry about currency conversion, because items purchased are usually charged in the local currency and then converted to U.S. dollars as part of the bank transaction

Money Matters

If you plan to use U.S. dollars in a country where they're accepted, take small bills rather than large ones. A merchant or taxi driver may not be willing or able to exchange a large bill, for one thing. Also, using small bills will minimize the amount of foreign currency that you accumulate as change.

process. The conversion is based on existing bank exchange rates and will usually offer the best local rate. Tourist-oriented hotels and restaurants almost always accept credit cards; small shops or restaurants may not, however, and may take only local currency. Depending on the destination, debit and cash cards may or may not be accepted. Refusal to accept such a card often happens simply because the infrastructure to perform instant banking transactions isn't available.

In Mexico and many countries in the Caribbean where diving is popular, U.S. dollars are widely accepted and can be used directly. Prices for items and services may be quoted in U.S. dollars. Still, in countries where this happens, change from purchases will usually be given in local currency. The financial exchange will be correct, but you can end up with a lot of foreign currency that you may not want. To minimize the amount of foreign money that you accumulate, carry dollar bills in small denominations so that you can come close to the full amount of the purchase price without receiving a lot of change. To find out if U.S. dollars are accepted for your planned destination, consult a detailed travel guidebook on the country you are visiting.

It's not advisable to carry large amounts of cash when traveling—and you certainly don't want to display large amounts of cash when making purchases. Larger hotels normally have safe deposit boxes that you can use to store valuables and reserve amounts of cash. Carry single dollars and other small bills at all times when traveling. You'll find these useful for tipping baggage porters at airports, taxi drivers, waiters, maids, and other service people, as well as for buying postcards, stamps, and similar small impulse purchases at airports and gift shops.

Before returning to the United States, you can usually exchange coins along with paper currency while still in your destination country. If you're in Australia, for example, you can trade in Australian coins along with paper money at a currency exchange booth or bank before you return to the U.S. When you reach the U.S., though, currency exchanges won't take the Australian coins—only the paper money.

Exchange rates for currency are usually best at banks, rather than at private exchange bureaus. Using airport cash machines to obtain local currency on a credit card may give you a good rate of currency exchange and a lot of convenience, but may carry additional bank and exchange fees that make the overall transaction more expensive. Similarly, currency exchange booths in airports are very convenient for changing cash into local currency, but may not offer as good a rate as a bank.

As a general rule, currency exchange rates are often better when you reach your destination. Still, you must allow for the possibility that if you arrive very early, very late, or on a weekend, currency exchange booths and banks may be closed and you may not be able to obtain local currency for a taxi or bus ride. Cash machines (ATMs) may or may not be available, depending on the destination. To guard against this, you may wish to take a small amount of destination currency for emergencies. A mix of cash and credit cards seems to work well and cover any eventuality.

If you use a credit card, be sure you have an adequate credit limit. Hotels and rental car agencies may place a hold on part of your credit card capability when initially processing your card, as insurance against final payment of your balance. Thus, that portion of your available credit is effective locked up and unusable. Some countries consider trying to make a purchase that will exceed your credit limit to be fraud, and the person who does this either knowingly or unknowingly may be subject to arrest. Know the balance and limit on your credit card.

Traveler's checks are normally accepted everywhere, although occasionally smaller shops or remote establishments won't take them. Some smaller banks may not cash traveler's checks.

Tipping varies from country to country. Some countries and cultures expect tips; some don't. Some are even offended if you offer a tip—they expect to provide you with service. Consult a detailed guidebook for tipping etiquette for the country you're visiting. It is customary, though optional, to leave tips for divemasters, dive boat captains, and instructors if you're pleased with their services. When paying restaurant and bar bills, check the itemized bill. In some cases the tip is already added and you don't need to leave an additional tip. In some countries it isn't.

*T*ips for Tipping

- Tipping varies from country to country; consult a detailed guidebook for tipping etiquette for the country you're visiting.
- When paying restaurant and bar bills, check the itemized bill to see if the tip has already been added.
- It's customary, though optional, to leave tips for divemasters, dive boat captains, and instructors if you're pleased with their services.
- You can leave tips that are split among all the dive crew, or you can leave a tip for an individual, if you wish.

Be prepared for any eventuality. I rode in a taxi in Sydney, Australia, on one trip and had a major credit card refused. It turned out that all the taxi companies were having a major dispute with this particular credit card company and would not honor the card, even though signs on the taxi window listed the card as acceptable for payment. Luckily I also had a different card, which was accepted. On another trip I planned to obtain local cash at a currency exchange in my destination airport, since I was to arrive at about 4:00 P.M. Due to mechanical problems and a delayed flight, however, I didn't get there until about 11:00 P.M., long after the currency exchange booths were closed. Fortunately, I had just enough coins from a previous trip to pay for a bus ride to the hotel. Admittedly the second of these situations could have been avoided by better planning on my part, but the first was unavoidable.

Language

Many of the premier dive sites around the world are located in or close to countries where English is not the primary language. Local tongues may range from Spanish (much of the Caribbean), to French (St. Martin), to the more challenging languages of the South Pacific. If you're comfortable with the language of the country you're visiting, or don't mind miming or making your needs known in sign language, then language shouldn't be a major barrier to where you wish to go.

Countries that cater to tourist populations generally feature signs in English or international symbols in major airports and tourist areas. Most of the larger resorts and hotels around the world in countries where English isn't the native language have at least a few staff members who speak it, thus making it possible to communicate most needs.

Personal Safety and Security

One area of concern for many international dive travelers is personal safety. This depends, in part, on the particular country you're visiting. Political conditions, especially in emerging nations, may change rapidly, as evidenced by stories in the news media. Check with your travel agent about safety in the part of the world you'll be visiting; he or she should be aware of any travel warnings for common tourist areas.

Another good resource for information on local political conditions is the U.S. Department of State, which publishes bulletins that contain any appropriate warnings for U.S. citizens in all countries. See appendix A at the back of this book for contact information.

It's also wise to check on local conditions after you arrive. Good sources of information are your local hotel or the local police. Some countries, such as the Cayman Islands, are extremely safe. Others require caution if you venture into unknown areas. Areas commonly frequented by tourists are generally safe, but it may not be wise to visit places off the beaten track without local advice on the area. Border areas between some countries may be volatile, and travel near or across borders, particularly at night, may be risky.

Wherever you are, take reasonable precautions, just as you would at home. Don't wear expensive jewelry (preferably leave it at home in a safe deposit box), don't flash large wads of currency, and don't expose an expensive camera more than necessary. Leave credit cards that you won't be using at home, along with other items from your wallet or purse that you don't expect to use. Avoid walking alone on dark streets at night; go in a group if possible. Keep an eye on your possessions at all times, and be aware of your surroundings.

As with any travel, don't forget to lock your hotel room and be sure that windows and sliding glass doors are locked. Don't leave jewelry, credit cards, money, or valuable small items lying around in your hotel room when you aren't there. Lock them in your suitcase or, in the case of very expensive items, put them in the hotel safe.

If you have a rental car, don't leave things in it at night. Always put valuable items out of sight during the day, or lock them securely in the trunk. I was on a dive trip in a small town in the western United States with one dive group, and someone from the dive shop left a large first-aid kit in a medical-type bag in the back of a station wagon overnight. The car was parked right outside a motel room, just a few feet from a ground-floor window where the dive instructors were sleeping. In the morning, however, the car had a broken window and the bag was gone. Leave nothing to chance.

Security of Your Home

When traveling, don't forget the security of your home and the possessions you leave behind. Remember to take precautions to safeguard your house or apartment if all the members of your family are gone. Notify neighbors or friends that you'll be away and ask them to watch the house for you. Don't draw the curtains or blinds shut, or close them halfway. Leave them open or arrange for someone to draw them every night and open them during the day.

Stop mail deliveries temporarily at the post office or have someone pick up mail at the house for you. Stop the newspaper while you are away, or arrange to have someone pick it up for you daily. A pile of newspapers outside the front door, undelivered mail overflowing the mailbox, and drawn curtains are sure signs to burglars that no one is home.

Leave a light on inside your house or apartment. Better yet, buy an electrical timer for a light and set it for approximately the times you would normally be using a light in the house at night, typically from about dusk to late evening. You can also have two light timers and set them in different rooms to operate lights at different times. Lights going on and off in different rooms gives the appearance of someone moving from room to room, perhaps to a bedroom to retire at night. Some people like to leave a radio or television on at a low level, so that it sounds like someone is home.

Use an answering machine on your telephone and record a neutral message for when it answers. For example, don't say: "We will be away for the next two weeks, call back after the twenty-third." This is an obvious message to a burglar who wants to know if anyone is home at night. It's better to say something noncommittal like, "We can't come to the phone right now; please leave a message."

Personal Health

Just as at home, injury or sickness is always a possibility while on a trip. Some key tips for healthy dive travel are given in the accompanying sidebar. For treating minor cuts and scrapes or minor illness, take along a small first-aid kit; appendix B in the back of this book includes a checklist of items that might be useful for minor health care. Add any items that you routinely use or may need.

Be sure that your health insurance covers emergencies and accidents while traveling in other countries. Some policies don't. If yours doesn't, buy some temporary traveler's insurance. Also, be sure you're covered for emergency air evacuation in case of decompression sickness (DCS) or other serious illness. Air ambulance service from remote locations is extremely expensive, typically costing many thousands of dollars.

Insurance against this eventuality can be purchased for a reasonable cost through organizations such as Divers Alert Network (DAN; see appendix A), or other dive and insurance agencies.

If you routinely use a prescription medicine, be sure that you have a large enough supply to last you through the entire trip, plus extra days for unexpected stopovers or travel interruptions. It's much easier to bring a supply for a few extra days than to try to get a prescription filled at short notice in a foreign country. Of course, always carry any prescription medications with

*T*he Essentials of Dive Travel Health

- **Make time on your trip for plenty of rest.** *Tiredness takes the pleasure out of a vacation, and fatigue may be a contributing factor to decompression sickness.*
- **Drink plenty of water.** *Dehydration, due to the dry air of airline cabin travel, caffeinated drinks, alcohol, or exertion, contributes to decompression sickness.*
- **Be careful about drinking local water.** *Be sure that it's safe to drink, or drink bottled water. Also be careful of ice used in drinks; it may have been made with local water.*
- **Don't eat raw fruit and food.** *Avoid raw foods, eat fruit only if you can peel it, and don't eat red or undercooked meat. Avoid mayonnaise and sour cream that have been sitting in a buffet line in the sun.*
- **Drink alcohol in moderation.** *Alcoholic drinks lead to dehydration. Diving with a hangover is a contributing factor to decompression sickness.*
- **Limit exposure to air-conditioning.** *Excessive use of air-conditioning can lead to sinus and throat congestion, which makes it hard to equalize your ears underwater. Air-conditioning can also blow fungi and molds into the air, both of which can cause further congestion in allergic individuals.*
- **Use insect repellent.** *Bug bites can be unpleasant and can become infected if scratched underwater. Mosquitoes can carry malaria, dengue fever, and other unpleasant diseases.*
- **Be careful if walking barefoot.** *Even the cleanest-looking sandy beaches may contain bits of glass, wood splinters, metal slivers, and bottle caps. Wear sandals on the beach. If you're wading in a lagoon, wear sandals, old tennis shoes, or dive boots with hard soles. Beaches and debris at the tideline also often contain biting sand fleas.*
- **Attend to minor cuts and scrapes right away.** *Warm climates and ocean dives can turn minor cuts into major infections. Wash cuts and scrapes well and cover them with antibiotic ointment.*
- **Wear a hat and sunscreen.** *Protect your head (especially if it's a balding one!), your neck, and the tops of your ears. Also protect white skin, such as the tops of your feet, knees, and upper thighs, which may not see sun for most of the year.*
- **Wear sunglasses.** *The intensity of the sun in the Tropics on waves and white sand can literally be blinding.*

you in your hand luggage, in case you and your checked baggage should become separated.

Travel on a dive boat may induce motion sickness in some susceptible individuals.

Popular over-the-counter medications are widely used by divers to prevent motion sickness. Also popular are decongestants to assist in unblocking the ears. The burden of safety lies with the individual diver. Drugs, such as decongestants, should be used with caution until you understand how your system reacts to these drugs underwater. For example, a common caution among many decongestants is that drowsiness may result. Remember again that you are responsible for your own life and safety. If you choose to use medications, be sure you understand how they affect you before you dive. Remember also that the effects of drugs may be influenced by depth during diving. What may be a minor effect on the surface can be amplified when the body is under increased pressure and breathing compressed air.

Many tropical islands contain mosquitoes and other small biting bugs, commonly known as no-see-ums or sand fleas. These can be a constant irritation in some areas and can raise a nice collection of welts by the end of a trip. Typically these bugs will be worse in islands or countries that receive a lot of rain and have high humidity. To minimize such bites, pack a good bug repellent. The most effective contain DEET (the chemical formula is diethyl-m-toluamide). The best are reputed to be the ones containing 100 percent DEET, but the higher the percentage of DEET, the greater the hazards of use. Read the label of any insect cream or spray carefully before using. Since bug repellents are never 100 percent effective, it's also advisable to bring along some cream or lotion to put on bites after they appear. Over-the-counter remedies are available in most drugstores.

If you're concerned about repeatedly using DEET or other insect repellents on your skin, one preventive for bites from microscopic gnats and sand fleas is to use a substance that leaves a layer of oil on the skin. Suitable substances include tanning oil, suntan lotion, a skin softening agent, or even vegetable oil. These substances provide a physical barrier that most tiny, irritating insects cannot penetrate to reach your skin.

Small biting insects typically create more of a problem in rooms or huts close to sandy beaches, particularly on small islands, since no-see-ums and sand fleas live in wet sand and ocean debris close to the water's edge. Unfortunately, the tendency is to select this type of room because it's the most picturesque. You can often avoid problems by picking huts on stilts and out over the water, where you're less likely to encounter insects.

If you're on the beach in buggy conditions, it may be possible to gain some respite by pulling a beach chair 4 or 5 feet out into the water before sitting down. Again, the bugs aren't found as commonly out over the water.

Malaria, encephalitis, and hepatitis are prevalent in some parts of the world, and they're still a major problem in many tropical areas. Generally this isn't a concern for divers, since many resorts are regularly sprayed to prevent mos-

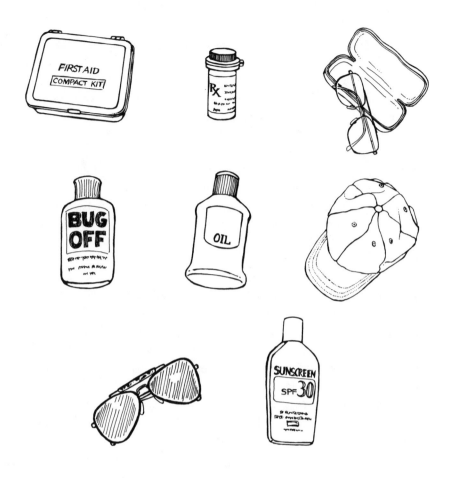

Things to not forget: small first-aid kit, prescription medicines, prescription reading glasses, hard protective glasses case, bug repellent, skin oil to prevent no-see-um bites, and protection against the sun—hat, sunglasses, and sunscreen.

quitoes from breeding, but it's wise to be cautious. If you think you'll be in a malaria-prone area, ask your doctor about preventive malaria medications, which may be easier than treatment of active malaria—a course of action that's often long and difficult. Mosquitoes are involved in the spread of yellow fever and encephalitis, and also carry dengue fever in Central and South America. Dengue fever is commonly called "break-bone fever," because it usually causes severe joint, bone, and muscle pain. The onset of fever, nausea, aching, or a rash after visiting tropical areas should send you promptly to a physician for treatment in case you might have picked up one of these diseases.

Though nobody likes to talk about it, there is still the ever-present possibility of a reaction to the local water. You should also be aware that many people have a reaction to some constituent of a different water supply than that to which their body is accustomed. Whether it is called Montezuma's Revenge or some other name, you should go prepared. An over-the-counter medication should be in your first-aid kit in case problems occur. If you expect more serious problems, discuss this with your personal physician and take a prescription medication with you.

I once stayed at a dive resort that boasted picturesque huts on stilts out in a lagoon. One evening my wife and I were standing outside on the balcony of our hut, watching for fish in the shallow water beneath, when I noticed, about 20 yards away, an underwater sewer outflow pipe from the main resort building oozing something emerald green into the water of the lagoon. Though unpleasant, this may be a reality in some countries that don't enjoy the standard of sanitation taken for granted in the United States.

The old adage "If you can't peel it, boil it, or cook it, don't eat it" may be simplistic, but remembering it may save you some grief on a trip. Don't eat uncooked food. Unless you're sure of the water supply, even at a hotel, drink bottled water, or bottled and canned beverages. Also use bottled water for brushing your teeth.

Because of the intensity of the sun in the Tropics, pack a hat and plenty of sunscreen. Areas particularly sensitive to sunburn are those normally covered by clothing, such as the tops of your feet. Sunscreen should be extra strength with a high sun protection factor (SPF) rating. An SPF rating of 30 or 40 should be suitable. Sunscreen should be water resistant, for obvious reasons. It should be applied liberally and often. A lip protector will help prevent lip dryness.

Before traveling to an international destination, obtain information from your doctor on precautions that you should take. Current tetanus immunization is advisable for all travelers. Be sure that routine immunizations are current. Check with your doctor for special needs before embarking on exotic travel. Most common dive destinations, such as Mexico, the Caribbean, and Australia, don't require vaccinations. Other destinations, however, such as the South Pacific, may require appropriate vaccinations. Yellow fever and cholera vaccinations are required by a few countries.

Departure Fees

Something that often catches first-time overseas travelers by surprise is payment of departure fees when leaving some international destinations. Many countries charge a departure tax when you leave the airport. The amount may be anywhere from $10 to $25 per person, payable in U.S. currency. Depending on the airline, this amount may be included as part of the original cost of the ticket, but it may not. If it isn't included in the price of the airline ticket, you'll have to pay it separately at the time and place of departure, often in cash. Typically U.S. dollars are accepted and may be preferred over local currency. Be sure to save some cash from your last-minute shopping and keep it handy for the government representative.

Electricity

Not all countries have the same operating voltage for appliances. Common voltages are either 110/120 volts or 220/240 volts, depending on the particular country. For example, most Caribbean countries use 110 volts, the same as the United States; Australia, however, uses 220 volts. Thus, depending on your destination, small appliances such as electric shavers and hair dryers either have to be manufactured to operate on dual voltages, or require the use of a voltage converter. Some hotels and resorts in tourist areas supply hair dryers in the rooms; some don't. Some hotels with a nominal voltage of 220 volts offer special low-power 110-volt outlets in the bathroom for use with electric shavers (only!).

As well as the voltage, find out about the frequency specifications of the electricity at your destination. Be sure that small appliances will operate correctly with whatever is available. The U.S. home voltage is 110 volts alternating current at 60 Hertz frequency (abbreviated Hz), which is the number of alternations per second. Other countries may use alternating current at 50 Hz. Even with the correct voltage, the different frequency can cause problems with chargers or devices that contain motors, such as hair dryers, designed to operate at 60 Hz.

On some small islands the 60 Hz supply may not be exactly 60 Hz, but slightly higher or lower. One consequence is that some electric clocks, such as your electric alarm clock or one supplied in a hotel room, may not give the correct time. Variations in the supply frequency may be enough to make the clock run slightly slow or fast over a period of time. I saw one hotel-room clock that routinely gained about ten minutes a day. Thus, be cautious when using such a clock for the precise time, such as if you need to wake up early to catch a plane home. Also, be aware that an unfamiliar hotel alarm clock may not work, may be set to P.M. instead of A.M., or may be subject to a power failure during the night. I always carry a small battery-operated alarm clock so I know the correct time.

Great Expectations—Caribbean Style

Sometimes visitors going to the Caribbean for the first time are surprised by what they encounter. The following comments are not all-inclusive, but may help you prepare for some common experiences during a trip.

- **Expect that you may get wet and/or be cold.** The Caribbean doesn't always have bright, sunny cloudless skies. At certain times of year, you may encounter violent tropical storms with lightning and thunder, and may experience drenching rains. Cool weather can occur on some islands, particularly in winter when storms have passed by, making it necessary to wear long pants and a sweatshirt.

- **Expect to be wet all the time.** Diving, by definition, is a wet sport. During a weeklong dive trip, however, it seems like you're constantly wet. Changing in and out of a swimsuit several times a day, preparing for dives in a suit still wet from the day before, continually showering and rinsing off after and between dives and snorkeling, the use of the swimming pool and beach—all can leave you, your bathroom floor, your towels, and your clothing wet all the time.

- **Expect hotel rooms to have tile floors.** This surprises some first-time travelers to nice hotels and may be initially perceived as a lack of luxury. But tile is an entirely practical way to deal with the sand and water that inevitably follow scuba divers every-where and would quickly ruin room carpeting. With tile floors, sand is easily swept up and water is easily mopped away.

- **Expect to wear casual clothing.** At most dive resorts, the uniform of the day is T-shirt, shorts, and sandals for both men and women, which makes it easy to choose clothes and pack. At some resorts that cater to vacationers other than divers, the level of dress may become more formal at dinnertime, but rarely rises above slacks and a colorful shirt for men and a summer dress for women. Some people like to dress up a bit, especially women in long skirts and fancy tops. This is fine, but not mandatory. There are some towns and resorts where dressing for dinner is required, but they're in the minority and must be sought out, if that's your desire. Some people like to wear long pants and long-sleeved shirts, with socks and shoes, when outdoors in the evening to cut down on bug bites on the ankles and legs.

- **Expect good food, but not necessarily gourmet food.** If you go with an all-inclusive resort or hotel plan, eating is often buffet style, but with a wide variety of dinner choices usually covering basic items—beef, pork, chicken, and other meats, seafood, pasta, and a supporting cast of soups, salads, and desserts. Breakfasts and lunches provide similar variety. At smaller resorts eating may be conducted family style, with everybody sitting at one large table and sharing plates of food. You may find that much of the food is relatively plain by U.S. standards and, while most of it ranges from very good to excellent, it may not reach gourmet expectations. Some resorts serve primarily local food, which may or may not be to your taste; check before booking if this would be a problem.

- **Expect to be bitten by bugs.** Walking on the beach without shoes can lead to bites on your feet and ankles. Sand fleas, sand flies, mosquitoes, and no-see-ums lurk everywhere, particularly in ocean debris and wet sand along the tideline. Biting bugs are often found on beaches and may come into non-air-conditioned rooms (the cold temperature of air-conditioning usually keeps them out). Bugs thrive very well in the wet, humid environments that are typical on tropical and semitropical dive islands.

- **Expect to spend more money than you'd planned.** Many dive trips are prepaid before you even leave home. Still, it's wise to plan for additional expenses during the trip, such as taxi rides, tips, exit fees, snacks, gifts and souvenirs, soft drinks, bar bills, meals out, and currency exchange fees.

The configuration of electrical outlets is also not the same worldwide. Check to see if you need an electrical adapter plug for the country where you're going. Adapter plugs may be obtained at department or travel-oriented stores before leaving home, or can often be purchased in gift and sundry stores in international airports during travel.

Electrical items that may not operate correctly during travel include rechargers for video cameras, camera strobe lights, and dive lights. Voltage supplied locally from a generator, particularly on small islands, may be erratic, either rising and falling, changing frequency, or containing uncontrolled spikes in the voltage. These variations can damage delicate electrical equipment. Dive shops often provide stabilized voltage outlets for charging strobe lights.

Odds and Ends

Before leaving on a dive trip, take stock of the items you might need that are easier to purchase at home. These are the little things you take for granted at home but may be difficult, or expensive, to find at a remote island: a favorite brand of sunscreen, batteries, aspirin, shampoo, or even your favorite facial tissues.

It's best to purchase flashlight batteries at home, along with other types of batteries used to power small items. For example, take along a spare battery if you need one to power your electronic camera. Specialty camera batteries may not be readily available at a remote resort, with the consequence that you may not be able to take any pictures until you can get another one. Even camera film, if there's a particular brand or type that you like and use, may not be readily available. If nothing else, having these small items with you saves the hassle of trying to find them during a vacation.

If bugs are a problem for you or at your destination, it may be helpful to ensure that your room has air-conditioning. Bugs that live in hot, humid environments typically don't like the frigid air of air-conditioning and will tend to stay out of the room. This can be helpful in rustic cabanas with thatched roofs that are open to the outside. One caution is that if the room becomes too cold, the bugs may become inactive and can fall out of their homes in the thatch into the room. Similarly, smoking can cause the bugs to fall into the room.

2

WORLDWIDE DIVE
DESTINATIONS

Scuba divers are found wherever there's water, and dive destinations can be found around the world. The majority of recreational divers go to warm-water destinations—Florida, Mexico, the Caribbean, and the Indian and Pacific Oceans. It's been estimated that more than a million divers go to warm-water diving destinations each year. Each person, however, has different priorities when it comes to preferences, budget, and time.

This chapter contains thumbnail sketches of popular dive vacation destinations that a majority of recreational divers enjoy. Given the diversity of the world's diving and limited space here, this chapter can only give a brief description of each spot. If one of the destinations sounds interesting, further details can be obtained from your travel agent, travel books in your local library, local dive shop, Web sites, and detailed dive guidebooks specific to a country, area, or island. Dive magazines also profile destinations around the world in various issues throughout the year.

One note of caution when choosing a destination is to check on the water temperature where you're going for the time of year that you'll be there. Some tropical areas in winter can have water temperatures as low as the 60s. If this isn't to your taste, either go prepared with a wet suit or pick a warmer destination.

Note that there are many dive destinations in the United States and around the world that aren't mentioned here. This is because these are destinations that are popular with only a limited number of divers, don't attract large numbers of divers for destination vacations, involve complex travel, or have inadequate or limited dive infrastructure for the average recreational diver. All the destinations listed here are relatively easy to reach, have highly developed dive operations, and have proven, over the years, to be popular with novice and intermediate divers. This situation may change in the future as other destinations develop their facilities further.

A large determining factor in choosing a destination is your budget. Obviously, prices increase with the degree of luxury and pampering you expect. A dive trip that involves driving to a nearby lake, with a stay at a budget motel, is very different from jetting off on a plane to a luxurious resort in the Caribbean. Both are fun in different ways; you just have to decide where dive travel fits into your budget.

A second determining factor is the time involved, which also relates to the amount of money to be spent. A local driving trip can be done over a two-day or extended weekend. Flying to a destination such as Florida or the Caribbean will add an extra day on each end of the trip for airplane travel. On a typical Saturday-to-Saturday trip to Belize, for example, you'll end up with seven nights of accommodations, six days of diving, and two days of travel. Travel to distant destinations, such as Australia or Fiji, will require two days of travel in each direction. Air flights from the West Coast of the United States direct to Australia require approximately fourteen hours of flying time. Thus, six days of diving in the South Pacific should be planned as at least a ten-day trip. If you go to the effort and expense to travel to places so exotic and far away, you may also want to take a few extra days for sight-seeing, thus extending the trip to two weeks or more.

Caribbean

A large grouping of popular dive destinations is in the Caribbean. Nearly all are international destinations, and some are relatively remote, thus adding a little complexity to travel planning. The most popular dive sites are the Bahamas, the Cayman Islands, and Cozumel Island. Abundant coral reefs, tropical climate, and warm sun in winter draw thousands of scuba divers to these islands.

A benefit of international dive travel is the opportunity to experience different cultures and adventures while enjoying outstanding diving. Caribbean destinations are all relatively easy to fly to from the United States and offer a full range of dive support, with accommodations ranging from the pampered ultraluxurious, through pleasant and comfortable, to guest houses and economical small motels. For those who enjoy exotic experiences, there are opportunities such as staying in grass-thatched huts, either on land or built on pilings over the water of a lagoon.

The locations described in this chapter are listed here because they've consistently been popular with divers over the years and offer the infrastructure, safety, comfort, and facilities expected by vacationing divers. As well as the islands specifically listed below, diving is also available on Antigua, Cuba, Barbados, Dominica, Jamaica, the Dominican Republic, Panama, and more.

Diving is generally good year-round in the Caribbean. The winter months tend to be a little cooler and drier. The lack of rain usually means better visibility in the ocean, because of reduced water runoff from the islands. The summer months tend to be hotter and rainier, and hence more humid.

Hurricane season in the Caribbean occurs in September and October, sometimes extending into early November. At this time of year, tropical storms originating off the coast of Africa sweep northwest across the Atlantic and occasionally hit Caribbean islands, where they have the capability to cause extensive damage. For this reason, some travelers prefer to avoid autumn trips.

Bahamas

The Bahama Islands consist of 700 major and minor islands and rock formations scattered over tens of thousands of square miles of ocean. Major islands, which include Grand Bahama, Eleuthera, Andros, Abaco, Chub Cay, and New Providence, are a short airplane flight or boat ride from Fort Lauderdale or Miami. The climate in the islands is subtropical, with water temperatures in summer between 75 and 85 degrees Fahrenheit and in winter between 70 and 75. Water visibility is usually around 80 to 100 feet, and sometimes more.

The capital of the islands, Nassau, on New Providence Island, is popular for golf, shopping, and casinos. The diving offers everything from shipwrecks to coralheads teeming with hundreds of species of colorful marine life. The surrounding ocean, off the southwest coast of the island, has often been used as an underwater location for motion pictures, such as Disney's classic 1954 underwater movie *20,000 Leagues Under the Sea* and several of the James Bond films. Many of the wrecks originally sunk for filming have slowly turned into artificial reefs with abundant fish and coral.

Andros, the largest island of the Bahamas group, is a popular dive destination that provides excellent diving all along the 110-mile Andros Barrier Reef, the longest in the Bahamas. Nearby is the Tongue of the Ocean, an underwater canyon 30 miles wide and 6,000 feet deep, which also offers excellent deep-sea fishing. The interior of the island consists of forest and swamp that's largely uninhabited and unexplored, but visitors can find interesting sites, such as Captain Morgan's Cave, which was supposedly the hiding place of the treasure trove of Morgan the Pirate. The interior of the island also contains many blue holes, which are underground sinks that are connected to spring and cave systems. Some are up to 350 feet deep and contain underwater currents that flow in and out at different times—thus divers should use caution exploring them. These are generally suggested for advanced divers only.

British Virgin Islands

These scenic islands, which were part of the inspiration for Robert Louis Stevenson's book *Treasure Island*, consist of fifty islands grouped closely together about 60 miles east of Puerto Rico. The two major islands are Tortola, which means "dove of peace," and Virgin Gorda, or "fat virgin." Tortola is the larger island. It has a population of about 9,000 people and combines the influences of Britain, France, and Holland. Island temperatures in summer range from 80 to 90 degrees Fahrenheit. Water temperatures range from about 75 in winter to 85 in summer.

This area enjoys a strong pirate heritage, including Henry Morgan and Edward Teach, better known as Blackbeard. The islands have never courted mass tourism, making them one of the best-kept secrets in the Caribbean. The islands themselves range from low hills covered with cacti and boulders on the south slopes to sloping mountains covered with green growth in the rainy season.

Diving here is exciting and varied. There are wrecks, reefs, walls, pinnacles, and a wide variety of marine life. The mail packet RMS *Rhone,* lying in 25 to 80 feet of water, is one of the best known of all Caribbean shipwrecks and was used as a filming location for the 1977 movie *The Deep.* A popular site to visit on the southern tip of Virgin Gorda is The Baths, where massive boulders, some as high as a house, form eerie grottos and pools of water suitable for snorkeling.

Because diving infrastructure is not as well developed on these islands as some of the other Caribbean islands, many of the sites are reached by live-aboard boats.

Cayman Islands

The Caymans are a group of three islands a little less than 500 miles south of Miami. The capital, George Town, is on Grand Cayman, the largest island.

The other two smaller islands—often called the Sister Islands—are Cayman Brac and Little Cayman. The three have different identities, but all have excellent diving. Nassau groupers, tarpon, turtles, jewfish, angelfish, and eagle rays are common at dive sites. Marine parks and replenishment zones around the islands protect the reefs and marine life.

Grand Cayman has most of the hotels, nightspots, and entertainment, though low-key accommodations and diving are also available at the east end of the island. Grand Cayman is famous for Stingray City, a very popular shallow dive of about 12 feet onto a sandy bottom where southern stingrays congregate.

Cayman Brac, about 90 miles to the east of Grand Cayman, is smaller and quieter. The island contains only a couple of resorts and a handful of condominiums. Diving is magnificent on the surrounding reefs, and includes the renamed MV *Capt. Keith Tibbetts*, a 330-foot Russian missile frigate sunk in 1996 in 110 feet of water specifically for diving. The stern deck of the ship is about 40 feet below the surface. The wreck broke in half during Hurricane Mitch in 1998, giving the site a surreal appearance—like a set from a science-fiction movie.

The island of Little Cayman, 5 miles away from Cayman Brac, is even more secluded, with an unlighted gravel runway at the airport and only about a hundred permanent residents. Though the island is small, it contains excellent accommodations and superb diving. Little Cayman is famous for its wall diving, including many dive sites on the world-famous Bloody Bay Wall and the area around Jackson's Wall, both in Bloody Bay Marine Park. The wall at Bloody Bay starts in only 20 feet of water.

Visibility in the water in these islands is commonly around 100 feet. They are very dry islands with little runoff into the ocean—thus the visibility in the water can range up to 250 feet on a clear day. The temperature on the Caymans averages 77 degrees Fahrenheit in winter, 82 in summer. Water temperatures are in the low 80s year-round.

Dutch Leeward Islands

These three islands—Aruba, Bonaire, and Curaçao—lie 50 miles north of the coast of Venezuela. They form part of the Netherlands Antilles and, because of their initials, are often called the ABC Islands. They're far enough south to be out of the Caribbean hurricane belt, which is a bonus for divers wanting to go in the fall months.

Curaçao has the largest population (160,000 residents) and a highly developed tourist infrastructure that includes casinos and nightclubs. Bonaire is the least populated (14,000) and has almost no nightlife.

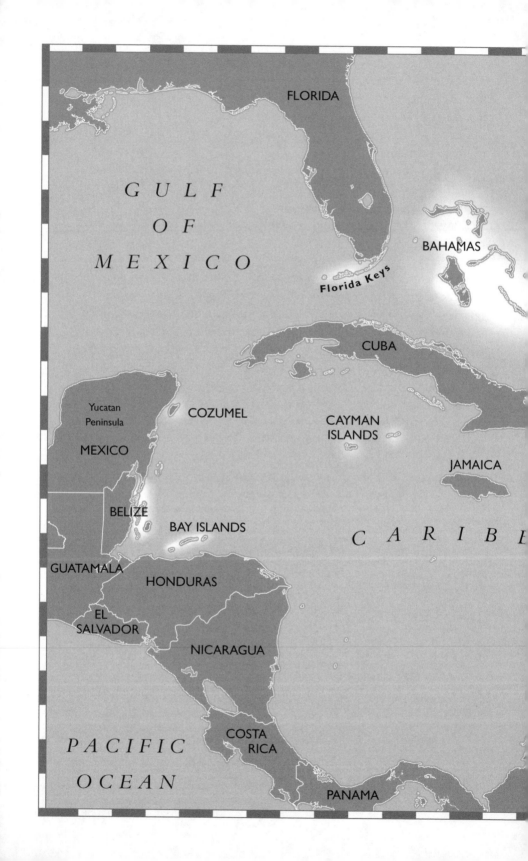

FLORIDA

G U L F

O F

M E X I C O

Florida Keys

BAHAMAS

CUBA

Yucatan
Peninsula

COZUMEL

CAYMAN
ISLANDS

MEXICO

JAMAICA

BELIZE

BAY ISLANDS

C A R I B E

GUATAMALA

HONDURAS

EL
SALVADOR

NICARAGUA

P A C I F I C

COSTA
RICA

O C E A N

PANAMA

N

A T L A N T I C

O C E A N

TURKS &
CAICOS

U. S. VIRGIN
ISLANDS

BRITISH
VIRGIN
ISLANDS

ST. MARTIN

HAITI   DOMINICAN
REPUBLIC

LEEWARD
ISLANDS

PUERTO
RICO

SABA

ST.
EUSTATIUS

E A N   *S E A*

ST. LUCIA

CURAÇAO

ARUBA   BONAIRE

WINDWARD
ISLANDS

OLOMBIA

VENEZUELA

Though all three islands offer diving, Bonaire is the most popular dive destination and provides some of the best diving in the Caribbean. Diving is in Bonaire Marine Park, which includes the entire ocean coast surrounding the island. Abundant coral gardens and reefs, with elkhorn coral, staghorn coral, and colorful sponges, greet the diver. Many divers specifically look for black coral and the brilliant orange elephant ear sponges. The reef and marine life of Bonaire is some of the most abundant in the world, and is reported to include 84 species of coral and 272 species of fish. Good diving is also found around Klein Bonaire, a 1,500-acre island about half a mile offshore, reached primarily by small boat.

A popular site for night diving is at the Kralendijk Town Pier. Because the pier is still in active use, diving requires a permit and a qualified dive escort. The extra effort, however, is worth it.

The island of Bonaire is 24 miles long by 5 miles wide, and is desertlike and very dry. Sight-seeing includes the Salt Works, huge mounds of salt dried from salt evaporation pans and awaiting export. Nearby are historic slave huts, used originally to house salt workers in the 1800s. On the northwest end of the island is Washington/Slagbaai Park, 15,000 acres of tropical desert with cacti and large, colorful iridescent blue lizards. On the coast inside the park, Boca Slagbaai, which means "slaughter bay," has a beautiful sandy beach that is a good area for a picnic and a shore dive. Also inside the park is the Gotomeer, a saltwater lagoon with hundreds of wild pink flamingos.

Diving is available in Aruba, and can be very good, with 100- to 130-foot visibility in the water. Aruba, however, does not have the spectacular reefs that surround Bonaire and Curaçao. Popular among divers is the *Antilla,* a 400-foot World War II German shipwreck that is the largest in the Caribbean, sitting in 60 feet of water. This site is also popular with snorkelers, since part of the wreck sticks up above the water. As well as diving, Aruba offers other ocean activities, such as Jet Skiing, parasailing, sportfishing, and sailboarding. On the island, Arikok National Park contains several caves with numerous colorful petroglyphs. Aruba also has a well-developed tourism infrastructure.

Curaçao lies 30 miles west of Bonaire. Much of the diving takes place in its underwater park. Divers can find a series of protected reefs with sponges, magnificent corals, and abundant fish life, along with steep wall dives. Many shallow wrecks are directly accessible from the shore. On shore you can explore Willemstad, the capital, which looks like a Dutch storybook town, and the Curaçao Seaquarium. Curaçao is a popular destination for cruise ships.

Dutch Windward Islands

The other group of islands that forms the Netherlands Antilles are in the northern Caribbean. This group of islands consists of St. Martin, Saba, and St. Eustatius. All three offer their own brand of diving in water that's around 76 to 80 degrees Fahrenheit, with visibility of up to 120 feet. Wreck, shore, and drift diving are popular.

The northern half of St. Martin is French and the southern, Dutch (Sint Maarten), though there are no formalities at the border between them. The reefs of St. Martin are not true coral reefs, but rather volcanic blocks covered with coral hydroids and sponges. Dive options include tunnels, 200-year-old swim-through wrecks complete with cannon and anchors, and prolific marine life.

Saba is a small island, only 5 miles across. Though it has rain forests, the island is formed from an extinct volcano and thus rises almost vertically from the sea. Because of this, most of the diving is deep, between 80 and 100 feet. There are no permanent beaches, and all the diving is from boats. The diving includes a pristine underwater park surrounding the island, underwater cliffs, steep walls, and many ledges, caves, and pinnacles. Saba requires that divers obtain a special permit to dive.

The diving around St. Eustatius includes old shipwrecks in Oranje Bay and at Wreck City, an artificial reef made from wrecks that were sunk relatively recently. Much of the diving is in St. Eustatius Marine Park, which was formed to protect marine life and historical artifacts. Snorkelers can explore the underwater ruins of the old city of Oranjestad, which was destroyed in 1781. The ruins are in 3 to 10 feet of water. Sight-seeing on the island includes an extinct volcano, called The Quill (originally called Kwil, meaning "pit" or "hole"), stone ruins, and old forts, complete with cannon and herds of wild goats. The locals call the island Statia, after St. Anastasia, the original name given to the island by Columbus. St. Eustatius does not allow you to dive wherever you like, but requires that you go with a local dive group.

St. Lucia

This island is often considered one of the Caribbean's most beautiful getaways.

St. Lucia, which is 27 miles long and 14 miles wide, is located among the Windward Islands of the Lesser Antilles. Its natural beauty stretches from low plains near the coast up to the summit of Mount Gimie, which is 3,120 feet high. One of the rainier islands, St. Lucia contains lush vegetation and tropical foliage. Earlier development promoted plantations to grow sugar, coconuts, coffee, and cotton.

Scuba Hot Spots at a Glance

Location	Type of Diving	Famous Dive Sites
Aruba	Soft and hard pillar corals; sloping reefs at 20–90'	• Wrecks: Antilla (50–60')
Australia (Great Barrier Reef)	Coral reefs (10–130+'). Live-aboards go to best sites on the outer reefs; closer day sites may be crowded. Good snorkeling. No shore diving because of murk and box jellyfish.	• Cod Hole (20–60') • Ribbon Reef system (15–60') • Heron Island reefs (10–70') • Wrecks: Yongala (80–100')
Bahamas	Walls starting at 30' and dropping to 130+'; shallow reefs to deep drift diving, as desired. Blue holes available for advanced divers.	• Andros reef system • Tongue of the Ocean • Wrecks: Tears of Allah, New Providence (40'); train wreck, Eleuthera (20')
Belize	Most diving is on outer islands and atolls (Turneffe Island, Glover's Atoll, and Ambergris Caye), rather than the mainland. Shallow coral gardens to deep walls. Most walls start at 20–40' and go to 100+'.	• Great Blue Hole (130+') • The Elbow—drift dive (45–130+') • Lighthouse Reef (25' to 130+')
Bonaire	Shallow reefs, gently sloping walls. Good shore diving.	• Town Pier/Customs Pier—night dive (20–40') • Bonaire Marine Park • Wrecks: Hilma Hooker (50–90')
British Virgin Islands	Coral reefs, pinnacles, and wrecks. Mostly shallow diving (less than 80'); no deep walls.	• The Baths, Virgin Gorda—snorkeling • Wrecks: RMS Rhone (25–80')
California (United States)	Shore diving from novice to advanced; requires shore diving and cold-water skills. Also boat diving to places such as Channel Islands National Park. Kelp forests. Fall and winter may give best visibility.	• Monterey Bay • Point Lobos State Reserve • Southern California coastal area • Santa Catalina Island—popular with novices • Wrecks: Wreck Alley, San Diego (70–90')
Cayman Brac (Cayman Islands)	Shallow reefs (30–60'), sand flats, and walls (40–100').	• Buccaneer Reef—night dive • Wrecks: MV Capt. Keith Tibbetts aka the Russian warship (40–110')
Costa Rica	Cocos Island (uninhabited) is a day-and-a-half boat ride off the Pacific shore; or live-aboard. More suited to advanced divers and strong sailors.	• Cocos Island—abundant large marine life, particularly sharks
Cozumel (Mexico)	Shallow reefs and coralheads to steep walls. Many dives at 20–60'; also deep dives at 90–130+'. Much of the diving is easy drift diving, but current and depth at some sites can challenge advanced divers. Most diving is around the southwest side of the island. No anchored sites; some shore diving. Very clear water due to the constant current.	• Palancar Reef system (15–100+') • Wrecks: airplane wreck (30–35')

Location	Type of Diving	Famous Dive Sites
Curaçao	Protected shallow reefs, steep walls (20–130+'), and sloping walls. Some shallow wrecks can be reached from shore.	• Mushroom Forest (20–100')
Fiji	Underwater currents from mild to roaring; strong currents more suited to advanced divers.	• Rainbow Reef sites—strong current
Florida Keys (United States)	20-minute boat ride to outer reef for best diving. Many shallow reefs (10–40') with no current make this good for beginners. Deep dives also available.	• Christ of the Abyss statue (25') • Key Largo National Marine Sanctuary • Looe Key National Marine Sanctuary • Wrecks: City of Washington (20'); Benwood (25–45'); Bibb and Duane (70–120')
Grand Cayman (Cayman Islands)	Most walls start at 50–60'; shallow reefs (15–50'). Most diving is on west wall and Seven Mile Beach area. East End often has currents and is more suited to advanced divers.	• Stingray City (10–20') • Eden Rock (30–50') • Wrecks: Oro Verde (25–50'); Balboa (10–40')
Great Lakes (United States)	Wreck diving. Suitable for advanced divers, this is very cold, deep water with murky conditions.	• Thunder Bay • Wrecks: Many excellent wrecks, but most are cold, deep dives
Guam	Coral reef gardens (10–130+'), vertical drop-offs, and WWII wrecks (50–130+').	• Wrecks: Double wreck of Tokai Maru and SMS Cormoran (50–110'); many other divable WWII wrecks
Guanaja (Honduran Bay Islands)	Barrier reef with steep drop-offs (15–130+'). Shallow coral gardens inside the fringing reef.	• Wrecks: Jado Trader (55–90')
Hawaii	No fringing reef, but many subtidal reefs (15–60'); impressive drop-offs to 130+'. Diving may involve swift current and drift diving. Diving may be better in calmer summer months.	• Kona Coast, Maui • Maui and Kauai—good snorkeling
Little Cayman (Cayman Islands)	Wall diving; sheer walls start at 15–20' and go to more than 130+'.	• Bloody Bay Wall (20–130+') • Walls at Jackson Bight (20–130+') • Wrecks: Soto Trader (30–50')
Palau (Belau)	Vertical walls outside the lagoon; coralheads and reefs inside the lagoon. Vertical walls start at 2–20' and go to 130+'. Strong currents may require advanced drift diving techniques.	• Jellyfish Lake—landlocked on Eil Malk island • Palau Lagoon • Wrecks: More than 30 WWII wrecks in the lagoon (25–120')
Red Sea	Shallow reefs (20–50') with calm, clear water. Shore diving at Eilat.	• Ras Muhammad
Roatan (Honduran Bay Islands)	Ranges from shallow reefs and channels to steep walls (to 130+'). Most diving done on the walls.	• Mary's Place—a winding crevice in the reef (20–100') • Wrecks: Prince Albert (35–65')

Location	Type of Diving	Famous Dive Sites
St. Lucia	Steep walls to 130+'. Most of the best diving is on the western shore, near Soufrière.	• Anse Chastenet Reef (20–130') • Wrecks: Lesleen M (35–65')
Saba	From shallow reefs to steep walls and deep-water pinnacles (starting at 90–100'). No shore diving. Mostly deep diving.	• Eye of the Needle
Truk (Chuuk)	Steep walls outside the lagoon; calm water inside. Greatest concentration of divable wrecks in the world, but many are deep (most in the 100+' range).	• Truk Lagoon has more than 50 WWII ships and aircraft (50–130+') • Wrecks: Shinkoku Maru (45–90'); Fujikawa Maru (30–90')
Turks and Caicos	Many shallow reefs (30–60'); good tongue-and-groove coral formations (40–110'); walls (50–130+').	• Grace Bay, Provo • West Caicos • Wrecks: Southwind (50')
U.S. Virgin Islands	St. Thomas and St. John have similar diving: fringing reef and coral gardens (20–80'); no spectacular drop-offs. Some sites are accessed from both islands. St. Croix is different from the other two—from gentle sloping coral reefs to walls and steep drop-offs. Walls start at 25–40' and go to 130+'.	 • St. Croix: Buck Island Reef National Monument (10–45') • Fredricksted Pier—small marine creatures (30')

Most of the popular diving is in the area of the fishing village of Soufrière, on the west side of the island. This is about an hour's drive from the airport at Castries, the island's capital. From Soufrière, dive sites are only a short boat ride. For divers staying on the other side of the island, the boat ride is an hour or more.

Unlike many Caribbean islands, St. Lucia does not have a fringing reef, but offshore diving includes an abundance of sponges and corals. The twin landmarks of the island are the Pitons, Gros Piton and Petit Piton, sharp spires that rise steeply up out of the ocean, just offshore, for almost 2,500 feet. Popular dive sites are in the nearby St. Lucia Marine Preserve on underwater reefs starting at 20 feet and dropping to 140 feet. Diving here requires you to go with a local dive company. Divers encounter squid, electric rays, lobsters, octopi, black coral, and barrel sponges, as well as all the other common Caribbean marine life.

Turks and Caicos

These are low-lying limestone islands formed by two mountains with relatively flat tops that rise from the floor of the Atlantic Ocean. They lie about

30 miles south of the Bahamas, about 570 miles from Miami. There are eight major islands and about forty small cays in this chain, many of them tiny and uninhabited. The larger islands offer a variety of resort and vacation options. Caico is a corruption of *caya hico,* which means "string of islands."

The largest island, 38 square miles, is Providenciales, or Provo, as it is more familiarly known. Divers will find sheer walls, tongue-and-groove coral gardens, and old shipwrecks. The walls at Northwest Point Marine Park start in 50 feet of water. The walls are remarkable vertical structures, covered with thick clusters of multicolored sponges. Schooling fish and rays are often seen, along with turtles, eagle rays, bottle-nosed dolphins, and manta rays. Atlantic humpback whales may be seen from late December to April, when they migrate past the islands. Summer water temperatures are usually between 82 and 85 degrees Fahrenheit, perhaps requiring a dive skin. Winter temperatures are usually between 74 and 78 degrees, requiring the use of a wet suit. Out of the water, the main attractions of the island are its long stretches of white beaches and the ocean. Salt ponds and marshes serve as a home for resident birds and a stopping place for migrating birds. There is sight-seeing at Princess Alexandria Land and Sea Park and Nature Reserve.

Grand Turk, the capital, is at the other end of the island chain. It offers wall diving with abundant black coral and friendly groupers. Another popular dive site is West Caico, an uninhabited island about 10 miles southwest of Provo, which offers some of the best diving in the islands. The island is known for West Caicos National Marine Park, a wall running for 2 miles along the western shore. Manta rays cruise its face, and dolphins are commonly seen in summer. Visibility in the water is often between 80 and 150 feet, and is frequently at the high end of this range.

U.S. Virgin Islands

This is a series of islands. The three principal ones are St. Thomas, St. John, and St. Croix, which is the largest. Diving includes walls, ledges, pinnacles, caves, canyons, wrecks, and abundant marine life.

The islands offer a wide variety of accommodations, ranging from luxury hotels and condominiums to guest cottages, and even camping. Dining is available in a wide variety of restaurants, and St. Croix and St. Thomas have an active nightlife. Charlotte Amalie, on St. Thomas, is one of the premier cruise-ship ports in the Caribbean and has excellent duty-free shopping.

For the nondiver, or for entertainment during the afternoon following a morning of diving, there are many land-based sports, such as golf and tennis, and water sports, such as snorkeling, sailing, sportfishing, and glass-bottomed boat trips. For the shopper, there are plenty of stores and boutiques. For the walker and hiker, there are hiking trails and tropical forests to explore.

The three islands are easy to reach, because there are frequent direct flights from the United States to St. Croix and St. Thomas. St. John is reached from St. Thomas by ferry boat, because it doesn't have the appropriate topography for a landing strip. About 10,000 acres of St. John is preserved as the scenic Virgin Islands National Park.

Because these islands form an American territory, many U.S. visitors feel that visiting them is an easy start to exploring the Caribbean without the added adventure of going to another country. Many vacationers visit all three islands on the same trip, since they are located very close together.

A popular snorkeling site is Buck Island Reef National Monument, an underwater park that is administered by the U.S. National Park Service. Buck Island is close to St. Croix and is easily reached by local boats. Water inside the lagoon is 8 to 12 feet deep and contains several underwater snorkeling trails. Diving outside the reef, the water is 30 to 45 feet deep.

Central America

Belize

South of the Yucatán Peninsula is the country of Belize. Off the coast of the mainland are mangrove and coral islands, and a variety of fringing reefs. This is the central portion of the Great Maya Reef, also known as the Great Western Barrier Reef, the second largest barrier reef in the world (after Australia's Great Barrier Reef). In Belize the Great Maya Reef is also called the Belize Barrier Reef. The major part of the reef is 12 to 30 miles offshore and runs in a north–south direction, paralleling the coast for about 170 miles. The outside of the reef is a near-vertical wall with sponges and black corals, while the inside contains smaller reefs and sandy plateaus.

Tourist attractions on the mainland of Belize include jungle, rivers, waterfalls, and the remains of the ancient Mayan civilization at El Picar. Ecotour destinations on the mainland include the Bermudian Landing Community Baboon Sanctuary, the Shipstern Wildlife Reserve, and the Cockscomb Basin Wildlife Sanctuary.

The primary dive destination is Ambergris Caye, an island 25 miles long and a mile wide off the northern coast. Activity on the island centers on the seaside town of San Pedro, which offers the most hotels and dive services.

Much of the diving in Belize is performed on or around three large offshore coral atolls, though other smaller cayes along the reef also have dive sites. Turneffe Island Atoll, located off the central coast of Belize, consists of a series of mangrove islands and is the largest coral atoll in the Western Hemisphere. The 25-mile-long and 7-mile-wide atoll starts about 15 miles from Belize City on the mainland, which translates into about a forty-five minute boat ride to the dive sites. There is wall diving here, as well as shallow coral gardens with plentiful marine life. Many of the dive facilities are located on small islands scattered around the atoll, since boats from the mainland take forty-five minutes to an hour and a half to reach major dive sites along the atoll and the outside the barrier reef.

At the extreme southern end of Turneffe Island Atoll is a popular dive site named The Elbow. At a point about a mile offshore, the surrounding currents mix and produce a steady upwelling of plankton, which attracts large numbers of fish. Large fish often come to the edge of the reef to feed, and eagle and manta rays, reef sharks, and other large animals may be seen gliding along just off the reef, in the blue of the deep ocean. The top of the reef drops to depths of 100 to 130 feet as the dive progresses. The steady current around The Elbow makes this a drift dive.

Glover's Atoll, reputedly the hideout of the English pirate John Glover, is the southernmost of the three atolls and the farthest (70 miles) from Belize City. It has few resorts located close by, and hence has the advantage of being less used by visitors.

About 40 miles off the central coast and to the east of the Turneffe Islands is Lighthouse Reef Atoll. The atoll forms a ring of reefs about 20 miles wide and 4 miles long, with almost vertical walls on the outside. Inside the reef, in the middle of the lagoon, is a popular and unusual dive site called the Great Blue Hole. The Blue Hole is a perfectly cylindrical crater in the ocean floor, nearly 1,000 feet in diameter and 440 feet deep, surrounded by a small coral reef. At a depth of 110 to 150 feet is a grotto of giant stalactites, some of them 35 feet long, that hang from the ceiling of an underwater cavern in the side of the vertical wall.

Costa Rica

Located between Panama and Nicaragua, Costa Rica is bordered by the Atlantic Ocean to the east and the Pacific Ocean to the west. Cocos Island, a national park located 300 miles off the west coast in the Pacific Ocean, is well known for its white-tip reef sharks, scalloped sharks, manta rays, and hammerhead sharks. Unfortunately for those who don't like long boat rides on the sea, the trip by boat from the mainland takes about thirty-two hours.

For divers, the Pacific coast of Costa Rica is generally considered better than the Atlantic coast, which is much shorter in length and not as well developed. You can see large marine animals on the Pacific side, such as hammerhead sharks, dolphins, whale sharks, eagle rays, and manta rays. Visibility in the water is usually in the 30- to 80-foot range, or more. Water temperature is typically between 75 and 85 degrees Fahrenheit.

Much of the Costa Rican countryside has been set aside as national parkland, and the mainland offers ecotour activities that range from visiting active volcanoes to exploring lush rain forests.

Honduras

The Great Maya Reef stretches from Mexico to Honduras; as noted, it's the second largest continuous barrier reef in the world. The huge reef starts in the ocean off Mexico's Yucatán peninsula, east of Cancún, stretches south past Belize, and then curves around to the east to run just north of Honduras. On the southeast end of the reef are the offshore islands of Honduras. They are collectively called the Bay Islands, and are located 15 to 40 miles north of the coast of the mainland.

The largest and most developed of the Bay Islands is Roatan, about 40 miles long by 4 miles wide. Dive sites on the reef are spectacular and contain a wide diversity of marine life. Roatan is also the site of the Institute for Marine Sciences, which offers a dolphin study and training program, with interactive dives with dolphins in a lagoon or in the open ocean. Visibility in the surrounding water is typically around 75 to 100 feet, with water temperatures around 78 to 84 degrees Fahrenheit. Visibility of 100 feet, or occasionally more, is not unusual. The average temperature on land is 80 degrees, but ranges up to 90 in summer.

Two smaller islands that are popular among divers are Guanaja and Utila, both of which have limited air service. Infrastructure on these two islands isn't well developed; transportation is by four-wheel drive or boat on Utila, and exclusively by boat on Guanaja because the island has no roads.

A stopover on the mainland of Honduras, on the way to the Bay Islands or back home, or a flight over to the mainland for a day tour can be arranged. Honduras has rivers, waterfalls, jungle, lofty mountains, lush forests, and sandy beaches. Mayan culture and history can be explored through the temples, altars and stairways at the popular ruins of Copán and El Sapo on the mainland. Copán, which has been named a UNESCO World Heritage Site, was an important Mayan ceremonial center from around A.D. 450 to 850.

Mexico

The most popular dive destination from the United States is Cozumel Island, an island 30 miles long by 10 miles wide located approximately 12 miles off the eastern coast of Mexico's Yucatán Peninsula. Cozumel is also a very popular destination for cruise ships.

Virtually all the diving around Cozumel is drift diving because of the swift Yucatán current that runs in the narrow channel between the island and the mainland of Mexico. This current also sweeps away silt and other ocean debris, resulting in extremely clear water and excellent visibility for diving. One of the top dive spots in Cozumel is Palancar Reef, often called the Underwater Grand Canyon. Made a marine park in 1980, it's a 20-mile-long fringing reef on the island's western side. Because the main part of Palancar Reef stretches for more than 3 miles, it offers many dive-site variations, such as Palancar Gardens, Palancar Deep, Palancar Caves, and Palancar Horseshoe. During time off from diving, many visitors arrange day trips to the mainland to visit Mayan ruins.

On the west coast of Mexico, between the mainland and the peninsula of Baja California, is the Sea of Cortez, which contains one of the richest diversities of marine life in the world, including hundreds of species of fish and thousands of varieties of invertebrates. Sponges, sea fans, and sea lions are common. California gray whales migrate from Alaska and the Bering Sea down the west coast of the United States, to bear their young in winter in the warm water surrounding Baja California.

Indian and Pacific Oceans

Most of these dive destinations are halfway around the world from the United States, thus requiring more planning and financial outlay. They also require a more extensive time commitment, because of the long distance to reach them. While a dive trip to Florida can be a quick weekend getaway, a trip to Australia will take a full day or more of travel time, and the westbound traveler will lose a day when crossing the international date line. Still, these exotic destinations can fulfill the dreams of a lifetime with an escape to an island paradise. For avid wreck divers, there are many exciting relics of World War II scattered throughout the islands of Micronesia. Human remains are still present on many of these wrecks, but they have been left in place both because of the danger of recovering them and out of reverence for the dead. Many of the destinations in the Pacific are known for their brisk currents, and drift diving is common.

As well as at the destinations described below, diving can also be found in Bali, Tahiti, Indonesia, Bora Bora, Thailand, Malaysia, and the Maldives, with the understanding that there may be less developed diving infrastructure in some locations.

Australia

Diving is available all around the Australian coast. You'll see a large variety of tropical fish, and may occasionally see manta rays. Popular places for diving are around Sydney, in southeastern Australia; around Perth in southwestern Australia; around Adelaide in South Australia, off Yorke Peninsula and Kangaroo Island; and around Darwin, off the north coast of the Northern Territories. Divers on the far north coast, around Darwin, and up and down the northeast coast in Queensland, must be aware of the possible presence of the box jellyfish, a dangerous stinging jellyfish. At certain times of year, these jellyfish are present in the ocean along the shore of the north coast and up the adjacent coastal rivers in the tidal zones. From October to May swimming in the ocean in areas not specifically protected from jellyfish by swimming nets in the ocean is prohibited. Swimming in these areas from June to September should be done with caution.

The premier diving in Australia, and one of the best sites in the world, is on the 1,430-mile Great Barrier Reef, off the coast of northeast Australia in the Coral Sea. The most popular diving facilities for the Great Barrier Reef are centered in Queensland, in the vicinity of Cairns and Port Douglas. Boats from coastal ports take about an hour to reach dive sites on the reef. Popular islands, such as Fitzroy Island and Green Island, may be reached from Cairns by day divers.

Another popular site is Lizard Island, north of Cairns in the Coral Sea, which is reached by either a thirty-hour boat trip from the Cairns area or a fifty-minute flight on a very small commuter plane, also from Cairns. There is a resort on the island, but most divers explore the surrounding area on live-aboards. About 20 miles to the east of Lizard Island is Cod Hole, located at Cormorant Pass, an underwater cut in the reef. This 30-foot dive site, at the north end of the Ribbon Reef system, is well known for its resident population of Australian potato cod (a giant grouper, also called the potato grouper), which may grow up to 7 feet long and weigh up to 400 pounds. The specimens typically seen on dives are in the 4- to 5-foot range.

Trips may also be arranged to excellent, but remote, dive sites on the outer coral reefs south of Cape Verde Peninsula in the Coral Sea, where the visibility may be greater than 150 feet. Farther south there are popular dive facilities based in Townsville, which is between Gladstone and Cairns on the central Queensland coast.

In Australian diving terminology, *bommie* refers to an isolated coralhead. This can either be quite small, as in an individual coralhead, or very large, as in a coral tower.

Because of the long distances from the mainland to the outer reef, which lies about 30 miles offshore and where the diving is best, you may choose to stay at hotels on outer islands. One such is the resort at Heron Island, which is considered to have some of the finest diving on the reef. About 50 miles from the mainland, the island is not reached by day boats; you arrive either by a two-hour catamaran ride from Gladstone, or by helicopter. The island, which is part of the coral reef, has dive sites all around. It's surrounded by other reefs that offer additional dive sites, but those considered the best are close to the island. Gladstone is also the gateway to the Capricorn Islands, which contain excellent diving on the reef just south of Heron Island.

Because Australia is in the Southern Hemisphere, the seasons are approximately reversed from the United States. Air temperature during the summer months of June to September—the Australian winter—may drop to around 75 degrees Fahrenheit. During winter (December to March), which is the Australian summer, the air temperature rises to 85 to 90 degrees, depending on the location. Water temperature varies between 65 and 80 degrees during the year at Heron Island, depending on the season, and between 75 and 85 degrees farther north by Cairns. Visibility in the water is usually between 30 and 70 feet.

Fiji

This grouping consists of a series of islands of which Viti Levu and Vanua Levu are the largest. A large reef system surrounds the islands and offers excellent diving everywhere. Diving experiences include underwater caves, wrecks, tunnels lined with soft corals, and hosted shark dives.

Hawaiian Islands

The island group that makes up Hawaii combines tropical diving with the convenience and infrastructure of America's fiftieth state. Because the underwater currents are brisk, diving in Hawaii is mostly drift diving.

The island of Hawaii has rain forests covered with orchids and other flowers, waterfalls, and an active volcano, Kilauea. Most of the diving is on the Kona Coast, where turtles and octopi may be seen.

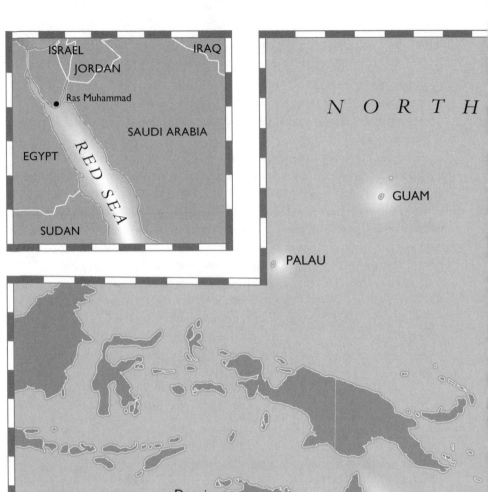

ISRAEL

IRAQ

JORDAN

Ras Muhammad

SAUDI ARABIA

EGYPT

RED SEA

SUDAN

N O R T H

GUAM

PALAU

C O R A

INDIAN

Darwin

OCEAN

Port
Douglas

GREAT BARRIER REEF

Cairns

Townsville

Gladstone

AUSTRALIA

Perth

Adelaide

Sydney

P A C I F I C   O C E A N

HAWAIIAN
ISLANDS

MARSHALL
ISLANDS

SEA

FIJI ISLANDS

S O U T H

P A C I F I C

O C E A N

N

TASMAN

SEA

Maui, called Hawaii's Valley Island, is known for excellent snorkeling on shallow reefs, many of which are easily reached from the shore. Maui combines resorts, mountains, jungles, and beaches. A popular place for sightseers is Haleakala, a spectacular 10,000-foot dormant volcano whose crest is often covered with mist and fog.

Honolulu and famous Waikiki Beach are on Oahu, an island of natural beauty with premium ocean surfing. Most of the diving is off the southern and western shorelines and includes wrecks, walls, caverns, and plentiful marine life.

Kauai, known as the Garden Island, has high, rugged mountains covered with rain forests, streams, and waterfalls. The Na Pali Coast, a spectacular stretch of shoreline, rises straight up from the sea and is so rugged that there are no access roads.

Micronesia

Guam is the gateway to Micronesia. The island is often used only as a stopping point for travel to the other islands, but it should not be overlooked for diving. Guam and Saipan are modern resort islands with luxury hotels and gourmet restaurants. Yap is known for excellent opportunities to view manta rays and its curious stone "money," which consists of stone wheels up to 6 feet in diameter.

Truk, whose correct present name is Chuuk, is a popular destination. The 8,000 square miles of Truk Lagoon contain sixty-six huge Japanese ships and 400 aircraft that were sunk in a decisive air battle during World War II. Two of the biggest ships, the tanker *Shinkoku Maru* (500 feet long) and the aircraft ferry *Fujikawa Maru* (440 feet), have become part of the marine ecosystem with gradual encrustation of corals and sponges. Eleven islands and many more small islets are located within the lagoon.

Palau consists of more than 300 small islands located in the triangle between the Philippines, Indonesia, and New Guinea. The diving includes shipwrecks, steep walls, and coral reefs, with sea fans, caves, and even sea horses. The inner lagoon has over thirty wrecks from World War II. A popular and unusual snorkeling site is Jellyfish Lake, a landlocked saltwater lagoon full of millions of *Mastigias* jellyfish that, through ages of evolution, have lost their ability to sting. Palau is also known for swift ocean currents, which often necessitate the use of reef hooks. These are large, barbless hooks that you hook on to dead coral in order to stop and observe something closer, or to take a photograph. When you're through, you unhook and continue to drift.

Pohnpei (formerly Ponape), often called the Garden Island of Micronesia, has eight nearby atolls with colorful reefs and drift-diving opportunities. The island contains lush, green virgin forests, ancient ruins, and remote reefs, and is complemented by a traditional lifestyle.

The Marshall Islands consist of twenty-nine atolls and five islands that include Bikini Atoll, the site of early atomic bomb tests soon after World War II. Bikini was closed to divers until 1996, when lingering radioactivity finally dissipated. One bomb test left a crater a mile wide and 200 feet deep in the reef. The seventy-two ships that were used as target vessels include the USS *Saratoga*. The underwater wreck of the aircraft carrier, which is 888 feet long, sits in 160 feet of water, though the superstructure is only 40 feet below the surface.

Red Sea

The reefs of the Red Sea, often considered one of the premier dive destinations in the world, contain a dazzling variety of colorful marine life. Visibility is crystal clear year-round and can reach a startling 200 feet. The land above water consists mostly of desert sand, arid landscape, and rocky mountains. Despite its undeserved reputation for terrorism, Egypt has a rate of serious crimes much lower than most major American cities. Opportunities for cultural and historical sight-seeing, such as Luxor, Cairo, and the pyramids at Giza, are plentiful.

Many of the premier dive sites are located around Ras Muhammad at the southern tip of the Sinai Peninsula. While excellent sites are available from land, many of the remote locations are best accessed by live-aboards. Summer is the best time for diving, when water temperatures rise to 80 degrees Fahrenheit. Winter water and air temperatures can drop to 60.

The high salt content in the water of the Red Sea increases buoyancy. You will usually need to add a few more pounds of weight than you'd need for Caribbean diving.

United States

Many divers start out in the dive destinations of U.S. coastal waters, which are easy to reach and relatively inexpensive for U.S. residents. For those divers not yet ready for the cost and added complexities of international travel, diving in the United States offers convenience and variety. California's waters are cold, but also convenient to major West Coast metro areas. Similarly, the water along the northeastern coast of the U.S. is cold, but easy to reach from the large population centers of the East. In contrast, the Florida Keys, in the southeast, offer warm-water diving, combined with the ambience and climate of the Caribbean.

Those living inland may be able to find quarries and artesian wells that have been developed for scuba diving, such as Bonne Terre Mine in Missouri, or the Blue Hole, an artesian spring in Santa Rosa, New Mexico.

California

The California coast is the second most popular dive destination in the United States (after Florida). California offers a variety of dive experiences centered on beach diving in southern California. Though much of the state's coast is not suitable for diving, there are many excellent dive sites located 100 to 150 yards or less offshore and accessible from public beaches. Shore diving, which involves techniques such as judging and negotiating coastal tides and rip currents, requires special training and experience. Charter dive boats are also popular and are available for dives at offshore sites, such as Channel Islands National Park, an island chain lying just off the southern coast.

California and the Pacific coast, as I've noted, involve cold-water diving and require a full ¼-inch wet suit with gloves and hood, or a dry suit. High temperatures at the water's surface in summer and fall are around 70 degrees Fahrenheit off southern California, and typically 50 to 55 degrees off the central and northern California coast. Winter and spring water temperatures in the south drop to around 50 to 65.

Visibility in the open ocean can be 60 feet in summer, but usually drops to 30 feet or less in winter and spring. Close to California beaches the visibility can be limited—typically only 10 to 30 feet, depending on the tide, water currents, and periodic blooms of algae. Ten feet should be considered the minimum visibility for a safe dive. Some of the best California diving is in the fall months of September and October, when the water is the warmest and the visibility is the clearest.

Farther north, the area around the Monterey Peninsula and the coast north of San Francisco, between the Russian River and Fort Bragg, offers some of the best diving in California. The ocean directly around San Francisco isn't commonly used by divers because of heavy surge, poor visibility in the water, and the common presence of great white sharks. Like southern California, the northern areas offer cold-water diving. While you can dive here in a wet suit and hood, a dry suit is more appropriate to the water temperatures.

Monterey Bay and the surrounding area provide an extremely rich and diverse marine diving environment. A majority of the marine mammals and fish that are found up and down the west coast may be found off this peninsula. This relatively small area, which includes the ocean off the towns of

Monterey, Pacific Grove, Pebble Beach, and Carmel, contains rocky reefs, kelp forests, and a variety of marine habitats. Ocean access is easy, so much of the diving is shore diving, though boats are required for travel to sites farther out in Monterey Bay. Water temperatures are about 50 to 55 degrees Fahrenheit in winter, and 55 to 60 in summer. When you're not in the water, you can enjoy golfing, restaurants, wineries, and the Monterey Bay Aquarium.

A popular place to dive in the Monterey area is south of Carmel, at Point Lobos State Reserve, the first underwater reserve in the United States. Whalers Cove, inside the reserve, offers diving in the local underwater marine environment while remaining protected from the open ocean. For those more adventurous, the cove is also the access point for nearby Bluefish Cove and the outer areas of the underwater reserve that are open for diving. Southern sea otters, harbor seals, and California sea lions may be observed while diving in the area. Like all of the west coast, this is cold-water diving. When I was there some years ago, the water temperature at the bottom of Whalers Cove, at around 50 feet, was only 42 degrees!

Florida

The most popular dive destination in the United States, Florida offers both saltwater ocean diving and freshwater spring diving, thus providing a wide range of underwater experiences. These include coral reefs and tropical fish, crystal-clear springs and sinkholes, and a variety of underwater wrecks.

Diving is available up and down both of the state's coasts, but the most popular dive destination is the Florida Keys. North-central Florida, the west coast, and the Florida panhandle have large groupings of divable springs and freshwater sinkholes fed by underground aquifers. The water temperature in most of these springs averages between 70 and 75 degrees Fahrenheit, thus requiring the use of a full wet suit. King's Bay, the Crystal River, Ginnie Springs, and Crystal Springs are all popular destinations for diving in springs. Many of the springs offer cave and cavern diving. The King's Bay and Three Sisters areas of the Crystal River, both in Crystal River National Wildlife Refuge, are good locations for viewing large herds of West Indian manatees, also known as sea cows, which enter into the warmer (72-degree) waters of the bay during the winter months.

South Florida offers coral reefs and a tropical atmosphere. Biscayne National Park, on the coast just south of central Miami, is easily accessible. More than 96 percent of the park is underwater, in a subtropical climate with warm, wet summers and mild, dry winters. Divers and snorkelers can explore underwater meadows of sea grass and turtle grass, coral gardens, and the mangrove-lined tidal habitat near the shoreline. The central part of the park has shallow reefs with colorful sponges, tropical fish, and a large variety of other underwater marine life.

The Florida Keys, which start about 60 miles south of Miami and then sweep to the south and west, make up one of the most popular areas in the United States for diving. The Keys consist of a series of more than 200 islands that stretch in a thin line for 100 miles from Key Largo on the north to Key West and the offshore Dry Tortuga Islands at the southern end of the chain. This results in more than 100 miles of reef and literally hundreds of dive sites. This offshore reef is the only living coral reef in the continental United States. Biscayne National Park contains the northernmost section of the reef. Wreck dives, walls, shallow coral reefs, and abundant marine life are everywhere. Concerns about water quality and numerous ships running aground in the Keys in the 1980s led to the formation of the Florida Keys National Marine Sanctuary to provide for expanded protection and preservation of the reef.

The Florida Keys provide good diving for beginners, because much of the diving on the reefs is at an average depth of 30 feet or so. Nevertheless, there's also plenty of deep and advanced diving for more experienced divers. You'll need a boat for the most popular dives, which lie about 6 to 8 miles offshore.

The easy drive from Miami to the town of Key Largo and Key Largo National Marine Sanctuary (designated in 1975) makes this a popular area to dive. Key Largo offers hotels, restaurants, and dive boats for every taste and level of budget, and there are probably more dive shops per capita in Key Largo than anywhere else in the nation. The reefs and wrecks of John Pennekamp Coral Reef State Park, southwest of the town of Key Largo, are a frequent dive destination. A local diving highlight is *Christ of the Deep,* also called *Christ of the Abyss,* an 11-foot statue solidly anchored in 25 feet of water at the edge of an outcropping in the coral reef. Water temperatures range from about 84 degrees Fahrenheit in summer down to a cool 70 degrees in winter.

Great Lakes

The Great Lakes are definitely a dive destination for those who enjoy cold-water diving. Still, they're very popular among divers because they contain a huge collection of underwater wrecks. Over the years divers have brought up countless artifacts, including brass and china items, from these wrecks. Lake Ontario contains the New York State David W. Mills Cultural Preserve and Dive Site to protect and preserve some of these wrecks.

3

AIRLINES, PACKING, AND LOCAL TRANSPORTATION

nce you've made your basic scuba travel decisions—where to go, when to go, and how long to be gone—you're ready to book your travel and arrange flights. There are several ways to do this.

Travel Agents

The easiest method is to call a professional travel agent and have him or her book the entire trip for you. Travel agents are experienced in matching travelers to destinations, in selecting airlines to meet individual needs, and in the myriad details that accompany booking travel, so you might as well take advantage of their knowledge and expertise. Travel agents in the past typically received their commission in the form of a discount from airlines and hotels, so it didn't cost a traveler any extra to use their services, though this is changing; some agents do now charge a small fee.

If you choose to use a travel agent, I highly recommend dealing with an agency that's familiar with diving or that specializes in working with scuba divers and dive trips. This type of agent will understand the needs and desires of divers, and will be able to provide you with up-to-date recommendations on dive resorts and conditions at the destination you choose. This can be particularly useful when traveling internationally, because the political climate of some smaller countries can change very quickly and you need to be aware of any unsafe or potentially disruptive conditions. Scuba travel agents should be familiar with the dive hotels and dive shops at the destination and be able to provide detailed information on them.

As an alternative, many international dive resorts have their own booking offices in the United States, and can also coordinate and arrange airline travel at the same time as hotel and dive bookings. This type of travel packaging can result in lower airfares—the agency may work through an airline consolidator to get a lower price than you might receive with an individual personal booking.

Another method for choosing and booking a dive trip is to consult your local dive shop. Most dive shops either book travel directly or work closely with a travel agency that books trips for them. Dive shops are usually well qualified to recommend places to go and, again, are usually very knowledgeable on the current social and political conditions of dive destinations, as well as the quality and arrangements at individual dive resorts and hotels.

Most dive shops also offer guided dive group tour packages, accompanied by one or more instructors or divemasters from the shop. If you feel uncertain about your ability to negotiate international travel to a dive destination, this may be a good option. Your travel is organized for you, and you have a guide to help you with the logistics of travel, such as negotiating strange airports, local transportation, and restaurants at your destination. Usually the accompanying guide from the dive shop will have been to the destination before and is familiar with local travel and customs. If you enjoy group activities, this type of travel also offers a chance to make new friends (usually from your hometown or local area) from a group of divers with similar interests.

The disadvantage of this type of travel for individuals who prefer solo or small-group activities is that these trips are obviously organized as and for a group, rather than an individual. You'll probably do everything as a group, including diving, sight-seeing, eating, and meeting in the bar in the evening. This type of camaraderie appeals to some—but not everyone. Choose wisely. If you find you don't like some of the members of the group, you may be stuck with them for the duration of the trip!

Passports and Visas

Generally, travel to an international destination will require a passport. This is a document issued by a national government to provide evidence that the holder is a citizen of that country. It's used to cross international borders.

If you don't have a passport, the application procedure is easy, but be sure to allow adequate time for processing of the paperwork before your trip. Application is made to one of the U.S. passport agencies located in many major cities. In large cities that don't have a separate passport agency, you can often apply at a local post office or other government office authorized to accept applications. Your local travel agent or a business that provides passport and identification photographs can provide further information. Typically the application and issuing process takes about four weeks; this may be longer or shorter at different times of year, however, so obtain current information from the U.S. passport agency or your travel agent. Passports are valid for ten years, then can be renewed by mail.

*I*dentity Check

- *Check to see if you need a passport for the country you're going to; some countries require a passport, others don't.*
- *A passport is the easiest and best proof of citizenship, even if it's not required.*
- *A driver's license is not considered proof of citizenship.*
- *If you take a birth certificate, be sure it's an original with an official seal; a copy probably won't be accepted.*
- *Married women may need proof of name change, such as a marriage certificate.*
- *Birth and marriage certificates must be original documents from an official government agency—not from a church, and not copies.*

Passports aren't always required for international travel. For example, Mexico and most Caribbean countries don't require a passport for U.S. citizens, but you must have a certified copy of your birth certificate, naturalization certificate, or voter's registration card as proof of citizenship with you when you arrive at your destination. A driver's license is not accepted as proof of citizenship. Some countries won't accept a voter registration card as proof of citizenship. Without a passport, a certified marriage certificate may be required for proof of name change for women. Since immigration regulations for different countries change periodically, always check with a travel agent or airline to be sure of the current requirements before assuming that you don't need a passport.

Even if a passport isn't required for the country you're visiting, it's easier to enter or exit international destinations if you have one. A passport contains a recent photograph and signature of the holder, and thus provides quick and easy proof of identification and nationality. Passports are requested for car rental in some countries and may be requested when checking into a hotel. Depending on the currency regulations of a particular country, a passport may also be required for foreign currency exchange.

If you already have a passport, check the expiration date before your trip. Some countries require that a passport remain valid for a certain period of time after the trip, often two to six months. If you return to the United States with a passport that has already expired, you may be charged a fee upon reentry.

If you lose your passport while you're traveling, or it's stolen, notify the nearest U.S. embassy or consul as well as the local police. They will advise you on the procedure for obtaining a replacement. A few minutes of advance planning may prove helpful if you're ever caught in this situation: When you receive your passport, copy the front page with your passport number and photograph. Then carry the copy with you when you travel, but separately from your passport. This copy will help speed up the paperwork process if you have to obtain a replacement in the case of loss or theft. Some travelers reduce the passport copy to wallet size and carry this in their wallet or purse. Travelers who have renewed their passports often also take their expired passport with them as proof of citizenship in case of loss of their current passport. This may also help expedite the replacement process.

Another method is to leave a copy of the front page of your passport at home with a relative or friend. If your passport is lost or stolen during your trip, you can have this copy faxed to you.

As well as a passport, check with your travel agent, airline, or other reliable source about whether or not you'll need a visa. This document doesn't replace a passport, but it may be required for travel to some countries in addition to a passport. A visa is a document issued by certain countries as official permission to enter a particular country. It comes in the form of either a stamp in your passport or a separate document attached to your passport. It shows that your travel documents have been reviewed and that you meet the requirements for entry into that country.

The need and requirements for a visa vary with the destination country and with your own citizenship. Requirements are different for different countries and change periodically. As of this writing, for example, U.S. citizens going to Australia to dive the Great Barrier Reef require an Australian visa; travel to neighboring New Zealand, however, does not require a visa. Australian visas may be obtained before travel by writing to your nearest Australian consulate, or can be obtained electronically by your airline or travel agent when making your airline booking.

Visitors with U.S. citizenship who are traveling to most Caribbean countries do not require a visa for short vacation stays. Be aware that those staying for extended periods or traveling for business purposes may need a visa.

Airlines, travel agents, and businesses that supply passport photographs should have information readily available on which destinations require a visa. Usually your passport must be submitted to a consulate of the country you intend to visit before your trip, so allow sufficient time before your travel date for mailing and processing. A visa may or may not have a fee associated with it.

C-Card and Logbook

There are two other important documents you must take with you whether or not you're bound for a destination overseas. The first is your C-card. Without your certification card, almost no dive operators will allow you to dive with them. Most won't rent equipment, and many won't provide air fills without it. The C-card should be on your list of essential dive equipment.

The second crucial document is an up-to-date logbook. Some divers don't bother with recording their dives; however, this is your only proof of diving experience. Depending on the dive shop, a logbook may or may not be required for diving. Some dive operators insist on inspecting your logbook to determine your level of dive experience. In some cases this information is used to divide large dive groups into equivalent levels of experience, so that advanced divers are not paired with divers on their first trip. In actuality, this method leads to a more pleasant dive experience for everybody involved.

Even if it's not required by a dive operator, a logbook is a useful source of reference information for your particular diving experiences. You can, for

*P*ut It in Writing

Some divers don't use logbooks; their loss. Here are some good reasons to use one:
- *On the fun side, you have a record and details of places you've been diving.*
- *You have a record of your dive profiles in potential cases of DCS.*
- *You have a useful record of equipment used, such as weighting, with various pieces of equipment.*
- *Logs contain useful information to plan future dives, based on past experiences.*
- *Logs can be useful in deciding when to fly after diving.*
- *You have a record of ability in case a dive shop requires proof of experience.*

*A*re You Certifiable?

If you plan to take a dive training course while on a trip overseas, you may be asked for proof of medical suitability to dive, or be required to furnish proof of an examination by a qualified dive physician. If you have health concerns, be sure to have medical certification with you or check with the dive shop in advance for their requirements.

example, record the weighting you used with particular dive gear or exposure suit. Then you just refer to your log the next time you meet similar conditions, rather than having to experiment to achieve the correct weighting.

Airlines

Those individuals who prefer complete control over their dive vacation plans often prefer to book their travel directly with the airlines. Making your own airline plans requires that you have chosen your destination, are willing to research the availability of lodging, and will coordinate local hotels and other facets of the trip at your destination. The booking process is quite simple and can be accomplished directly over the telephone with an airline, through airline Internet sites, or through various brokers that offer package services or destinations on the Internet.

This method of travel planning often requires that you select charter airlines or international airlines with which you may not be familiar. A comforting thought is that all airlines, including non-U.S. airlines, have to meet the same safety requirements as U.S. airlines if they fly to or from airports in the United States. Thus, you can feel just as secure traveling on these airlines as you would on major U.S. carriers. Be aware, however, that some smaller foreign domestic airlines or planes flying among islands overseas may not be subject to these same requirements.

Airline security has been increased recently. Some considerations for travelers are listed in the accompanying sidebar.

If you choose a package airline flight that originates at a typical international gateway airport, such as Los Angeles, Miami, or Houston, remember that you will have to add the price of airfare from your hometown to the gateway to the total flight cost. It can add up.

Be aware that some airlines charge an additional fee for scuba equipment, even if your luggage is within the airlines' weight or bag limit—typically three

Travel between islands may involve small planes.

Airline Security

Heightened levels of security are in place at airports. While this generally isn't a major problem for travelers, there are some considerations you should be aware of.

- **Arrive early at the airport**—*at least two hours for domestic or international flights. Large international airports may require longer because of long lines at check-in counters, departure immigration, and lengthened lines and delays at security checkpoints. When returning to the United States, allow plenty of time to go through immigration and final checkpoints into the overseas departure lounges, because security lines sometimes move very slowly and you may miss your flight.*
- **Be sure to be at the departure gate in time to board the aircraft.** *Most airlines are requiring passengers to be in their seats well before the plane departs. Last-minute arrivals at the gate may not be allowed to board.*
- **Say good-bye to friends and family before reaching security checkpoints.** *At most airports, only passengers with boarding passes are allowed onto the concourses. Likewise, arrange a meeting place before you leave if folks are picking you up, since they probably can't meet you at the gate.*
- **Expect to be the subject of a random search during passenger screening.** *Pack your hand luggage in such a way that it's easy to search and put neatly back together. In some airports you may have to send your shoes through X-ray machines and walk barefoot through the metal detector. Belts with metal buckles and shoes with staples or metal shanks are among some of the more unexpected items that may trigger metal detectors.*
- **Expect to be asked to put keys, wallets, and jewelry through X-ray machines.** *Some male travelers prefer to put their wallet and money clip inside their carry-on bag for safety when going through the metal detector, so that it's not mislaid at a checkpoint. Some women put their metal jewelry in a zipper-top plastic bag; then the entire bag can be inspected or put through the X-ray machine while minimizing the possibility of small items, such as earrings, becoming lost.*
- **If you carry a computer, it will be X-rayed separately, so have it out of its carrying case, ready for inspection.** *Be prepared to turn it on for inspection. Be sure to retrieve it after going through the metal detector, because it's not uncommon for a passenger to pick up other bags and forget the computer.*
- **Cutting implements or sharp objects, whether made of metal or another material, are not allowed on your person or in hand luggage.** *This includes knives, scissors, nail files, and knitting needles, but may also include diverse items such as safety razors and umbrellas. These should all be packed in checked luggage. Divers should always pack dive knives in checked luggage. At some airports these items will be confiscated if in hand luggage and will not be stored or returned. Medications requiring needles should be accompanied by a physician's prescription. If in doubt about a particular item, check with your airline well before departure.*
- **Keep your passport and boarding pass handy.** *You'll need them at various security checkpoints. For domestic flights, a driver's license is acceptable identification.*

bags. You may wish to check with the particular airline you will be using for its policies on scuba equipment. Otherwise an unpleasant and expensive surprise may await you at the airport check-in counter on your day of departure.

Most small island-hopping commuter planes have severe baggage weight and size restrictions. You may wish to check on baggage policies with any small airlines you may be using. They typically limit the number of pieces of carry-on baggage and count all pieces of carry-on baggage, including briefcases and purses, in your total weight limit. Total baggage over the weight limit is charged an additional fee—at a hefty per-pound rate. Overweight luggage may be delayed to fly later than you, or may continue only on a space-available basis. Try to minimize what you bring if you'll be taking one of these flights.

If you travel internationally, the name on your airplane ticket must exactly match the name on your passport. Do not use nicknames or abbreviations on the tickets. Also check to be sure that your airline ticket is correct, with

$\mathcal{S}$taying Healthy in the Air

Dehydration
The process of pressurizing an aircraft cabin produces air with extremely low levels of humidity, which may result in dryness of the throat and mouth, and may irritate the eyes of contact lens wearers. Adequate hydration is of particular concern to scuba divers, since dehydration has been linked to the incidence of decompression sickness.
To reduce the effects of dehydration on the flight, do the following:

• Drink water or juice as much as possible, particularly on long flights.
• Limit the drinking of alcohol, coffee, and tea, since these are diuretics and increase body dehydration.
• Use eyeglasses instead of contact lenses if your eyes become irritated.
• Though not a specific factor in dehydration, it's also wise to avoid overeating or eating large amounts of fatty food just before the flight. It's harder for the body to digest food when it's inactive, and a feeling of bloating may result.

Deep Vein Thrombosis
Sitting upright and immobile for long periods of time in an aircraft seat can increase the risk of a condition called deep vein thrombosis (DVT), which is the formation of blood clots in the legs. The compression of blood vessels and a reduction of fluid flow in the legs while sitting may result in stagnation of blood in the lower extremities. These blood clots can break loose and circulate in the bloodstream, causing heart attacks or stroke. The risk may increase by personal factors such as obesity, recent surgery or injury to the lower limbs, clotting disorders, hormone therapy (including oral contraceptives), increasing age, or particular medications. Risk can also be increased by dehydration. If you feel that you might be at risk for DVT, seek advice

the correct dates of travel, the correct connecting airports, and the correct destination. If you have a paper ticket, as opposed to electronic, be sure all the flight coupons are present in the ticket package. I once flew on a last-minute business trip to Greenville, North Carolina, and didn't realize until I was at the connecting gate in Charlotte that the travel agent had mistakenly booked me to Greensboro, North Carolina. Luckily the two towns are in the same state and had similar connecting flights. Always check for mistakes.

When flying internationally, it's very important to reconfirm your flight plans with your airline. Typically this is done forty-eight to seventy-two hours before your flight by making a local phone call to the airline, or arranged through the front desk of larger hotels. Reconfirmation of seats isn't necessary for flights within the United States, but it's critical if you're flying in other countries and with non-U.S. carriers. If you don't reconfirm your flight, you may find that your seat has been given away to another passenger, particularly on popular flights. I once saw two young men who hadn't felt a need to reconfirm their flight show up at an international airport to return to the U.S., only to find that their seats had been given away; they had to wait for available space to show up on another, later flight.

Some health considerations for air travelers are given in the accompanying sidebar.

Suitcases and Bags

Choosing luggage that best meets your travel needs involves considering a wide range of options. You'll find large suitcases and small suitcases, hard-shell suitcases and soft-sided duffel bags, luggage with shoulder straps for carrying, suitcases with handles, suitcases with wheels, and so on, and so forth. Only you can decide what works best for you, but the following are some factors you may wish to consider.

from your physician. While risks appear to be minimal for most healthy travelers, it's wise to consider preventive measures, particularly if anticipating a long flight. To reduce the risk of DVT, do the following:

- *Move your legs and feet vigorously for five minutes every hour while on the flight.*
- *Do in-seat leg workouts, such as rotating your feet and ankles in circles or up and down, alternately lifting the heels and toes of your feet from the floor, or lifting your legs up and down.*
- *Get up and move about the cabin or move about in open area, such as in the back of the plane by the galleys or lavatories.*
- *If you're at risk for DVT, consult your physician about the use of surgical compression stockings during flight. These elastic leg stockings, available from drugstores or surgical supply companies, may improve the blood flow from the legs back to the body.*

First is size. A friend of mine embraced the philosophy that all the dive gear that he and his wife owned should fit into one dive bag. And he made sure that it did. Unfortunately, however, the undesired side effect was that the fully packed dive bag was so heavy and bulky that it became essentially unmanageable and required two people to lift it. Thus, it may be more convenient for carrying purposes to split dive equipment and clothing into two or more smaller, but manageable, suitcases or bags. Some airlines will only take bags that are less than a specified weight, due to the difficulties of handling bulky or heavy bags.

There are two common schools of thought on the type of baggage to purchase for air travel. One is to buy cheap luggage and plan on replacing it often due to wear and tear. The other extreme is to buy very expensive heavy-duty luggage and assume that it will last for a long time. The reality probably lies somewhere between these two extremes. My advice is to purchase baggage sturdy enough to protect the contents, but assume that it will soon show signs of wear, especially after frequent travel. Airlines typically don't assume responsibility for "normal" wear and tear of luggage (whatever that is!). Such wear and tear—which may include rips, small holes, and missing handles, tow straps, and wheels—is considered the traveler's responsibility. Thus I recommend buying luggage with the idea that you will have to replace it periodically.

Another consideration is that you may not want to reveal the fact that you're carrying expensive dive equipment. Though unfortunate, it's a reality that baggage and its contents are occasionally stolen somewhere along the journey. Commercial dive bags often serve as an advertisement that they're full of dive equipment—and thus valuable. It isn't unknown for an expensive dive bag featuring the logo of a well-known dive equipment manufacturer to disappear en route. Depending on your confidence in people and where you're traveling, you may wish to use bags that don't have a dive logo on the outside.

One approach to bag security is to buy older bags and suitcases from a local thrift store. They won't look like they contain expensive dive equipment—and they'll be cheap. You can add an inexpensive bag strap, which often can be obtained with a lock, around the outside of the bag in order to secure the contents inside. A few years of airline handling may mean that these bags have to be discarded and replaced, but further inexpensive replacements from a thrift store are again ideal.

An interesting approach to prevent petty pilfering is to have suitcases or bags individually wrapped in polyethylene film. Vendors in some airports offer this service. The bag is tightly wrapped in multiple layers of continuous plastic film. While this doesn't stop theft of the bag itself and doesn't totally deter thieves, the plastic film makes it harder for inquisitive people to pop the locks, look through the bag, and extract anything that may be of interest to them.

Bags with combination locks, either as part of the locking mechanism or as a separate small travel lock, have an advantage over key locks in that you don't have to carry a key. You do, obviously, have to pick a combination that you can remember easily and reliably!

Packing

The biggest mistake in any type of travel is taking too much with you. If you pack things you don't need and won't use, you'll end up with more baggage than you can handle conveniently. The basic strategy in packing for any travel is to try, within reason, to cut down on what you're taking. You needn't scrimp so much on what you take that you spend your whole Caribbean vacation wishing you'd brought that extra pair of sandals or shorts, but do try to be sensible about what you take. In other words, don't take four pairs of shorts if you can reasonably expect to wear only two.

Here's an example to illustrate this point. Some years ago I accompanied a colleague on an overnight business trip. This particular man lugged along a huge suitcase, a giant folding garment bag, and a large briefcase. I had a thin, folding garment bag and a thin, soft-sided briefcase. After the two of us had unpacked and settled into our respective rooms, I noticed that my friend had packed four business suits (plus the one he was wearing), five pairs of shoes, and the associated sundry neckties, shirts, and other accessories. When I asked why he'd brought all these clothes, he replied that he didn't know what he was going to wear the next day for the business meeting. So he brought everything he thought he *might* need. The moral of the story is, make these decisions at home, and bring only what you *do* need!

For many temperate-climate U.S. destinations, you can bring the amount

Pack It Right

- *Don't take anything you don't need.*
- *Don't put items you can't live without in checked luggage.*
- *Be sure that you can carry all your bags.*
- *Be sure to put a label on the outside and inside of each bag.*
- *Secure all bags so they don't open during travel.*

and type of clothing that you'd usually wear at home. For warmer destinations, such as Florida, Mexico, or the Caribbean, lean more toward shorts, T-shirts, sandals, and other warm-weather clothing. For guidance, appendix B in the back of this book includes a list of representative clothing required for a dive trip to a warm destination, as well as a checklist of dive equipment items. Working from a list of things to take may seem childish, but it's a convenient way to be sure you remember everything you need.

After you've decided what and how much to take, think about breaking the total amount down into manageable suitcase-sized chunks. Instead of packing everything into one huge suitcase, it may be better to pack two or more smaller bags. For example, you may find it easier to maintain your balance while walking if you carry one bag of roughly the same size and weight in each hand, rather than walking lopsided with a giant suitcase in only one hand. Also, each of the two will be lighter than a single bag.

The best way to think about packing and the number of suitcases you'll need is to imagine that you have to carry, cart, push, or lug all these cases by yourself through airports or into a hotel without any luggage carts. More often than not, this is what actually happens at some point in a trip. Also, remember that when you come back into the United States from abroad, you'll have to bring suitcases through immigration and customs by yourself in most airports. You may be able to take baggage carts through customs, but in some instances you may have to leave them in a secure area and carry the bags yourself.

If you'll be continuing on domestic flights to other U.S. destinations after returning from overseas, most airlines have special baggage check-in counters immediately outside customs so that you can recheck your bags after inspection without having to go to the ticketing counters. This is convenient, but you may still have to carry them for some distance.

Finally, consider what should be carried in checked baggage. In general, items that are rugged and can withstand dropping, such as clothes, shoes, fins, and wet suits, are appropriate for checked bags. Delicate and fragile items, like masks or flashlights, can be wrapped in clothing or wet suits and placed in the center of a bag, between layers of clothing, to give them another layer of protection and shock resistance. Fins can go on the bottom or top to add another layer of protection and strength to the sides of the bag. Wrap anything that may leak, such as shampoo or suntan lotion, in paper towels and seal in heavy-duty zipper-lock plastic bags so that it won't spill on clothing or other items during the trip.

Many divers prefer to carry very delicate or breakable items, such as regulators and dive computers, with them in carry-on baggage in the cabin of the aircraft. Though regulators and gauges are generally rugged enough to withstand the bumps and bounces of travel, remember the cardinal rule that says you are responsible for your own life and safety. You don't want vital life-supporting dive equipment to be damaged. Checked bags, particularly heavy pieces, are often swung, hefted, or dropped onto conveyor belts and baggage carts on their way to the aircraft. Though baggage is generally handled with reasonable care, it's not unknown for suitcases to fall off conveyor belts, fall off baggage carts, have other heavy bags piled high on top of them, or sustain random bumps and bangs from handling. On several occasions, while gazing casually out of the window of a plane before a flight, I've observed baggage falling several feet onto the tarmac from the conveyor belt that transports bags into the luggage hold. Again, this isn't common—but it does happen, and it may be preferable to err on the side of caution when you travel with life-supporting equipment, such as a regulator. For the same reason, I prefer to carry all delicate equipment, such as compasses and dive computers, in a carry-on bag. Special padded carrying cases are available for regulators, if you wish to pack them separately and carry them with you onto the plane as hand luggage.

Lost Luggage

A crucial consideration with baggage is of course to ensure that it gets to your ultimate destination with you. Traveling within the United States is luckily quite straightforward; it's unusual for luggage to be "lost" for more than a few hours, at worst. Baggage almost always arrives when you do, unless a flight has been canceled or delayed, then it may arrive on the next flight before or after you. Missing baggage should always be reported immediately to your airline. To avoid potential mistakes at the check-in counter, examine your baggage receipts to make sure that the destination and any connecting airports are correct and match your ticket itinerary.

It's also wise to avoid short connection times at connecting cities and not to change flight itineraries after your baggage is checked in. On international flights, ask if your baggage is checked all the way through to your final destination, or if you have to reclaim it at an intermediate connecting airport along the way. Usually bags have to be reclaimed at the first airport of entry into a country (this includes your return to the United States) in order to go through customs with you. After this, if you're traveling further, baggage is rechecked for the final destination.

The most frequently chosen U.S. dive destinations are Florida for warm-water diving, and the California coast for cold water. These are generally straightforward trips. International dive destinations, on the other hand, tend to be farther away and are often in relatively remote parts of the world.

Essential travel paperwork: passport, airline tickets, C-card, dive insurance card, and regulator warranty card.

Journeys may involve multiple flight segments, and often include changes of airlines. The reality is that, even though baggage almost always arrives with you without delay, there are no guarantees that it will do so. I learned this lesson the hard way when I had a flight to a Caribbean island delayed, rescheduled to another airline, then finally canceled completely. I had to reclaim various pieces of baggage that were strewn across three connecting airports along the rest of the journey. Strangely enough, one bag even arrived unaccompanied at my hotel on the day before I finally arrived! Assume that lost luggage may take twenty-four to forty-eight hours to catch up to you.

To avoid complete panic and a delay in diving and beach activities if your baggage does go temporarily astray on a trip to a tropical destination, it's advisable to add a few essentials to your carry-on baggage, such as a few toiletries, a T-shirt, and a swimsuit, so that you can at least function until your luggage shows up. Some divers like to also carry their mask and regulator in hand luggage, so that they can dive with their own equipment. Most equipment can be rented for a few days in case luggage doesn't arrive when you do, but you may wish to hand-carry items that would prevent diving if they don't arrive. Suitcases rarely become totally lost, but it can be a real inconvenience if your dive gear takes two or three days to catch up with you at the beginning of a dive trip and you have no swimsuit.

Other items that should be carried in hand luggage on the airplane are those that would cause you difficulty if you lost them or were without them for any length of time, such as prescription drugs, prescription eyeglasses, money, passports, and credit cards. Appendix B includes a list of items that you may wish to take in your hand luggage when traveling by plane. This list is not all-inclusive; you should modify it according to your personal needs and preferences.

*T*he Bare Essentials

If most items are inadvertently left at home, they can be replaced at your destination—or else their absence won't ruin a trip. Some items, however, are critical. Among them:
- *Passport*
- *Airline tickets*
- *C-card*
- *Cash, credit card, or traveler's checks*
- *Prescription medications and eyeglasses*

As well as luggage tags on the outside of your bag, place one on the inside with your name, home address, and phone number. In addition, list your flight information and destination information, such as your hotel or resort. If your bag becomes completely lost and the outside tags are missing, this may help in its return, or may help it to catch up to you on your trip.

Transportation at Your Destination

Once you arrive at your destination, you'll have to make your way to your accommodations. If you've arranged a dive package at a hotel or resort, land transportation is often included and arranged for you. Either a hotel shuttle will pick you up, or other arrangements will have been made to transport you and your luggage to your hotel or resort.

After arrival, if you wish to see more of the area, you'll need to check out local transportation options. For maximum freedom and flexibility, you may wish to rent a car. Most major car rental companies offer overseas rentals, either directly or through an affiliate, so reservations can usually be made at home with a local or toll-free telephone call. Be sure to check with the car rental agency at the time of booking about insurance requirements, minimum age limits for drivers, driver's licenses, and any other special terms you may need to be aware of. Some rental companies require a minimum age for renting, or even driving, a car overseas, along with a good driving record. Be sure that you or any other potential drivers can meet all the requirements.

Usually an international driver's license isn't necessary to drive a car overseas. In most cases a valid driver's license from your home state or country is all you need, but check ahead to be sure. A passport may be required for identification. Some countries require that you buy an additional temporary driver's permit or license while you're there.

In some countries, such as the Cayman Islands, St. Lucia, and Australia, you drive on the left side of the road as is the British custom; if you are not comfortable with that, you may want to rethink driving a rental car. One tip that makes driving on the "other" side easier is to rent a car with an automatic transmission instead of a manual. The small extra expense is worth it in terms of not having to worry about shifting gears when driving on the left side of the road. This helps free up your concentration for remembering to stay on the correct side of the centerline!

Other options for transportation at your destination include taxis (often expensive!), motor scooters, local buses, bicycles, and even walking. Guided tours and tour buses may be available. Obviously the degree of complexity and the cost are directly related.

Always ask the price of a taxi ride, and negotiate if that's the local custom, before entering a taxi. International airports often have taxi dispatchers. Ask them to tell you the typical price of a ride to your destination. Depending on the safety of a town or local area at night, you may want to take a taxi after dark rather than using other local transportation.

Ask whether the hotel or resort where you're staying offers complimentary transportation to and from nearby towns, tourist attractions, local shopping, snorkeling beaches, or other local areas. I encountered one friendly grocery store on a small island that would pick up grocery shoppers at their time-share condos, drive them to the store, and then deliver them back with their load of groceries after shopping.

For those who enjoy a stroll, very often there are shops or restaurants within walking distance of a hotel or resort. For example, I stayed at one resort in Bonaire that was conveniently located within about a two-minute walk of the central shopping area of Kralendijk, the capital of the island.

Bicycles and motor scooters can be very enjoyable ways to see a small island at a leisurely pace. They can provide an interesting afternoon's diversion and sight-seeing, or help provide entertainment on days that you take off from diving.

4

MASKS, FINS, SNORKELS, AND EXPOSURE SUITS

Because scuba diving is a highly technical sport, it's only logical that you'll find a high level of emphasis on equipment. This chapter will discuss various facets of the equipment basic to scuba diving, such as fins and a mask. Chapter 5 focuses on other essential equipment, such as regulators and computers; chapter 7 details accessory equipment that isn't mandatory but makes diving easier and more enjoyable.

By the completion of your open-water training course, you will typically have purchased your own mask, snorkel, and fins. If you haven't yet done so or are considering upgrading your equipment, this chapter provides tips for choosing them and other basic equipment. Reviews of new scuba equipment appear regularly in mass-market newsstand periodicals devoted to diving and are good sources of information about products and their features. Manufacturers' catalogs and Web sites are other good resources to check.

New divers often rent equipment for their first few dives. This saves money while you begin what is an expensive sport. It also allows you to try different brands of equipment to determine what best meets your needs and preferences before you commit to a major outlay of money. There are advantages and disadvantages to renting versus owning your own equipment.

The Rent-Versus-Buy Decision

Purchasing dive equipment is more expensive in the short term than renting, but it provides several advantages, such as always having your gear ready for use, intimate knowledge of the equipment you dive with, and familiarity with its condition. Some of the considerations for renting versus buying are listed in the accompanying chart.

One of the most important considerations is fit. When you purchase your own equipment, you know that it fits correctly and is always available. Renting at a dive shop, particularly at a remote island site, you may find that the equipment available doesn't fit correctly. As an extreme case, if you have special needs—perhaps you require extra-large equipment or are very short—you may find that there's no BC or exposure suit available at the shop that fits. Or you may find that the one size XXL available has just been rented out to someone else.

One point to remember about the cost of equipment is that, even after you've made the initial purchase of your own equipment, there will be some additional, ongoing expenses for maintenance and general upkeep. In particular, regulators should undergo annual maintenance, even if they're seldom used. While not particularly expensive, this annual service adds to the price of the equipment over its lifetime. If you're an infrequent diver, it might make more economic sense to rent a regulator for occasional use than to purchase one.

If you're on a tight budget, one option for expanding your dive equipment inventory is to purchase rental gear instead of new equipment. Many dive shops periodically sell off their rental gear, perhaps every year or so, and replace it with new equipment. Buying used rental equipment, of course, costs less than purchasing it brand new. This equipment will have been used frequently for dive classes and rentals, but should be well maintained and relatively new. If you should purchase used equipment from an individual, such as from a friend upgrading equipment or ceasing to dive, be sure to have it first inspected and serviced by a dive shop to ensure that it's in good working order.

A second way to save money is to look for price reductions on discontinued, demonstration, or inventory close-out equipment. For example, dry suits are often supplied for cold-water diving classes, such as ice diving, and then sold to students afterward at a discount. It's possible to save considerable money by purchasing equipment in this manner. For some equipment, such as wet suits, the fact that it may have been used a few times will not affect its functioning.

Rent or Own: Which One's for You?

Feature	Rent	Purchase
Cost	Lower initial cash outlay, but continues to add up as long as you continue to rent	Higher initial cash outlay, but it's over all at once
Maintenance	Equipment is serviced and maintained by the dive shop	Regulators require annual maintenance, thus increasing the total effective cost over the lifetime of the regulator; BCs should be serviced at two-year intervals; scuba tanks require annual visual inspection and periodic pressure testing
Convenience	Have to pick up and return the rented items to the dive shop for each rental	Always ready for use at home
Equipment condition	Heavy use and previous careless users may mean the equipment isn't in as good a condition as you might like	Condition of the equipment is whatever you want it to be, determined by how well you care for it
Availability	Unusual sizes of equipment, such as exposure suits or BCs, may not be available at the rental site or may be already rented by others	You always know that your equipment is available and ready to use
Fit	Some equipment may not fit as well as you'd like	You have the fit you like all the time
Familiarity	You could be renting unfamiliar equipment, which requires some initial orientation; you may not be as comfortable with the features in an emergency	The more you use your own equipment, the more familiar you'll be with its features and operation, particularly in an emergency

Masks

A dive mask is placed over the nose and eyes while diving to provide clear visibility, because human eyes are intended to operate correctly on land with air in front of them, not water. A mask provides an air interface between the eyes and the underwater environment. Swim goggles should never be worn for scuba diving, because they have no capability for equalizing the pressure inside the goggles, which can lead to eye squeeze.

Diving masks are made in many shapes and sizes, and the one that's right for you is a very individual decision. It's important that your mask fit you correctly; if it's the wrong size or configuration for your face, it will be uncomfortable, it may leak, and it can obstruct your vision.

Some divers prefer a small-volume mask that sits close to the face and has a small residual air volume in front of the eyes. Other divers don't like having the front of the mask close to the face, or prefer a wide viewing angle. These divers may prefer a mask that has a larger front volume, with the lens sitting farther away from the eyes. The corresponding disadvantage of such a mask is that it will hold more air; you may thus have to exert more effort both to clear water from it and to equalize mask pressure. Some people prefer a mask with side windows to reduce any claustrophobic feeling.

You will have learned in your open-water pool classes to clear water from the inside of your mask by tilting it away from your face and simultaneously exhaling into it. This method works easily and effectively. For diver convenience, some masks are available with one-way purge valves built into the skirt to allow clearing of water from inside the mask with a strong exhalation. This offers some convenience, but the valve must be kept clean and free from sand and debris or it may leak small amounts of water into the mask during a dive. Purge valves also tend to wear and require periodic replacement.

Modern masks are constructed with a skirt made from translucent white, or opaque black, silicone rubber to seal to the face. Some divers prefer the translucent silicone, which provides a feeling of light in front of the face. Other divers prefer the black version because they feel that it directs all the light through the front lens. This is an individual preference.

Some older masks use an opaque, black neoprene rubber for the skirt material. Neoprene rubber tends to have a strong, distinctive smell, as opposed to silicone rubber, which doesn't. Neoprene will eventually crack and split after prolonged exposure to sunlight and to many chemicals, such as skin oils; silicone rubber has a higher resistance to cracking and splitting. Finally, neoprene rubber can cause allergic reactions when in contact with the skin of some sensitive individuals.

Vision correction is available in many masks by replacing the clear tempered glass with corrective lenses according to your individual prescription. Corrective lenses may be either standard models available in fixed diopters or custom lenses that also correct for other vision problems, such as astigmatism. For those who require bifocal reading glasses to clearly distinguish fine print, lenses are available for masks in standard, nonprescription bifocal magnifying configurations to aid the older diver in reading gauges and computers. For those who require only a small amount of correction or minimal magnification under water, there are supplementary flexible soft-plastic magnifying lenses that can be placed on the inside of the glass of a mask and peeled off again if you need to change them. Those divers who absolutely need a prescription mask to function underwater may wish to purchase an extra mask so that they aren't incapacitated in case of mask breakage or loss.

Different types of mask strap can be used to hold the mask onto the head, and this style may be a part of your purchase decision. Most straps on new masks are made from translucent silicone rubber. This type of strap stretches and adheres well to the head to hold the mask in place; still, some

If you can't pull your mask about an inch from your face, the strap is too tight.

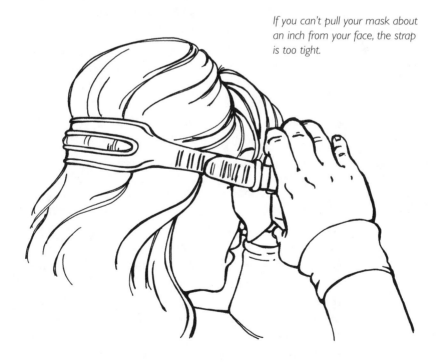

people feel that a silicone strap binds in their hair and is difficult to position easily. A neoprene-and-nylon strap, often called a slap strap, can be used instead and will slide easily over the hair. By the same token, some divers feel it also slides off too easily, perhaps leading to mask loss underwater. Again, it's a matter of personal preference.

Whichever type of mask and strap you prefer, the mask should fit and seal well to your face, and should feel comfortable on your head. The traditional test for mask fit and seal is to place the mask up to your face without putting the strap around your head, inhale gently through your nose, and carefully let go of the mask with your hand. If the mask fits and seals well, the suction of the inhalation should hold the mask in place on your face without your having to hold it with your hand. However, be careful when testing a new mask with this method, because a dive shop may not appreciate it if the mask doesn't seal and falls off onto the floor!

Masks should also be comfortable. For most people this means that the mask should only touch the face around the skirt, and shouldn't press on the bridge of the nose. When a new mask is purchased, it usually has an oily film on the glass left over from manufacturing. This film should be cleaned off before use. Toothpaste or common household scouring powder, applied lightly with a rag or sponge in a swirling motion to the inside and outside glass surfaces, can be used to remove this film.

Dive masks are also available with tinted glass, instead of the usual clear lenses. The color of the tinting compensates for the color shift of light with deeper depths of seawater; as with sunglasses, however, the tinting will also reduce the intensity of the light transmitted to the eye. Tinted lenses are generally suitable for shallow, sunlit diving, but they may reduce the light intensity too much for easy viewing while deep diving, night diving, or diving under cloudy conditions.

Snorkels

Snorkels aren't particularly complicated and come with fewer options than masks, but there are still a few choices to be made. In general, the shorter the snorkel barrel and the larger the diameter of the barrel (the bore), the easier it will be to breathe through it. The bore should be at least ¾ inch in diameter for ease of breathing. But note also that the larger the bore, the more effort will be required to blow water out of the barrel to purge the snorkel. The barrel should be 12 to 14 inches long in order to adequately clear the surface of the water above you, yet still allow easy breathing. Modern snorkels are manufactured with silicone mouthpieces to avoid the taste of the neoprene rubber that was used in older models.

Snorkels are made in various configurations. Basic choices are a fixed J-shape, a fixed L-shape, a contoured shape that looks like the J-shape with an angled barrel at the top, or a snorkel with a flexible, corrugated connection between the barrel and the mouthpiece. When using the J-type, L-type, and contoured type, the mouthpiece is turned away from your mouth when diving to avoid interfering with the regulator in your mouth. You then turn the mouthpiece back to your mouth when you use it as a snorkel on the water's surface. The type of snorkel with the corrugated hose allows the mouthpiece to fall out of the way when you release it from your mouth and use a regulator. You should have seen all these types when you took your open-water training course, and should have tried them at least once in order to make the best selection for you.

Most modern snorkels have a built-in purge valve at the lowest part. Theoretically, when you blow air into the snorkel from your mouth, the water will be purged automatically from the valve. In practice, some of the air blows out the top of the snorkel and a residue of water often stays at the bottom of the J and sloshes back into your mouth. You will have to decide if this type works acceptably for you. I've found that an efficient method to purge water through the purge valve while snorkeling is to reach up and cover the exposed end of the snorkel with my hand before blowing. This action forces all the water out of the purge valve and leaves the snorkel barrel empty.

Some snorkels don't have a purge valve, but are purged by blowing a strong, hard breath of air into the mouthpiece. If you have this type of snorkel, you may have to breathe carefully on your next breath to avoid inhaling any residual water. You may have to purge the snorkel several times to successfully blow all the water out.

Fins and Boots

By the completion of your open-water training, you should have decided on and purchased a pair of fins. Fins are used to increase the efficiency of the diver's forward motion while swimming through the water. Fin swimming is two or three times more efficient than swimming with bare feet; thus you need less effort for the same motion through the water.

Fins are made by many manufacturers in designs that use different types of vents, channels, composite materials, stiffness, and other features to produce different swimming characteristics. There are so many brands and designs of fins that, in most cases, the choice will be a personal one. There are a few generalities, however, that can be discussed.

One factor to consider is that the length of the fin blade will determine the amount of power applied to propel you through the water. Put simply, the larger, longer, and stiffer the fin blade, the more force will be generated to move you through the water. While this is desirable, the disadvantage is that the longer and stiffer fins also require more leg force during use, which directly translates into the amount of energy that you have to put into each fin kick. Thus, in general, men and stronger women will tend to choose fins with longer blades to propel them faster through the water, and smaller women and children, with less strength in their legs, will tend to choose smaller fins that require less effort to kick. In practice, unless you wish to race through the water as fast as possible or require fins with large blades for kicking against heavy currents, the size of the fins won't make much difference for recreational diving. The newer split-blade fins with are reported by some divers to require less effort to move through the water, but others feel they offer less power against underwater currents. Again, a personal decision has to be made based on your type and desired level of diving.

Remember also that the objective of recreational scuba diving isn't necessarily to race through the water as fast as possible, but to enjoy the underwater environment as much as possible. You'll see more of the underwater environment by slowing down and concentrating on the details of what you're swimming over.

There are two major types of fin: full-foot fins and open-heel fins. As the name implies, full-foot fins have a closed foot housing, or shoe, molded into the rear. The fin is then slipped onto the foot like a shoe. As with any shoe, full-foot fins must fit well on your foot. Some divers wear an old pair of socks on their feet with full-foot fins to prevent chafing of the bare skin by the fin pocket. Special dive socks are also made for this purpose.

Open-heel fins, in contrast, do not have an integral shoe, but have a pocket in the rear of the fin for the foot to slip into, with a strap placed around the heel to hold the foot in the pocket. Open-heel fins are usually worn with neoprene dive boots that fit snugly into the fin pocket. Neoprene boots are made out of the same material as wet suits. They usually have solid rubber soles to provide some foot protection against stepping on sharp objects in the water, though some boots don't and are more like neoprene socks. Open-heel fins can be used with bare feet and no boots, but they're more comfortable with boots, which prevent the fins from chafing the feet. Heavy wool socks can also be used with open-foot fins but don't work as well as boots. The straps on the backs of open-heel fins are adjustable and can be used to compensate for differences in the fit of boots to the fins.

One tip if you're purchasing open-heel fins is to purchase them *after* purchasing boots, not the other way around. A fin that fits a particular brand and type of boot may not fit a boot from a different manufacturer, even if the boot size is the same, because boots are not all the same outside size and configuration.

Full-foot fins generally have blades that are smaller and more flexible than the open-foot type. Thus, full-foot fins are better suited for snorkeling and warm-water diving, where foot protection, insulation, and power aren't required. Open-heel fins, with dive boots, are always used for cold-water diving (below about 70 degrees Fahrenheit), because insulation is required on the feet in order to conserve body heat. For extreme cold-water diving, such as ice diving, a dry suit with integrated boots is used, thus requiring the use of open-foot fins.

If you wear neoprene dive boots, it can be difficult to slide in your foot when the boots are dry, since the lining doesn't slide easily on skin. There are two ways to overcome this. One is to put on the boots when they're wet. The water will act as a lubricant and allow the boots to slide more easily onto your feet. The disadvantage is that you'll be sitting around in wet boots until you dive.

Another way to make putting on neoprene boots easier is to wear something slippery, such as nylon, on your feet to allow the boots to slide on more easily. This can be accomplished by wearing a nylon dive skin with attached feet, nylon socks, or a pair of women's ankle-high nylons. Some divers, including men, wear women's full-length panty hose under their dive skin or wet suit because this layer of slippery nylon also makes it easy to pull on neoprene wet suit pants. As well as making it easier to pull on dive boots and wet suits, this thin layer of material adds a small measure of thermal protection by trapping an additional layer of water next to the skin. Wearing a nylon dive skin underneath a wet suit will achieve the same purpose.

Another approach to making boots easier to put on is to purchase boots with zippers in the side or rear, which allows easier entry. Zippered boots are easier to put on and remove, but are slightly colder for the wearer due to heat loss through the zippers. Of course, this isn't a problem in tropical waters.

One further consideration that you may wish to think about when deciding between open-heel or closed-foot fins is their use during snorkeling. Very often when snorkeling in the ocean, you need to walk out into the water for a small distance before putting on your fins, because the water at the shore is too shallow to swim in and you need more depth before lying down in the water. Some snorkeling sites may feature rocks, coral, or eelgrass close to shore to navigate over, or through, before swimming. If you use full-foot fins, you will be walking through this shallow water in your bare feet before putting on your fins. As you do so, it's quite easy to unknowingly step on rocks, coral, seashells, broken glass, fishhooks, bristle worms, and other items that can cut or otherwise injure your feet. Often these hazards will be invisible in eelgrass or buried in the sand. Many snorkelers, therefore, prefer to use open-heel fins with boots instead of closed-foot fins. This way they're wearing dive boots while walking out to deeper water, which helps protect the feet from cuts and other abuse from submerged hazards.

Dive Skins and Wet Suits

Though glamour photographs often show female models diving in bikini swimsuits at resorts in the Caribbean and the South Seas, the reality is that most divers will want some additional thermal insulation to protect them from cool water. Various choices, in order of ascending thermal protection, are a dive skin, a jacket-and-pants wet suit, a Farmer John (or Jane) wet suit, a Farmer John with gloves and dive hood, and a dry suit.

The typical core body (deep internal) temperature of human beings is 98 degrees Fahrenheit, with the skin temperature being about 10 degrees lower. Thus, immersion in water that's less than 88 degrees means body heat will flow out from you into the water. After a period of such heat loss, you'll start to feel cold. Water is an excellent conductor of heat, conducting heat away from the body approximately twenty-five times faster than air. This is why standing in the open air in a T-shirt and swimsuit at 70 degrees is comfortable, but standing fully immersed in 70-degree water feels extremely cold. Wearing only a swimsuit in 80-degree water is the same as standing in a swimsuit in open air of about 40 degrees.

Heat flows quite rapidly from a warm, unprotected body into cooler water as the water moves over the diver's skin and carries away the heat. Thus most divers—particularly on shallower dives, which may involve spending up to an hour in contact with the water—wear something to insulate themselves from this continual heat loss. Divers often also tend to feel colder when making a second or third

> ## $\mathcal{S}$uiting Up
>
> *Most people prefer to wear more than just a swimsuit, even in tropical waters.*
> - *A dive skin, particularly a lined one, provides additional warmth.*
> - *A dive skin provides protection from jellyfish and stinging coral.*
> - *Add a shorty wet suit on top of the dive skin if you get cold easily.*
> - *Add a hood for additional warmth, particularly if it's cold on a night dive.*

dive on the same day, because they have already lost body heat during the first dive.

Even so-called warm-water diving involves temperatures lower than that of the human body. The waters of the Caribbean Sea, for example, may be in the high 80s in summer and in the low 80s in winter. A temperature of 82 degrees Fahrenheit, which is typical for Caribbean winter diving, is approximately 8 to 10 degrees lower than skin temperature, which means you're continually losing heat to the water. Thus, a feeling of cold in the extremities is a sign that you need to leave the water and warm up.

If you start to shiver during a dive, your body is cooling down too rapidly, and heat loss is reaching a critical level. A continued loss of body heat will lead to a lowering of core body temperature and eventually to hypothermia, a situation in which the core body temperature drops so low that continued heat loss will result in death. Shivering consists of a series of involuntary muscular contractions that are initiated when the body is trying to generate heat to offset excessive heat loss through the skin. One of the early signs of approaching hypothermia is continual uncontrollable shivering as the body tries to generate additional heat. The onset of such shivering is a good sign to immediately terminate a dive, exit the water, and regain warmth. Unrecognized hypothermia is one of the common contributing factors in diver deaths.

Most divers find that at least some minimal thermal protection in the form of a dive skin is desirable. A dive skin is a one-piece stretch bodysuit that covers the torso, legs, and arms with a thin layer of Lycra or some similar material that clings to the body. Suits may also be lined with Polartec or fleece for comfort and additional thermal protection. You can choose a front or back zipper for closure—whichever is your personal preference.

The dive skin serves a dual purpose. First, it slows the transfer of heat into the water from the body by retaining a thin layer of warmed water next to the body to act as insulation. The second purpose is that even a thin suit helps to protect the body from minor encounters with underwater objects, such as coral that can abrade the skin or produce cuts and scrapes. As well as mechanical protection from cuts, a dive skin can protect you from undesired animals that sting, such as fire coral, bristle worms, or jellyfish.

An increased level of thermal protection beyond a dive skin is gained by using a wet suit, which adds another layer of insulation to reduce heat loss. Wet suits are typically made from neoprene foam rubber with nylon or Lycra bonded to the outside and a fleece lining on the inside for comfort and ease of dressing. The neoprene is manufactured with a foaming process

that traps tiny bubbles in the rubber material to increase its insulating capabilities. Some people are allergic to neoprene and may break out in a minor
skin rash after wearing it next to the skin. You can avoid this by wearing a
nylon dive skin or T-shirt under the wet suit.

A wet suit is correctly named an exposure suit, but divers loosely call this
garment a wet suit, because the inside of the suit, next to the skin, is wet. The
principle behind its use is that the outer suit material traps a thin layer of
water next to the body but retards circulation of this water in and out of the
suit. Thus, the trapped water warms to skin temperature and adds a further
layer of insulation from the cooler surrounding water. Hence the feeling
when jumping in for the first dive of the day that someone has poured cold
water down your back. That is exactly what has happened as the cooler
water trickles in through the neck of the suit. Then, as this water warms to
skin temperature, its coolness becomes more bearable.

Wet suit thickness depends on the degree of protection required.
Common suit thicknesses are ⅛ inch (3 millimeters) for general use, ¼ inch (6
millimeters) for cooler use, and up to ⅓ inch (9 millimeters) for very cold
water. When deciding on a suitable thickness for diving, be aware that the
material in neoprene wet suits compresses with increasing depth during a
dive. A ¼-inch wet suit can compress by a factor of four at 100 feet to produce an effective thickness of only ¹⁄₁₆ inch compared to its thickness at the
surface. This compression results in a loss of buoyancy and insulating value. The
suit will expand again to its original thickness when you ascend to the surface.

Wet suits are made in different styles and thickness, and come in both
men's and women's shapes. Full wet suits, which are intended primarily for
cold-water diving, consist of either a two-piece suit or a Farmer John (Farmer
Jane for the ladies!) style. The Farmer John/Jane style is so named because the
underneath portion looks like a farmer's bib overall with a chest covering
and straps over the shoulders, rather than a simple pair of pants. Thus, this
style of suit provides an additional layer of protection over the chest when
the jacket is worn.

The two-piece suit, as its name suggests, consists of a wet suit jacket and
pants. Some jackets have a lower portion that covers the buttocks at the
back and the lower abdomen at the front, with a piece at the back that goes
between the legs and fastens with Velcro at the front. This piece, and type
of jacket, is called a beaver tail, since the connecting portion resembles the
triangular-shaped tail of the common beaver. Alternately, the jacket may have
short legs, like a pair of shorts that come partially down the thighs. This style
of jacket is often called a shorty. Either type of jacket is worn over the pants

and gives extra insulation to the lower abdomen and groin area, which is one of the areas of high heat loss on the body's surface. The Farmer John/Jane gives a higher level of thermal protection to the torso, and would typically be worn for diving in very cold water.

There is an old saying among mountain climbers to the effect that, "If you're cold, put on your hat." The same is true of diving. If additional thermal protection is required for diving in cold water, a neoprene dive hood or beanie can be worn on the head. This addition will slow down heat loss considerably. Depending on the circumstances, up to 50 percent of the body's heat loss occurs from the head, because there is a disproportionately large flow of blood through the head and scalp, thus leading to high levels of heat loss by radiation. Adding a layer of thermal insulation to the head and neck in the form of a dive hood will drastically cut such heat loss—by 25 to 50 percent, depending on the surrounding water temperature. For additional insulation, dive hoods are available with an attached vest that fits over the chest. This garment adds a layer of insulation to the upper torso.

A dive hood should fit snugly, but not tightly. If the hood fits too tightly, it may seal itself securely to the side of your head and make it difficult to equalize your ears. A hood that's too tight can also put excessive pressure on the carotid arteries on either side of the neck and cause an unexpected underwater blackout by compressing them, reducing blood flow to the brain.

A dive hood should always be worn in water cooler than 70 degrees Fahrenheit. Insulated dive gloves should also be worn in very cold water, in order to cut heat loss through the hands and fingers and to help make the diving experience more comfortable. Either a mitten-style model or gloves with separate fingers can be worn; the mitten-style is warmer.

The level of thermal protection that provides warmth and comfort varies with the age and physiology of the individual diver, the type of diving being performed, and personal preference. Some folks find that they require a heavy layer of insulation in order to feel warm even in tropical water. Others can dive in comfort without an exposure suit. Older divers, whose circulation has started to slow down, will often be more comfortable with additional layers of protection.

It is certainly no indication of weakness to wear whatever makes you comfortable. If you require a full wet suit to be warm and comfortable in the Caribbean, then that's what you should wear. I have always worn a dive skin and wet suit jacket in the Caribbean in winter. A little ribbing from companions and divemasters is trivial compared to a cold dive with the potential for hypothermia.

Here are some rules of thumb. Most divers in the Caribbean wear a dive skin year-round for minimal protection; in winter many also add a shorty jacket or wet suit top. Note, however, that some divers feel comfortable in summer waters of 82 to 84 degrees Fahrenheit in only a swimsuit and T-shirt. For cooler waters, such as Florida in winter, most divers will wear a wet suit top for comfort. Cold waters, such as the ocean off the coast of California, require a full wet suit at least ¼ inch thick at all times of year and, probably, a dive hood. In general, a dive hood and gloves should be worn if the water temperature is less than 70 degrees.

Beating the Cold: Thermal Protection for Various Dive Conditions

Type of Conditions	Temperature Range	Typical Locations	Typical Exposure Protection Required
Tropical and warm water	80–90° F	Caribbean in summer; Indian Ocean	Dive skin
Cool water	70–80° F	Caribbean in winter; Great Barrier Reef	Dive skin with ³⁄₁₆" or ¼" (4–6mm) wet suit top; or 2–3mm full-length wet suit; or plush fleece-lined dive skin
Cold water	55–70° F	Southern California; many inland lakes, springs, and rivers in summer	Farmer John/Jane ¼" (6mm) exposure suit with jacket, gloves, and hood
Very cold water down to freezing conditions	32–55° F	Northern California coast; British Columbia; Great Lakes; inland and high-altitude lakes in summer; low end of the range is ice diving conditions	Dry suit with thermal underwear

Note that these are only rough guidelines. Personal warmth and comfort will depend on your physical characteristics, metabolism, age, and level of exertion, as well as the length of the dive, depth of the dive, weather conditions, and other personal and environmental conditions.

Diving the northwest coast of the United States, toward Canada, or diving in mountain lakes and springs in the West, requires a Farmer John/Jane with wet suit top as well as a hood and gloves. Very cold diving, such as ice diving or prolonged diving in northern lakes and quarries, requires a dry suit with hood and gloves. Some divers who spend long periods of time in cool waters prefer to wear a dry suit to prevent the continued loss of body heat that occurs with lengthy immersions. I once went lake diving in 35-degree water in just a wet suit with hood and was able to function without problems, but I would have been far more comfortable (and sensible!) in a dry suit.

Dry Suits

The ultimate thermal protection for recreational diving is a dry suit. As the name implies, a dry suit is dry inside. It consists of a full bodysuit made of foamed neoprene rubber or of rubberized fabric, with fully integrated boots and cuffs around the wrists and neck to seal out water. Unlike a wet suit that relies on warming a thin layer of water for insulation between the suit and the diver's skin, a dry suit keeps all the water out and uses an additional thermal undergarment for insulation against cold water. The suit has either an attached or a separate diving suit hood. Dry suits use a low-power inflator and an exhaust valve to add and release air to the inside of the suit.

Diving with a dry suit requires special training for getting in and out of the suit, for buoyancy control, to be able to handle potential emergencies should there be a malfunction of buoyancy or suit valves, or should the suit become flooded. Dive shops in parts of the country that may require dry suits offer in-water training in these techniques.

Marking Equipment

Before going on a dive with other divers, it's wise to mark your equipment with your name or some other type of identifying mark. This may not seem important until you're on a dive boat and realize that two other divers have the same brand and model of fins or mask that you do. It's also surprising how many BCs look the same. It's easier to have your equipment distinctly identified. Marking pens with permanent ink, typically used for laundry, can be used for this purpose. Some markings on plastic, such as on fins, may wear off in seawater and need to be periodically renewed. Special marking pens for dive gear may also be used.

5

BCs, Regulators, Tanks, Weights, and Dive Computers

ask, fins, and a snorkel are considered basic equipment for snorkeling or diving. As well as these fundamental items, however, some other technical items are required for diving. This chapter will discuss BCs, tanks, weights and weight belts, and dive computers.

Buoyancy Compensators

The modern buoyancy compensator (BC), also known as a buoyancy compensating device or buoyancy control device (BCD), has evolved from the personal flotation devices (PFDs) used by early scuba divers to act as emergency flotation devices at the surface. The modern BC is a nylon jacket with a sealed polyethylene bladder inside, used to maintain neutral buoyancy at depth while diving and to assist in creating a controlled ascent by inflating and deflating the bladder from the air tank as required. This is the same principle as that used by fish to achieve neutral buoyancy. Most bony fish have a swim bladder—a soft-walled cavity in their abdomens that is inflated and deflated by adding or removing gas from their bloodstream and is used to achieve the desired buoyancy.

For humans, the BC is also used to provide positive buoyancy for improved flotation and support at the surface. It should be remembered, however, that BCs are not life jackets and should not be used for that purpose.

Modern BCs combine a tank backpack, for securing the tank to the jacket, and an inflatable jacket in one unit. Older separate backpacks and horsecollar PFD units are rarely seen today.

A BC should have a power inflator control. This uses low-pressure air from the first stage of the regulator to inflate the BC. There will also be a method of inflating the jacket orally, in case of an out-of-air situation or a malfunction of the regulator. The power inflator also contains a deflator control button and valve to let air out of the BC to control buoyancy. An emergency dump valve, or rapid exhaust valve, is used to quickly deflate the BC in an emergency.

At one time BCs were equipped with a detonator inflator, which released the contents of a small CO_2 (carbon dioxide gas) cartridge into the BC for instant inflation. These devices have fallen into disfavor because they produce almost instantaneous and complete inflation of the BC, often leading to an out-of-control ascent to the surface. Rapid ascent is dangerous because of the potential for lung rupture and the rapid formation of bubbles that can cause decompression sickness.

The ABCs of BCs

- Most important: Be sure your BC fits comfortably.
- Also be sure that it fits over whatever you wear underneath, such as a bulky wet suit.
- Some people prefer a streamlined design with buckles on the shoulders, while others prefer a full bladder type; get what's comfortable for you.
- Decide whether front buckles or a Vecro band is more comfortable for you.
- Be sure that all the features, such as inflator and pockets, are readily accessible.
- Women's styles may be more comfortable for women than unisex BCs.
- Decide whether you want integrated weights or not.

Another problem is that sealed CO_2 cylinders may not be transported on aircraft, such as when traveling to a dive destination.

In recent years the trend in buoyancy compensators for use in warm water has been to minimize and streamline the jacket design. This is based on the fact that warm-water diving requires less of the BC to be inflated for adequate lift than does cold-water diving. Thus, many BCs intended for warm-water diving eliminate the front part of the inflatable air bladder, placing the inflation chamber primarily at the rear of the BC. The inflatable volume that has been removed is replaced by chest straps and buckles for comfort and ease of entry and exit. Chest straps are adjustable to provide a customized fit. This makes the BC more comfortable to wear, although it also has equivalently less lift than does a jacket style of BC with a full bladder located in front of and behind the chest.

For cold-water diving, it's still preferable to have a BC with a full inflation bladder distributed throughout the jacket. For extreme cold-water diving activities, such as ice diving, the extra lift provided by the full jacket may be critical for safety.

If you regularly wear a wet suit to dive, this will provide some limited padding between the tank backpack and your back. For those who dive without a wet suit, a padded BC may be preferable for comfort.

One BC option to consider is the design of the chest strap. Some divers prefer the standard nylon chest strap with a snap buckle. Others prefer a wide, soft chest cummerbund that fastens with Velcro. Try both styles to determine which one you prefer and which is more comfortable to wear.

Simply making a BC smaller for women may not produce a correct fit for a woman's body. Therefore, some manufacturers make BCs specifically designed to accommodate a woman's torso; these may be more comfortable for women than unisex models. When choosing a BC, try it on with a tank attached. This will give you a good idea of how the chest and shoulder straps will feel while diving.

Regulators

A regulator consists of a combination of two pressure-reduction stages that provide air from the diver's tank at a pressure suitable for breathing underwater. The first, or high-pressure, stage attaches directly to the tank valve and lowers the high pressure of the compressed air in the tank, which is initially about 2,500 to 3,000 pounds per square inch (PSI) at the start of a dive, to a lower, intermediate pressure of about 100 to 140 PSI. The second stage of the regulator, which is attached to the first stage via a flexible rubber hose, provides air to the mouth at the pressure required for breathing.

Modern regulators for recreational diving use a single-hose design, which means there's a single hose between the first and second stages. Double-hose regulators and other designs are sometimes used for specialized diving situations, but are beyond the scope of this book and will not be mentioned further. Technical details on the operation of regulators should have been covered in your open-water training course and so will also not be discussed here.

Regulator first stages use what is called either a balanced or an unbalanced design. Modern regulators almost always use a balanced first-stage valve. Balanced regulators produce a constant output pressure, regardless of the incoming tank pressure. Thus, balanced regulators provide the same ease of breathing at all depths, because the air valve floats inside the regulator housing. Unbalanced regulators are affected by decreasing tank pressure as the air is used, and thus become increasingly difficult to breathe through at greater depths in the water. Still, some divers actually like this apparently negative feature and use it as a safety warning to tell them they're starting to run low on air.

When purchasing a regulator you may also note that it's described as either a diaphragm or a piston design. This terminology refers to the specific design style of the mechanism of the air valve in the first stage. Both types have advantages and disadvantages, but these are really more technical than practical. In modern regulators, both designs should be comparable in performance.

Modern regulator systems also have an auxiliary second-stage regulator attached to the first stage to provide a spare supply of air in case of an emergency. This auxiliary second-stage regulator is called an alternate air source, an octopus regulator, or, most commonly, an octopus. It looks like the normal regulator second stage but is usually colored bright yellow for visibility and has a longer hose so that it can be used to supply air to another diver if an emergency arises.

The regulator first stage usually has several hoses attached, to either high-pressure or low-pressure ports. A high-pressure port supplies air at direct tank pressure; a low-pressure port supplies air at a reduced pressure from the first stage. One low-pressure port and hose goes to the second stage of the regulator to supply air for breathing. One low-pressure port and hose is connected to the octopus as a spare air supply. A third low-pressure hose attaches to the BC and has a manual valve that's used to control inflation and deflation of the BC. If you expect to be diving with a dry suit, be sure there's an additional low-pressure port to attach the dry suit's inflator fitting. The final hose is attached to a high-pressure port, and goes to the dive console to a submersible pressure gauge (SPG), which is used to monitor the amount of air remaining in the tank. Some modern scuba systems use a wireless transmission link to replace the SPG and hose from the tank. A low-power radio transmitter on the tank sends a direct reading of remaining tank pressure to a wireless receiver that is integrated into a wrist-mounted dive computer and displays the tank pressure on the computer screen.

The second stage of the regulator contains a soft silicone mouthpiece that provides air for breathing. This stage is attached to the first by a flexible rubber hose. A purge valve is used to expel water from the breathing chamber with low-pressure air and also to relieve pressure in the second stage and hoses after the tank valve is closed.

When choosing a regulator, it's important to make sure the mouthpiece fits your mouth comfortably and securely. What fits your spouse, dive partner or another diver may not fit you. A mouthpiece that's too big will always feel like it's coming out of your mouth, and can even become dislodged if you're doing a giant-stride entry into the water or by surf conditions. If you like a certain regulator and the mouthpiece doesn't seem to fit well, it can be changed for one that fits better or for a custom-molded mouthpiece.

Some second stages incorporate an adjustment control on the side that allows you to adjust the air flow for varying breathing requirements underwater. This can be used to change the breathing characteristics of the regulator at different depths or when differing amounts of underwater effort are involved during a dive. Some divers like the ability to make this adjustment; others prefer a regulator without this feature so they don't have to be bothered with it.

When purchasing a regulator, look to see if there are protectors on both ends of each hose where it's crimped into the threaded fitting. Hose protectors are vinyl or rubber sleeves used to provide strain relief, since hose cracking and wear occur primarily at the ends. If the hoses don't already have protectors installed in both places, have them installed by a dive shop. This will help make the hoses last longer. The vinyl type of protector is harder to install than the rubber type, but will last longer.

Console and Instruments

The instrument panel or dive console is a rubber housing that contains instrumentation to monitor dive status and safety. Instruments commonly found in the console include a dive computer, a submersible pressure gauge (SPG), a compass, and a mechanical depth gauge. The pressure gauge for determining the air supply remaining in the tank may be found in the console or on the dive computer display for air-integrated models.

In the United States, SPGs read the pressure of the air remaining in the tank directly in pounds per square inch (PSI). When the needle of the gauge reads below 500, it typically enters a warning area marked in red, since that's the lowest pressure recommended for exiting a recreational dive.

In European countries or other countries following the European system of measurements, the dial may be marked in bars, which is the metric measure of pressure. To convert bars to PSI, remember that 1 bar equals 14.5 PSI.

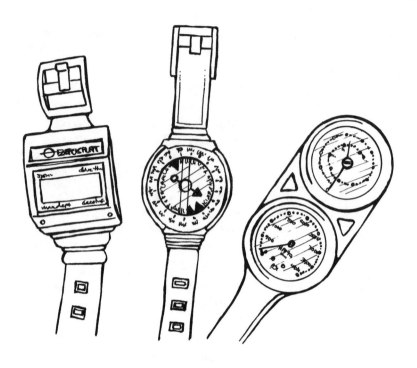

Basic diving instrumentation consists of a computer, a compass, a pressure gauge, and an optional analog depth gauge.

Depending on your mathematical ability, you may be able to multiply bar readings in your head by 15 to get PSI. For example, if a gauge reads 100 bars, a quick approximation is to multiply that figure by 15 for an approximate equivalent of 1,500 PSI. For very rough, in-your-head conversions when underwater, though, a factor of 10 can be used. Thus, a reading of 200 bars is *very* roughly 2,000 PSI. This difference in dial readings isn't actually as much of a problem as you'd think. A large tank, when full, will read about 200 bars, which is approximately 3,000 PSI. Metric gauges also show low-pressure readings in red on their scales, but the warning area starts at 50 bars, or about 750 PSI, instead of 500 PSI.

The console may also contain a thermometer, which isn't an essential piece of dive equipment but does provide helpful information about water temperature. You can use this to plan whether or not to wear a wet suit or add a dive hood and gloves. The thermometer reading may also just provide interesting information about your dive.

Tanks

Depending on the type of diving you do, you may or may not wish to purchase your own air tank. If you live close to water and dive frequently in local areas without airplane travel, you'll probably want your own tank. If your diving experience involves only flying to distant destinations to dive, then you probably won't. This is because tanks are heavy and difficult to transport.

Tanks filled with compressed air cannot be taken on airplanes. If transported on an airplane, a scuba tank must be completely empty and the tank valve either removed or fully open. Because of this, dive shops and resorts supply tanks as part of their dive packages. If you aren't diving with a commercial dive operation that supplies a tank to you, you can rent full tanks at a local dive shop at your destination.

If you decide to purchase your own tank, consult with your local dive shop on the best size and type for your needs. Dive tanks are made from either steel or aluminum (actually an aluminum alloy). The most popular size of tank is either the 71.2-cubic-foot steel tank or the 80-cubic-foot aluminum tank. Larger and smaller models are available. All tanks have a number stamped on the neck, below the valve, to indicate the service pressure of the tank. Double tanks are used for demanding applications, such as cave diving.

Steel tanks are initially more expensive than aluminum tanks, but will last virtually for a lifetime if given proper maintenance. Aluminum tanks are cheaper and more popular, but their potential lifetime has not yet been fully assessed. Metal fatigue due to constant filling and refilling may result in a shorter lifetime than for steel tanks. Both types require regular inspections to ensure safe operating performance. Estimates based on manufacturers' cycle tests place the service life of a metal tank at about 100,000 cycles of fill and refill.

Modern dive tanks use what's called a K-valve, which is a simple faucetlike open-and-shut valve mechanism that provides air directly to the regulator and relies on an attached submersible pressure gauge in the dive console to indicate the amount of air remaining. Older tanks used a J-valve, which contains an additional spring-loaded shutoff valve that's used to preserve a small amount of reserve air in the tank. When the tank is close to empty, the position of the valve is changed and the reserve air is made available to the diver. With the use and popularity of the modern submersible pressure gauge to continually monitor the diver's remaining air supply, this type of valve isn't commonly used.

Note that tanks should never be repainted or refinished with a process that requires heat. This will weaken the tensile strength of aluminum tanks, possibly causing them to explode when refilled. Always consult with the manufacturer before refinishing a tank.

All compressed air tanks require periodic maintenance, consisting of an annual internal visual inspection for corrosion on the inside of the tank, and also a static pressure test at intervals of no more than five years. You should have learned the basics of air tanks and their handling during your open-water training, so no further discussion will be included here.

Weight and Weight Belts

It isn't necessary to have your own weights. Weights and a weight belt are usually supplied in dive packages. Because of this you don't have to carry heavy weights on an airplane as part of your baggage. The exception is if you have unusual requirements, such as using one of the newer BCs with special integrated weights, or if you use lead shot weight in pouches instead of the traditional blocks of lead. In these instances you may have to carry your own weights. Of course, if you do local dives without using a commercial dive operation, you'll need to purchase your own weights and weight belt.

Lead weights are sold by the pound and are inexpensive to purchase. Dive weights are available as blocks of lead in different sizes, typically two through six pounds. To arrive at the total weight that you need, simply mix and match different sizes of weights. More will be said in chapter 6 about the specific amount of weight to be used to correctly achieve neutral buoyancy.

Block lead weights have two slots in them for threading onto a weight belt, though some lighter weights have only one slot and are intended to be spaced evenly around a belt. It's better not to use one or two very heavy weights to make up the total weight required, but instead a larger number of smaller weights. In this manner it's possible to distribute the smaller sizes of weight more evenly around your waist and achieve better balance.

Placing a large weight at the back of your weight belt may be uncomfortable and interfere with the tank or backpack of your BC. To achieve symmetrical balance while diving, don't place different sizes of weight on different sides of the belt. For example, don't use one six-pound weight on one hip and one three-pound weight on the other. This arrangement will unbalance you when you are swimming through the water.

What works quite well is to balance the same size of weight evenly on each hip and put whatever is required to make up the balance at the small of your back. If you need ten pounds of weight, then, rather than use two five-pound weights, it may be more comfortable for you to use a four-pound weight on each hip and a two-pound weight at the back.

The two slots in lead weights are, as noted, used for threading onto the weight belt. One problem with this is that the weights can slide back off if you pick up an unbuckled belt by the buckle. Lead weight is heavy and, if the weight slides off and falls on your (or someone else's) foot, a broken toe can result. To prevent this, use weight clips to hold the weights in place. Another easy method for preventing weights from sliding off the belt is to secure the last weight on the belt when initially threading them: Place the end of the belt through the first slot on the last weight, then make a half turn of the belt before putting the belt through the second slot. When pulled tight, this half turn will lock the last weight firmly in place and prevent all of them from sliding off again if the belt is unbuckled.

Some divers find BCs with integrated weights easier and more comfortable to use; be aware, however, that there are other considerations involved in the use of integrated-weight BCs. For example, integrated weights may not be as easy to ditch in an emergency as a weight belt. Also, if you take off your BC in the water and hand it up to someone on a boat, a BC with integrated weights is much harder for both diver and boat captain to handle. And if you have to take your BC off underwater to correct a problem, such as a tank that has slipped out of its band, you are left without weights and may have more difficulty in staying down while working. Your best bet is to look around and consult with your local dive shop to see what's most comfortable for you.

Very large divers may also prefer to distribute some of their weight as ankle weights, in order to keep their feet down in the water when swimming. Achieving the correct ankle weighting may require some experimentation, since too much will leave you swimming in an upright position, which is awkward and inefficient.

Divers with apple-shaped figures—a waist larger than their hips—may have trouble with their weight belts slipping off when they enter the water. To avoid this you can use weights that are integrated into your BC and thus are stabilized against slipping off during entry into the water. Another approach is to use a weight harness—a device that looks like a pair of men's trouser suspenders and fastens with clips to a regular weight belt. The harness will transfer some of the weight from your hips to your shoulders, improving the belt's stability.

Even thought weight belts are usually supplied as part of a dive with a commercial dive operation, I recommend that you invest in your own. The cost is only a few dollars, and having your own belt may save some problems. This recommendation is based on two factors. One is that the selection of rental weight belts on a dive boat may or may not fit you very well.

What's available may be too long or too short. If you have your own weight belt, you can adjust it to your own size and know that it will fit you correctly each time.

A weight belt should have no more than 6 to 8 inches of excess belt protruding beyond the buckle, with weights attached and when fastened in place around your waist, in order to prevent tangling in a BC or other equipment. Weight belts are made from heavy nylon webbing and can be shortened by cutting the end to the desired length with scissors or a sharp knife. Then heat the end of the belt, where it was just cut, with a candle, cigarette lighter, or other open flame to melt and seal the end to prevent it from fraying.

The other, and more important, reason to own your own weight belt is that rental weight belts or belts supplied on a dive boat receive a lot of use, which may lead to excessive wear of the latching mechanism and possible unlatching during diving. For example, I once used a rental weight belt that was so worn, it unbuckled underwater and fell off, starting me on an unexpected and very rapid ascent to the surface. Luckily I was close to the anchor chain and able to grab it to hold myself down while I retrieved the belt from the bottom. I've also seen several well-used weight belts that unbuckled themselves when the divers made a giant stride into the water from a boat.

Dive Computers

A dive computer is considered an essential piece of equipment for modern scuba diving, due to its ease of use and the ability to continually and accurately calculate remaining bottom time during multilevel dives. Traditional dive tables can be, and are, still used for calculating bottom time, but the convenience, added safety, and ease of use of dive computers has all but relegated the tables to the classroom.

Another reason for using a computer is that, in the unlikely event that you should undergo decompression sickness, the computer will have stored a log of your preceding dives; this will assist the attending physician in the course of treatment. The computer doesn't forget or confuse maximum depths or bottom times, as a diver might when under stress.

An important point to make is that a dive computer is an instrument to be used by one individual. If one diver of a dive pair uses a computer, the other diver must also use a dive computer, because computers base the amount of remaining bottom time on the individual diver's profile in the water. Most recreational dives are multilevel, and a computer can only track the ascents and descents for one individual. If two individuals try to base their dive on a single computer, the diver without the computer runs the risk of decompression sickness because of differences in dive profile between the divers that will occur during the dive.

If you should borrow or rent a computer, it must be completely clear of any ongoing calculations from the previous diver. Depending on the brand of computer, twenty-four hours is usually a safe recovery period.

The most obvious difference among dive computers is that some are worn on the diver's wrist, while others are mounted in the instrument console. The choice between a wrist-mounted and a console-mounted

*D*ive Computer 101

- *Choose a dive computer that fits your style of diving: conservative or aggressive.*
- *Decide whether you prefer a console- or wrist-mounted style.*
- *Be sure you know how to operate the computer.*
- *Be sure you know what the readouts mean.*
- *Each diver in a team must have his or her own computer.*
- *Never use someone else's computer unless it's been cleared of the previous diver's information.*
- *Replace the computer battery at intervals recommended by the manufacturer.*
- *Be sure you can work dive tables in case of computer failure.*

computer is a matter of personal preference. The trend in recent years has been toward mounting all dive monitoring equipment, such as computer, SPG, and compass, in the dive console, thus providing a single compact monitoring unit. Some divers prefer the convenience of having all their monitoring equipment mounted in the console. Others prefer their computer and compass on their wrist so that a quick glance provides their dive profile and direction at the same time.

Wrist computers may be relatively large, with large easy-to-read displays, or as small as a wristwatch, with the resulting displays in a very compact size. Whichever style you prefer, be sure that the numbers on the display screen can be easily read and positively identified. Some wrist computers, and console computers that display large amounts of information, may have very small numbers that are hard to read and decipher.

Some computers display only essential information, such as current depth, maximum depth of the dive, remaining no-decompression time and ascent rate. Others display additional information that's nice to know—water temperature and nitrogen-loading profile, for instance—but isn't essential for a safe dive. Choose a style of display that you can easily read and provides all the information you want to know during a dive.

Some computers activate automatically when you enter the water; you don't have to remember to activate them. Some require manual activation, usually via a pushbutton. Choose whichever type is comfortable for you.

Beyond the obvious physical aspects, the major difference among dive computers lies in their internal algorithm, or mathematical method of computing the dive profile and allowable residual bottom time. Some brands use very conservative algorithms that lean toward safety when computing allowable bottom time. Other computers take a more aggressive approach to computing nitrogen absorption and release by the body tissues, thus creating a more liberal allowance for bottom time during the dive. These differences result either in a shorter dive that has an increased safety margin or in a longer time at the bottom and the acceptance of a higher risk of decompression sickness. Before purchasing a computer, you may wish to consult one of the articles published periodically in recreational dive magazines that compare brands and their calculations, from aggressive to conservative.

One of the most important facts to remember is that, as with the calculations made from manual dive tables, *no computer can guarantee complete freedom from decompression sickness.*

If you plan to dive at altitudes other than sea level, another consideration in choosing a computer may be whether or not it incorporates compensations for high-altitude diving. Be aware that the term *high-altitude diving* doesn't necessarily refer to diving in lakes high in the mountains of Colorado or California. *High altitude* in scuba diving is generally defined as anything over 1,000 feet in elevation. This elevation may be quite easily reached in some Midwestern states. Of course, if you plan to dive in the Rockies, the mountains of the Northwest, or the mountain lakes of California, it's essential that your computer adjust dive profiles according to the altitude.

A feature that many divers want is the ability to download data from their dive computer to a personal computer (PC) after the dive trip. This requires making a connection between the computer and the PC through a cable, typically one that plugs into a communication (COM) port on the computer. The PC uses special software that interrogates the dive computer through this link, downloads data, displays the results on the PC screen, and logs the dive profile and other information by individual dive. For the ultimate in convenience, some dive computers have the capacity to store underwater profiles for an entire dive trip with no need to use a handwritten logbook. This data is downloaded at home after the trip and added to the diver's logbook.

To eliminate the need for a separate hose to connect the pressure gauge in the console to the tank, some computers use a wireless link from a tank-mounted transmitter to send air pressure status to the computer. These are referred to as air-integrated computers. This configuration reduces clutter by eliminating one hose and displays air pressure readings on the computer for monitoring convenience.

Even if you're using a dive computer, it's a wise precaution to take along a copy of the standard dive tables that you used in your dive class in case the computer fails or for any reason the need arises to manually compute a safe dive. For convenience, a simple rule to remember about the tables—for the *first* dive only—is that no-decompression depth plus maximum bottom time below 60 feet approximately equals 120. Thus, the tables will indicate a no-decompression dive of 60 feet for a maximum of 60 minutes, 80 feet for 40 minutes, or 100 feet for 20 minutes. This is only a rough guide, but could be helpful if your computer fails during a dive or you need the information in an emergency and don't have a copy of the dive tables. This seat-of-the-pants rule doesn't apply to repetitive dives, because it doesn't account for residual nitrogen time (RNT) from previous dives. Many divers performing deep dives carry a copy of the dive tables during the dive and add a backup mechanical depth gauge in their console in case of computer failure.

One feature to think about when purchasing a computer is whether or not the display is lighted for night diving. Without a lighted display, you must direct a dive light at the face of the computer to monitor dive depth and time. To avoid this inconvenience during night diving, some computers have a backlit screen option that glows and displays the required information without additional light. If you don't have a computer that lights up, you can use a luminescent analog depth gauge or pressure gauge as a backup.

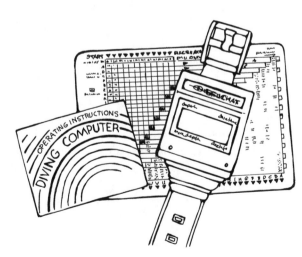

Read and understand your computer instruction book thoroughly, but also know how to work the dive tables.

*D*ive Computer 102

A final consideration is that U.S. computers display dive depth in feet, while European versions read in meters. This consideration is mostly of concern to those who may rent a computer at a distant dive site, such as in Australia, and unexpectedly find that they're dealing with a different depth scale. The conversion is quite easy to do in your head, since 1 meter approximately equals 3 feet. Actually 1 meter is closer to 3.3 feet (3.281 feet, to be precise), but a quick conversion of multiplying meters by 3 to get feet is close enough for most purposes. More to the point, though, not having a familiar depth scale may be a concern for those who aren't fast at conversion math or who don't want the stress of making mental conversions while underwater.

There are two possible solutions. The first is to always dive with your own equipment. While this may mean potential inconvenience in travel, you're always dealing with gauges and a computer that are familiar. The second solution is to have a computer that's separate from your dive console—for example, one configured in a wrist mount. This way you can take along your dive computer, since it's small, but don't have to take your regulator and other gauges.

There may still be situations where it's more convenient to rent equipment. As an example, a businessperson on a two-week trip may manage to squeeze in a day of diving on a day off. He or she might not want to carry around a regulator for two weeks for a single day of diving; renting is probably easier.

Of course, it should go without saying that whatever your brand and model of computer, you should read the manual and understand how it operates. I returned from one dive to find one member of my dive group, who had come back to the boat early, sitting on deck puzzling over his computer display. Though not a novice, he had just purchased a new computer, but hadn't bothered before diving to fully understand how it worked and what the displays meant. He'd come up early because he thought he had a decompression violation and was trying to recall his dive profile from the computer. He never did figure it out. Luckily, he wasn't bent—but he did spend the rest of the day and evening reading the computer manual instead of diving!

6

WEIGHTING AND
BUOYANCY

I n addition to compass and navigation skills, a subject that usually doesn't receive enough attention during initial dive training is the skills related to proper weighting and achieving neutral buoyancy. Thus I've chosen to place this topic in a short chapter by itself.

Weighting

You and your equipment should not be dragging along the bottom. This can damage underwater life such as corals and sponges, or may damage your equipment.

Buoyancy control and achieving neutral buoyancy under the water are thus important scuba diving skills. Positive buoyancy means an object will rise in the water; negative buoyancy means it will sink. Neutral buoyancy means the object will stay level at a constant depth in the water, neither rising nor sinking. One of the skills taught in scuba training is to how to use inflation and deflation of the BC to fine-tune for neutral buoyancy at different depths.

As you will have learned in your open-water dive course, proper buoyancy control starts with the correct weighting. If you don't wear enough weight, you'll be unable to descend. If you carry too much, you'll either be rapidly pulled down under the surface of the water, perhaps faster than you wish to be, or drag on the bottom during the dive. Another symptom of excess weight is that you'll be constantly inflating and deflating your BC during the dive to try to maintain neutral buoyancy underwater.

Watch Your Weight

- Novice divers tend to overweight; remove weight if you constantly sink or are inflating your BC.
- Add a little weight if you start wearing a wet suit.
- Weighting may decrease over a week's time as you become more relaxed diving.
- Decide whether you want integrated weights. Remember, you can't ditch integrated weights as easily as a weight belt in an emergency.
- Record your weighting in your logbook so you know how much to wear next time.

The goal of achieving and maintaining neutral buoyancy is to become proficient at managing ascent, descent, and swimming underwater without constantly adding and venting air from the BC. Most experienced divers rarely inflate or deflate a BC during a dive, only inflating it at the surface in adverse conditions or diving emergencies. These divers are able to maintain neutral buoyancy and swimming conditions without relying on their BC. Small buoyancy changes are made by controlling breathing. A deep breath increases buoyancy by increasing the volume of the chest, thus allowing you to rise in the water. A deep exhalation will decrease buoyancy and let you sink. Remember, however, never to hold your breath at any time. Breathe continuously underwater to avoid the lung expansion injuries that can occur if you hold your breath.

The principle of weighting for scuba diving is quite simple. The additional weight required on a weight belt by a diver to achieve neutral buoyancy is the difference between the weight of the water displaced by the diver's body and equipment, when fully immersed in the water, and the combined weight of the diver and his equipment before entering the water. This complicated-sounding statement will be made clearer by an example. Assume that a particular diver displaces 3 cubic feet of seawater when fully immersed in the ocean. Each cubic foot of seawater weighs 64 pounds; thus 3 cubic feet of water will weigh 192 pounds. In order to achieve neutral buoyancy, the weight of this particular diver's body and equipment, plus weight belt, must be 192 pounds. If this diver and equipment, without weight belt, weighs 180 pounds, then an additional 12 pounds of weight on the weight belt will provide neutral buoyancy in seawater.

A cubic foot of salt water weighs 64.0 pounds. For the same calculations involving fresh water, a cubic foot of water weighs 62.4 pounds. The heavier weight of seawater is due to its dissolved salts.

Weighting is very simple in theory, but becomes a little more complicated in practice. The first difficulty is to determine how much water a diver displaces. In practice, divers don't try to find out, but add and subtract weight experimentally in the water until neutral buoyancy is achieved. The general rule of thumb to determine initial weighting requirements is to use about 10 percent of your body weight, if you're wearing a full wet suit. Beginning divers usually require more weight than experienced divers, because they tend to be nervous and breathe faster and shallower. This creates a larger displacement of water, because of greater inflation of the lungs; additional weight is needed to offset this effect. As divers gain more experience and learn to control their breathing, the requirement for the additional weight decreases.

A second complication is that weight requirements vary with different dive conditions. Buoyancy is affected by wearing a wet suit, and by the thickness of the wet suit material. A full Farmer John/Jane model with jacket will produce about fifteen pounds of additional buoyancy, as compared to wearing no wet suit. This additional amount of lift will decrease as the suit ages and starts to become permanently thinner, due to repeated compression–expansion cycles.

Neoprene wet suit material compresses as you descend through the water, due to increasing surrounding pressure on the suit. Compression can be to as much as 25 percent of the original surface thickness at a depth of 100 feet. A wet suit that is ¼ inch thick at the surface may compress to only ¹⁄₁₆ inch at 100 feet. Thus, the volume of water that you displace at the surface will decrease with increasing depth during the dive. As a result, buoyancy will decrease with increasing water depth when wearing a neoprene wet suit, and weighting requirements will change.

When you ascend, wet suit material will start to expand again to its original thickness at the surface. As it does so, a greater volume of seawater will be displaced, and buoyancy will increase. You compensate for this increase by slowly venting air from your BC to reduce overall buoyancy. If performed properly, this results in a slow, stable ascent to the surface.

Since it isn't practical to change to different weights at different depths, inflating and deflating the BC to displace a higher or lower volume of water is used to compensate for these changes. To offset a loss of buoyancy with increasing depth when wearing a wet suit, you can add a slight amount of air to the BC during descent, in order to increase volume and maintain neutral buoyancy at all depths.

Novice divers will find that their weighting requirements change as they gain experience. This may also happen to more experienced divers who dive infrequently, such as those who take a single one-week dive vacation each year. As the week goes on, they may find that they can use less weight. The common situation in both these cases is that the divers are hyperventilating as they start to dive. Then, as they become more comfortable in the water, breathing slows down and becomes more regular, thus reducing the need for additional weight to overcome the added buoyancy.

Buoyancy will also change depending on the type of tank used for a particular dive. And it will change from the beginning to the end of a dive, due to consumption of the air in your tank. Steel and aluminum tanks in the 80-cubic-foot size weigh about thirty to thirty-five pounds when empty and out of the water. In the water steel tanks are several pounds negatively buoyant and will sink; aluminum tanks are several pounds positively buoyant and will float. Thus, changing from steel to aluminum tanks will mean adding anywhere from five to eight pounds of weight to offset the difference in tank buoyancy.

Another factor involved in correct weighting under different dive conditions is making an adjustment for the type of water encountered. I've mentioned that salt water weighs 64.0 pounds per cubic foot; fresh water, 62.4 pounds per cubic foot. Thus, salt water is 1.6 pounds heavier per cubic foot, or approximately 2.5 percent denser, than fresh water. Consequently, salt water will produce more buoyancy for the same displacement than fresh water. Because seawater is more buoyant than fresh water, you'll generally require less weight when diving in fresh water. As a rule of thumb for quick calculations, the amount of weight to be removed when changing from salt to fresh water is roughly 3 percent of the combined weight of the diver, equipment, and weights (3 percent is easier to calculate quickly in your head than 2.5 percent). For example, if you and your equipment weigh 180 pounds—plus an additional 12 pounds of weight for diving in seawater, for a total of 192 pounds—then in fresh water, remove 3 percent of the total, or about 6 pounds, when wearing the same exposure suit.

On very shallow observation dives, such as Stingray City on Grand Cayman (15 feet) or Cod Hole on the Great Barrier Reef (20 feet), add about 20 percent extra weight to your normal weighting so that you can stay comfortably on the bottom without constantly floating upward.

When making minor adjustments in weighting due to a change from one type of water to the other, or when diving in different conditions or with different equipment, be sure to record the weighting you use in your diving logbook for future reference.

Neutral Buoyancy

The goal of correct weighting is to achieve neutral buoyancy underwater. You will have learned the basic technique to achieve correct weighting during open-water dive training. Be sure to experiment with this until it's correct. Otherwise you'll spend all your time on a dive fighting buoyancy problems, alternately dropping to the bottom and rising uncontrollably toward the surface. Neutral buoyancy should be achieved without having to constantly inflate and deflate your BC.

Most instructors teach beginning divers to achieve neutral buoyancy while floating at the water's surface. The goal of this exercise is to carry just enough weight on your weight belt to float at eye level while holding a normal breath with no air in your BC. When you exhale, you should sink below the surface. When you inhale, you should rise back to eye level at the surface again.

Make a buoyancy check in the water, such as at the dock, before going out on a boat. It's easier to figure out the correct weighting in calm water by a dock

*B*uoyed Up

- *Aim for neutral buoyancy—neither sinking nor floating.*
- *Buoyancy will be affected at different depths when wearing a wet suit.*
- *Buoyancy is greater in seawater than in fresh; thus you'll need a little more weight in the ocean.*
- *Buoyancy will be affected to some degree by tank size and material.*
- *Check for neutral buoyancy at the surface before trying to dive.*

or in a lagoon than rising and falling in the ocean while the rest of the group is champing at the bit to dive. Fine-tuning of weighting during a dive is acceptable, but doing a buoyancy check before jumping into the ocean will at least allow you to be close.

One technique for adjusting initial weighting while in the water is to put all the expected weight on your weight belt, except for a couple of pounds. If you don't know how much weight you'll need, start with about 10 percent of your body weight. Carry a few remaining weights in your BC pocket. In this manner, you can hand this extra weight from your pocket to someone on the dock or boat to decrease your weight slightly if you need to fine-tune your buoyancy. Similarly, if you're slightly underweighted, have someone hand you small weights and put them into your pocket until you have achieved the correct buoyancy. Then, after you exit the water, reassemble the weights on your belt to the correct amount.

Other divemasters teach that neutral buoyancy should be achieved at 10 or 15 feet under the surface, often with a nearly empty tank with only 500 PSI or so of air left in it. Achieving neutral buoyancy at this depth helps offset the initial effects of compression of the wet suit, for wet suit divers, when under the water. Since this compression will result in an increase in negative buoyancy, this causes you to sink. More importantly, achieving neutral buoyancy at 15 feet with an empty tank will make it easier for you to make a safety stop at the end of a dive. Being neutrally buoyant during the safety stop is much

The Weighting Game

- *You should be neutrally buoyant at the surface if you're weighted correctly.*
- *Put an extra weight in your BC pocket for quick buoyancy adjustments.*
- *Add a couple of extra pounds of weight if you're diving in seawater rather than fresh.*
- *Add about 20 percent more weight on very shallow observation dives (10 to 20 feet) if you need to stay solidly on the bottom.*

easier than having to struggle to stay at the constant safety-stop depth.

The principle of achieving neutral buoyancy at 10 feet is the same as achieving neutral buoyancy at the surface, except of course that the target level for neutral buoyancy is 10 feet down. Thus, you adjust your weight belt to float motionless in the water while at a depth of 10 feet, rising when inhaling and sinking when exhaling. This method is a little more difficult to accomplish, because the weighting adjustment is made underwater. It's more often used by people who've been diving for a long enough period of time to be very comfortable there.

After practice, many divers who routinely wear wet suits weight themselves to be neutrally buoyant at the deeper depths where they commonly dive, such as at 40 or 60 feet. With experience, these divers don't have to add or release air from their BC to adjust their buoyancy as they descend to the depth at which they wish to dive. This should only be attempted after learning to be neutrally buoyant at the surface.

If you commonly wear a wet suit and wish to try this, first become comfortable with the correct weighting at the surface. Then subtract a slight amount of weight to compensate for wet suit compression at the deeper depths. The amount of weight you remove will depend on the amount of weight you use initially and the type of wet suit you have. Usually a pound or two is appropriate.

The disadvantage of this method is that you may be slightly positively buoyant at the surface and can have difficulty descending for the first few feet until the wet suit compresses to offset this. You can overcome this by kicking downward using a headfirst descent, until excess buoyancy is overcome. Of course, if you don't wear an exposure suit while diving, then changing depth will not affect buoyancy and correct weighting at the surface will be suitable for all depths.

If you have achieved neutral buoyancy for a long period of time while diving, but find that your buoyancy has unexpectedly changed from one dive to another or are having trouble initially descending in the water, make sure all the air is out of your BC. Some divemasters automatically put a little air into your BC on the boat while setting up your gear. Alternately, be sure that there wasn't some air remaining in your BC after the last dive, or that the heat of the sun hasn't expanded any air remaining in your BC and partially inflated it. A third possible cause is that water has leaked into your BC during a preceding dive and needs to be dumped out to return to neutral buoyancy.

CO_2 Inflators

If your BC has an emergency CO_2 inflator, it should only be activated at the surface to provide positive buoyancy under emergency conditions. If a CO_2 inflator is activated underwater, either intentionally or accidentally, it will result in immediate and complete inflation of the BC. This will lead to an uncontrolled ascent to the surface, with the associated danger of lung expansion injury. Most modern divers remove the CO_2 cylinder from their BCs, if they have one, and don't use it. If you prefer to keep a CO_2 cylinder attached to your BC when you dive, be aware that gas cylinders, which include small CO_2 cylinders, may not be transported on airplanes, because of the danger of explosion or rupture of the cylinder at the reduced pressures during flight.

7

DIVE EQUIPMENT ACCESSORIES

E quipment is fundamental to diving. Discussion of essential equipment items required by all divers was the subject of chapters 4 and 5. In addition to the basic equipment, such as fins, mask, and regulator, many dive-related items aren't essential to diving but will make it easier and more enjoyable. These items are usually added to your dive equipment collection as you progress in your diving skills and enter new areas of diving through training.

Gear Bags

A useful and inexpensive first accessory to take on a dive trip is a roll-up gear bag. The bag may be solid, such as a waterproof canvas or nylon tote, duffel, or carry bag, or it may be constructed from a porous mesh material to allow water to drain out of it when carrying wet gear.

A mesh duffel bag is a useful way to carry dive gear—such as BC, fins, and regulator—around the dive site or between your car or hotel room and the dive boat or shore dive site. When staying at a dive hotel or resort, the dive shop will often supply a mesh gear bag for each diver during his or her stay. The bags are numbered and are used to identify the equipment to be loaded onto a particular boat for a particular diver.

Still, I've seen several instances of resorts that were very full running short of gear bags. As a result, some unfortunate guests (including me on one occasion!) had to carry bits and pieces of gear around by hand until another guest left and there was an extra bag available. Some resorts don't supply

Double-Bagging It

You should have two kinds of equipment bag:
- A soft- or hard-sided dive bag to hold and protect all your equipment while traveling.
- A soft, roll-up mesh bag to carry equipment to and from the dive boat or dive site.

gear bags at all. To guard against this possibility, it's easy to roll up a mesh bag and stuff it into a corner of your suitcase. Having your own bag is also convenient for carrying dive gear to and from the dive boat or shop on your first and last days, either before you get a bag or after you've turned it back in.

A mesh bag can also be very convenient for carrying equipment for snorkeling, or taking gear to an off-resort dive site. A large duffel bag that uses two loop handles on top for carrying can be used as a temporary backpack by putting an arm through each loop. This can be a useful and convenient way to carry equipment when using a bicycle or scooter to go to a dive or snorkeling site.

A multipurpose item for carrying wet gear, and other uses during dive travel, is a common trash sack. Large, heavy-duty plastic trash sacks, such as those used around the garden, are ideal for carrying clothes and equipment, and can be used for packing wet items in a bag or suitcase when you come home. This allows you to pack a swimsuit still wet from a last-minute swim in the ocean without soaking everything else in the suitcase. Large trash sacks are also commonly used by folks who do a lot of beach or shore diving. The sacks can be spread out on the beach like a blanket to protect dive gear and clothing from sand and dirt during equipment setup and disassembly. A clean work area is advisable for protecting regulators against sand entering important parts.

Dive Watches

With the advent of modern dive computers, many divers no longer use a dive watch underwater for timing their dive; still, a dive watch is often easier to use for timing safety stops than a computer, and thus makes a useful beginner's accessory. Though there's something to be said for the psychological freedom of not wearing a watch while on a dive vacation, you don't want to be late for the dive boat or for dinner!

For those who prefer to keep track of their day, there are many styles and types of dive watch to choose from. Some divers prefer digital readouts, whereas others like a watch with conventional hour and minute hands. Some dive watches not only display the time but also incorporate specific dive-related features, such as a depth gauge or water temperature indicator. Dive computers are also available in watch-sized units that have all the features expected from a watch, plus those of a larger, conventional dive computer. One consideration for the purchase or use of any of the units with digital displays is to be sure that you can read all the displays. Watch-sized dive computers that display large amounts of information sometimes feature numbers so small that they can be difficult to read.

Also, be sure the dive watch you choose is indeed waterproof. Actually, no watch is totally waterproof; it's rated rather by its degree of water resistance. Watches useful for scuba diving will have a rating such as "water resistant to 600 feet/200 meters." Even though recreational divers don't go to these extreme depths, some of the watches rated for lesser depths—say, 150 feet—may not consistently withstand the water pressures created during recreational diving and, as a consequence, may leak water into the housing.

This apparent inconsistency in water resistance versus depth rating comes about because watch housings are rated as water resistant for static pressure, which is an application of water pressure with the watch held motionless during the test. Higher pressures may be generated on the housing if the watch moves through the water during a dive. This is called dynamic pressure, and it results in a higher pressure on the watch than the static pressure to which the watch housing is rated. Thus, if the static pressure rating of the watch housing isn't high enough, the watch seal may leak while in use underwater.

Another factor in water resistance is that underwater operation of the control buttons on a watch, such as to change the function of the display, may produce leakage around the seal of the button if the watch isn't rated at a depth high enough for scuba diving. Be aware that some watches rated for lesser depths may leak if the control buttons are pushed while underwater. Water-resistant watches with low depth ratings may still be suitable for other uses, such as during swimming at the surface or snorkeling, in swimming pools, or while showering.

Octopus Holders

Some divers place their octopus into a pocket of their BC and then close the pocket so it won't fall out. This isn't a good practice, because it also means that the octopus may not be easily visible or available if you or your dive partner needs to use it quickly in an emergency.

Therefore, an inexpensive, but very useful, dive safety accessory is an octopus holder that fastens to your BC. This is a plastic holder or clip that holds your octopus in a fixed position on your BC. It's usually made from soft

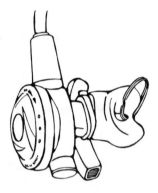

An octopus holder is used to hold the octopus out of the way, but leaves it readily accessible for emergency use.

plastic and shaped either like the regulator mouthpiece for a snug fit, or perhaps like a ball. It may also be in the form of a clip that fastens to your BC. An octopus holder is usually made from one of the easily visible fluorescent safety colors, such as orange or lime green, so that it's readily apparent to a diver swimming toward you.

An octopus holder serves two purposes. First, it prevents the octopus from dangling beneath you in the water and dragging either in the sand or across a coralhead as you swim. If the octopus drags in the sand it may become clogged, or sand grains may enter the mechanism and cause the octopus to free-flow. The holder keeps the octopus close to your body, thus preventing damage to both the reef and the octopus. An octopus holder also prevents possible entanglement of the octopus hose (which is usually longer than the hose on the primary regulator) around your legs or BC.

The second purpose for an octopus holder is to keep the octopus in a known and stable position on the body where it can be easily reached by you or your dive partner, if it's needed quickly in an emergency. Many divers attach their octopus holder to a strap or clip in the middle of the BC at chest height. This places the octopus out of the way of entanglement, but keeps it in a convenient location for you or another diver, if it's needed. A quick pull on the octopus and it's freed for use.

Compasses

Basic compass work and direction finding usually forms one element of introductory scuba courses—but the purchase of a compass is often glossed over as an option that you may wish to make later. I have strong opinions that a compass should always be part of a basic dive outfit and that one should be purchased and used by divers of all skill levels. If you're swimming toward a dive goal—whether it's a buried anchor, a swim-through, or a particular coralhead—it's easy to misjudge the direction of swim slightly and totally miss your goal. Also, when swimming back after a dive, it's easy to miss your dive boat or shore entry point if the visibility is poor. Knowing the direction of the dive boat at all times also provides a feeling of security and comfort.

Some divers argue that a compass isn't necessary because it's difficult to become totally lost while diving. Indeed, it is rare that divers, except those on a drift dive, swim more than a couple of hundred yards from the dive boat; except in extremely choppy weather, you'll be able to easily spot the dive boat from the surface. Still, I'd argue that you should take a compass with you on every dive, even if you think you may not need it. It's easy to lose sight of a boat in murky conditions, and knowing the direction of the boat underwater will give you a sense of security. Also, having to ascend one or more times to the surface to locate the boat or point of dive entry is an inconvenience, may violate decompression rules, and wastes air and effort.

Proper compass technique is best developed in class and through practice. For simple out-and-back boat or shore diving, however, the technique is really quite simple. Before you enter the water, line up the lubber line (reference line) of your compass in the direction that you wish to go. On a boat, this will typically be the direction that starts you swimming into the current. From the stern of the boat this will be the direction of the bow, though you should check underwater to verify that the underwater current is the same as the surface current. When you're underwater, follow the compass heading that you made on land or on the boat.

When you've completed the first part of your dive—usually when your total air supply is about one-third consumed—reverse the compass bezel (the rotating part with the degrees marked) by 180 degrees (a half turn),

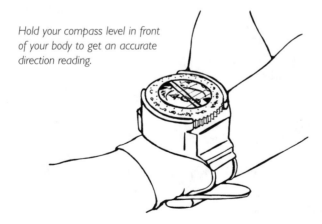

Hold your compass level in front of your body to get an accurate direction reading.

turn around, and follow the compass heading back to the boat. While swimming back, keep watching for the anchor line, or look overhead for the boat, so that you don't swim past it.

If you lose your sense of direction while diving in the ocean, the accepted practice is to ascend slowly to the surface, then orient your compass and bearings on the direction of the boat or the dive entry point on shore, and swim toward it.

The fundamental use of a compass is covered in basic and advanced open-water scuba classes. Once you grasp the basic principles adequately, then practice is all you need to achieve familiarity and proficiency with navigation and direction finding. If the introductory classes don't provide you with enough comfort in using a compass, then classes in navigation are available as specialty courses.

Dive Lights

A dive light is mandatory for night diving; however, it can also be used during daylight hours. When diving walls and reefs, it's often desirable to be able to bring additional light to holes and crevices that are in shadows under overhangs. These holes are typically locations where lobsters and crabs hide during the day. A bright flashlight will allow you to see them clearly when in the darkness of a hole in the reef. A dive light can also be useful in conditions of poor visibility or to illuminate the inside of wrecks.

Console instruments, such as an SPG or analog depth gauge, usually have luminous faces. To activate their luminous properties for night diving, hold your dive light directly over the console and shine it on the dials for a minute or so. The dials should glow for some period of time after the light is removed. When the luminosity fades, reapply the light, or apply it for a longer period of time to maintain the glow for longer. Alternately, simply shine the dive light at the dial to read it in the dark.

Dive lights are also fun to use on shore at night. Walking out on a dock or walking along the shoreline at night and shining a light into the water will allow you to see sea life, such as lobsters, octopi, rays, and fish, that come into the shallows to feed in the evening.

*L*ight Show

• A dive light used during the day will reveal the true colors of corals and fish.
• In daytime a dive light can be used to look under ledges and in crevices.
• Some divers attach a chemical or electronic light stick to a valuable video or dive camera on a night dive. If the camera is dropped, the attached light makes it easier to find.

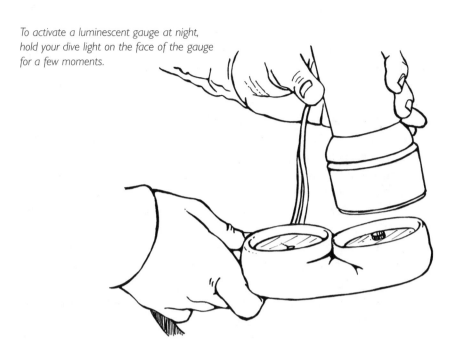

A good rule of thumb is to buy the brightest light that you can afford and can conveniently carry underwater. At night you'll need a bright light underwater to be able to see clearly. During the day a bright light allows you to see farther into crevices and cracks in reefs. One consideration is that some of the very powerful dive lights can only be operated underwater, because they use ambient water for cooling to prevent overheating and failure of the bulb. If you purchase a very powerful light and plan to also use it on land, check to be sure that it doesn't require water cooling. Dive lights should always have a wrist strap or a lanyard, so that they won't fall to the bottom or become lost, if dropped.

Perversely, a very powerful light may be less effective in murky water than a less powerful light. The backscatter of light due to reflection of the beam by particles suspended in the water may reduce the effectiveness of a very powerful light.

For night diving it's also a good idea to carry a backup light. This needn't be as large and powerful as your primary light, but should be of sufficient lighting capability to carry you through the dive if your primary light fails. A small secondary light that can be carried in the pocket of a BC or snapped to a D-ring somewhere on your BC is suitable. It's also a good practice to stay close to your dive partner during night dives, in case your primary light fails.

You can often dive at night with your light turned off, even though this statement sounds contradictory to the previous paragraphs. If you're diving from a boat, the captain may lower a location light into the water that provides enough visibility to see clearly. In a group of divers, the reflected glow from their dive lights may be enough to allow you to see clearly without your own light being turned on. If the moon is out, enough light may filter down from the surface to dive without a light.

If you wish, you can also turn your dive light off and on underwater as you need to use it. Still, if you choose not to use a light when diving at night, always take your flashlight with you and hold it in your hand ready for immediate use, if circumstances dictate. If you are uneasy underwater at night without a light, then keep it turned on at all times.

Before diving at night with a nonrechargeable light, it's a good rule of thumb to always replace its batteries. The cost of a new set of batteries is minimal compared to the other costs associated with diving and the risk of having the light fail partway through a dive. Using new batteries for each dive will ensure that you have a strong light when starting the dive and that it will last for the maximum amount of time. Of course if you have a rechargeable light, be sure it's been fully charged before the dive.

Rechargeable batteries have a high initial cost but can be economical over time if you use your light frequently. Remember that they don't last forever. Most nickel-cadmium rechargeable batteries will have to be replaced after a year or two of use, because the useful service life of the cells decreases after multiple charge–discharge cycles.

One disadvantage of nickel-cadmium rechargeable batteries is that they tend to operate at full power, or almost full power, and then suddenly fail totally when the charge is exhausted. The light produced by replaceable batteries will die away more gradually, thus giving some warning of failure. For this reason it's preferable to power backup lights with alkaline batteries.

The longest and brightest output from lights with disposable batteries will be obtained by using alkaline batteries. So-called standard cells or heavy-duty cells (both are carbon-zinc type) won't last as long, and the light output will quickly become dimmer and more yellow in color as the batteries discharge.

Before a night dive, or at least before a trip that may include a night dive, it's a good idea to clean the O-ring seal (or O-rings, if there's more than one) in a dive light and lubricate it lightly with silicone grease. One grain of sand in the wrong place on the O-ring can cause the housing to flood with water. If a light does flood underwater, disassemble it immediately after the dive and flush the inside well with fresh water. Dry thoroughly. Discard any batteries that have been exposed to water.

It's also wise to bring along a spare bulb for your particular light on a dive trip, in case you can't find a spare where you're staying. The cost of carrying a spare bulb is inconsequential compared to the nuisance of looking for a new bulb just before a dive. Carry one or two spare sets of new batteries for your light, too: You'll have them at hand if you need them, and they're probably less expensive if purchased at home before a trip than in a small island dive shop. If you replace batteries while on a trip, it's environmentally friendly to take the used batteries home with you, because many small islands don't have suitable facilities for disposing of old batteries.

The type of bulb you use will determine the amount of lighting power available—but the brighter the light, the shorter the battery lifetime. Conventional tungsten-filament flashlight bulbs are the least expensive and are considered the "standard" bulb. Krypton flashlight bulbs will provide a brighter, whiter light, at the expense of somewhat shorter battery life. Halogen bulbs are very bright, providing about three to four times the lighting power of tungsten-filament bulbs, but they tend to drain batteries much faster, typically in about half the time. Modern high-intensity xenon lamps can provide extremely bright light with reasonable battery life. These issues can only be addressed in general statements, of course, because brightness and battery life are highly dependent on the specific bulb and battery combination.

When replacing high-intensity light bulbs, such xenon or krypton types, do not allow your fingers to directly contact the glass of the bulb. Handle the bulb indirectly with a facial tissue or gloves. If you do touch the glass directly, wipe the fingerprints off right away. Residues of skin oil from the fingers on the glass of these types of bulbs may cause high-intensity bulbs to smoke, or can cause the glass to crack, melt, or otherwise fail prematurely.

Shore diving at night requires additional lights as well as training in specialized light techniques, such as placement of shore lights, the use of strobe lights above and below water as markers, and various other safety procedures. These techniques are more detailed than space here allows. Performing your first few night shore dives with other experienced shore divers is a good idea.

Other Lighting Devices

Other lighting devices may be useful for you. Small dive lights are available to attach to your mask strap, so that the light points in the direction you're looking.

A similar setup features lamps mounted on a headband for underwater use. They have the convenience of hands-free use, and point the beam of the light in the direction you're looking. Since these lights are small and low powered, they're typically used only for illuminating slates and underwater gauges.

An optional lighting device for night diving is the disposable light stick, also generically called a cyalume stick. This is a plastic cylinder about ½ inch in diameter and 4 to 6 inches long; it contains separated chemicals that are mixed to activate the light just prior to a dive. The purpose of a light stick is to create a chemically fueled glow for an entire dive, indicating the location of divers to those both underwater and on the surface. Once activated, these sticks last for five or six hours, and are then thrown away. The plastic housing of the stick is usually bent or struck on a hard surface to break the internal separator and mix the chemicals.

Light sticks are available in various colors, such as red, green, and blue. Different colors are sometimes used to separate and identify multiple dive groups in the water at the same time.

Light sticks are commonly fastened to a diver's tank by a rigid tab that protrudes from the base of a stick's plastic housing. This plastic tab is placed underneath the yoke screw that holds the primary stage of the regulator to the tank valve. In this way an activated light stick is easily visible to other divers behind the one wearing it. It often isn't visible to a diver in front, however, because the stick is hidden behind the wearer's head. To overcome this, some divers tape the light stick to the top of their snorkel, where it's higher than their head and thus visible to divers approaching the wearer from any angle. Attachment devices, commonly a modified snorkel keeper or a special plastic clip, are available to fasten a light stick to your snorkel.

Alternately, some divers fasten the light stick to their equipment with a rubber band so that it can be detached, if necessary, during a dive. In an emergency, if a primary light fails during a night dive, a cyalume stick will provide enough light to read gauges and a computer without having to abort the dive. If your night vision is good, a light stick will also produce enough light to navigate safely back to the boat or shore.

Instead of using a chemical light stick, there are also small, low-powered red, green, or white electronic lights that can be attached to your tank yoke or snorkel to indicate your presence in the water on a night dive. These lights are either incandescent or electronic light-emitting-diode (LED) lamps that are illuminated for the duration of the dive. Some of them flash, and others give off steady illumination. Flashing lamps attract more attention but are also more irritating to other divers.

You may or may not be required to use a light stick or other indicator device during a night dive. Some divemasters and dive operations insist that every diver use a light stick during a night dive. Other dive operators consider light sticks optional, and some don't use them at all. One negative aspect to using them is that more and more used light sticks are washing up on shore, producing nondegradable plastic trash on the beaches. So if you use one, be sure you bring it back with you and dispose of it properly.

Some divers attach a chemical or electronic light stick to a valuable video or dive camera on a night dive. If the camera is dropped, the attached light makes it easier to find on the bottom.

Dive Knives

Most women consider knives, especially big dive knives, to be a "guy thing." To some extent this is probably true; still, knives do have a useful place in diving. Recognize that a dive knife is not intended to be a weapon or used for underwater defense. The primary use for a knife is for cutting—for example, cutting underwater hazards that might entangle a diver, such as fishing line, netting, or kelp. Additional uses are to pry, poke, dig, and pound. Prying and pounding should be performed with care so that the cutting edge of the knife is not damaged. A knife can also be used as a crude measuring device if the length is known.

Some divers feel no need to carry a dive knife. Like policemen and their guns, most divers will never have an occasion to draw their knife. However, like a policeman and his gun, if you ever need your knife in a difficult situation, such as becoming entangled in fishing line, it may literally be a lifesaver. Thus a knife is useful, but may not ever be needed on dives in calm conditions in the open ocean.

It isn't necessary to have a large knife, but you do need a sharp one. If you have to cut through something in an emergency, you want a knife that cuts well. If the primary purpose of the knife is for cutting rope or netting, a serrated edge will cut more effectively—but this type of edge is also harder to sharpen than a knife with a flat edge.

Though the blade should be sharp, a dive knife doesn't necessarily need a sharp point. If the primary purpose is to poke and pry, it's actually a disadvantage to have a sharp point on the end. Many dive knives are flat at the end with a blunt tip that resembles the blade of a large screwdriver. Some dive knives have a metal butt cap at the top of the handle to bang on the side of a tank underwater as a method of attracting a dive partner's attention.

Dive knives are generally manufactured from a high-quality chromium stainless steel. It's important to note that this doesn't necessarily prevent a dive knife from rusting. Many novice divers have been appalled when their shiny new knife starts to show some discoloration spots of reddish rust after their first dives in the ocean. This shouldn't be a concern. High-quality steel dive knives contain a high percentage of carbon in order to harden the steel so that it will hold a sharp cutting edge. This carbon content may cause the knife to show some rust spots if it's immersed in seawater and then isn't thoroughly rinsed and dried after use. In fact, if a dive knife *doesn't* show minor rust under these conditions, it's a good indication that it's not the type of stainless steel that will hold a good, sharp edge.

To remove any light rust discoloration, rub the rust spot with steel wool and then rinse clean. Following this, rub a light coating of silicone grease on the stainless steel to help avoid such discoloration in the future. Some dive knives are made from titanium alloys; these don't rust and combine good strength with light weight.

A dive knife is commonly strapped in a sheath on the inside of the lower leg, just above the top of the dive boot. In this position it's stored out of the way, but can be easily and quickly reached for use in an emergency. Knives are occasionally worn on the forearm or upper arm for ease of reach. Small knives may be carried in the pocket of a BC.

*P*rotecting Our Fragile Reefs

- Be neutrally buoyant and don't let anything touch the reef.
- Use an octopus holder and hold up your gauges to prevent them from dragging on the reef.
- If you have to touch the reef, use only a single finger.
- Don't wear reef gloves; the temptation to touch things may be too great.
- Be careful with your fins; don't kick the reef—or other divers!

Reef Gloves

Reef gloves are lightweight gloves worn to protect the hands. The use of reef gloves while diving is controversial. The argument for wearing them is that they provide protection for the hands—for example, so that a diver won't be cut or stung when diving around coral. The argument for not wearing them is that gloves can encourage touching coral and other marine life. Many dive operators don't allow divers to wear reef gloves while diving, in order to avoid the temptation of touching things underwater.

Touching many undersea organisms will damage or even kill them. For example, touching a live coral reef while wearing gloves will kill some of the

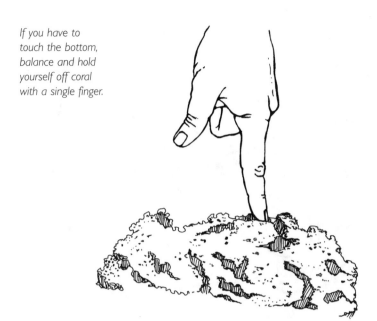

If you have to touch the bottom, balance and hold yourself off coral with a single finger.

coral polyps. Also, touching fish while wearing gloves will injure them. The bodies of fishes are covered with a protective film of mucus. Touching or stroking fish with gloves will scrape off part of this protective coating, thus leaving that area of the fish's skin open to infection or disease. This situation would be similar to a human having outer portions of the skin abraded away, leaving the lower layers of flesh open to invasion by bacteria or other germs.

Signaling and Communication Devices

Communication equipment is a catchall term that includes visual devices, such as underwater dive slates, and audible devices, such as tank bangers, rattles, and whistles.

The most common method for communicating underwater is with a dive slate. This is a thin, flat piece of white plastic, somewhat like a miniature office whiteboard, with an attached lead pencil. Dive slates are available in different sizes and shapes. Small ones mount on the back of a dive console or on your wrist. Larger slates are clipped to your BC with a short lanyard and hang by your side during a dive, until needed. Messages are written on slates underwater with a common lead pencil, and then the writing is erased after the dive so that the slate is ready for reuse during the next dive.

Dive slates are a convenient way to communicate with your dive partner or another diver while underwater. After you attract your partner's attention,

Writing on a dive slate with a pencil is a convenient way to communicate underwater.

you can write a message on the slate and show it to your partner. Alternately, you may wish to write notes for yourself, such as the name of the dive site, your times in and out of the water, dive depth, what you saw on a dive, and other details that you may want to record in your dive logbook when you finish the day's dives.

After use, there are several ways to erase lead pencil writing from a dive slate. A conventional rubber pencil eraser may be used. There are also special cleaners that remove the writing. One of the easiest, and cheapest, methods is to use common toothpaste to wipe off the writing. Squeeze a small amount of toothpaste onto the writing surface of the slate and rub it around either with your finger or with a facial tissue. The mildly abrasive powder in the toothpaste will scour off the writing. Then rinse the slate clean with running water. Household scouring powder may also be used for the same purpose.

Another way to communicate underwater is with sign language. During dive training you will have learned some of the basic signals divers use to communicate underwater. Important ones to know are the common hand signs for low-on-air, out-of-air, the okay signs with the hand and with the arm, ascend-to-the-surface, and stop-there. There are also many others that may be reviewed in your dive manual. If you're diving with a new partner, it's important that you both review at least these basic signs, and make sure that you both use the same sign to mean the same thing.

A dive slate and sign language are useful for visual communication under-water. Before using them, however, it's often necessary to attract another diver's attention. You may also wish to call your dive partner's attention to something interesting, so that you can share the underwater world together. A common way of attracting attention underwater is to make a noise with a tank banger or underwater rattle.

A tank banger is a device made from surgical rubber tubing, with an attached plastic ball, that's stretched around the bottom portion of your tank. To attract attention, you pull the ball away from the tank and then release it to allow it to rebound and hit the tank. Repeat this several times, if neces-sary. The action of the ball banging on the metal tank will make enough noise to attract another diver's attention. Though a tank banger is effective and inexpensive, there are two disadvantages to its use. One is that it's awkward to reach up behind you to the tank to use the banger. Also, dive boat crews don't always see that you have a banger on the bottom of your tank when they change tanks between dives, and it may get lost in the shuffle. In prac-tice, not many divers use them.

Another type of tank banger is a metal device attached by a lanyard to your BC. When you need to attract your buddy's attention, you retrieve the metal object, reach up behind you, and bang it on your tank. This type is also somewhat awkward to use, since you have to reach behind you to bang on the side of the tank.

Rather than specialized banging devices for underwater communication, some divers use the haft of their knife to bang on the side or bottom of their tank. As noted, many models of dive knife have a metal butt cap on the top of the handle for this purpose. One caution when using this method is to remember that you'll be flailing away behind you with an unsheathed knife, or perhaps even holding on to the blade while banging on the tank. Be care-ful not to cut yourself, your BC, or a nearby diver while doing this, since dive knives are very sharp!

A different, but similar, type of attention-getting device is an underwater rattle. This is a closed, cylindrical housing that contains ball bearings or other metal parts that move against each other inside. To attract attention, you shake the tube back and forth to produce a clacking or rattling sound. This type of device can be conveniently hung with a clip and lanyard on your wrist or on a D-ring on the front of your BC, where it's readily accessible for use.

After some trial and error, you may be able to attract a diver's attention underwater by simply banging one fist sharply into the palm of the other hand. The sound this produces isn't very loud underwater and may become

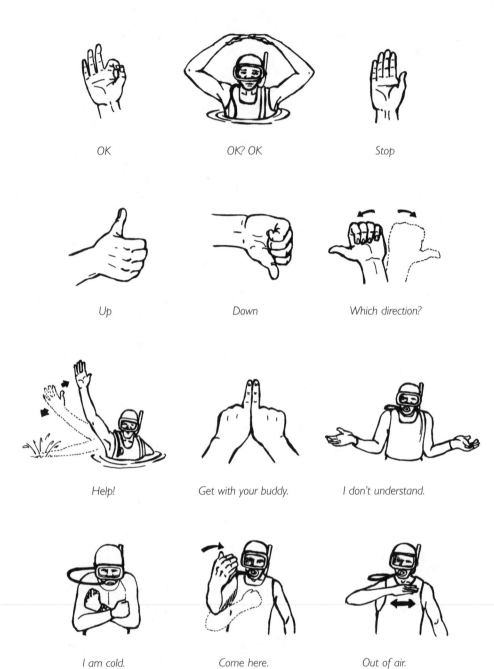

Common hand signals for underwater communication.

lost in other underwater noises, but it's something to try if you don't have a tank banger or other signaling device.

A useful audible communication device for attracting attention on the surface is a whistle. A small plastic whistle is often attached when you purchase a BC. If you're trying to attract attention on the surface, blow the whistle in groups of three times to indicate an emergency situation. More powerful whistles are also available as accessories from dive shops. Whistles can be especially useful for attracting attention on the surface in rough seas.

Other underwater audible attention-getting devices are available. There are air-operated devices that use air from your tank to create a noise underwater, typically a low-pitched buzzing or quacking noise. These devices attach between your low-pressure inflator hose and the BC inflator valve. The effective radius of the sound from these devices underwater is on the order of 10 to 25 feet. Similar air-operated devices are available for use as a loud alarm horn on the surface for signaling, instead of a whistle. These will produce a penetrating blast of sound to attract a dive boat or signal for help. If you use one of these two types of signaling device, be sure to get the correct one for your purpose. Underwater signaling horns are typically not intended or efficient for surface use and vice versa, since sound does not transfer well between air and water.

A common way of signaling other divers during night dives is to shine the beam of your light where their light is shining, and then move it rapidly up and down, or from side to side. Moving the beam in a circle is sometimes used for the okay signal. Don't flash your light in a diver's eyes to attract attention; this will be annoying and will destroy his or her night vision.

Occasionally a dive boat crew needs to attract the attention of divers in the water. Typically this is used to recall divers to the boat in case of an emergency. Common methods range from activating an underwater siren to banging hard on a tank underneath the boat.

Voice Communication Devices

One of the difficulties with trying to speak underwater is that you have a regulator in your mouth. If you've ever tried talking above water with your regulator in your mouth, you'll appreciate the difficulty of speaking words, let alone being understood, in the underwater environment. To overcome this there are several types of devices that allow voice communication underwater. This equipment basically involves a full-face mask with an integrated second-stage regulator. The regulator is mounted on the mask to create an air space in front of the face, so that the regulator doesn't have to be kept in the mouth to breathe. With an air space and no regulator in your mouth, you can talk normally underwater. The voice is picked up by a microphone and then transmitted through the water to an accompanying transceiver unit worn by another diver. These devices aren't commonly found among recreational divers because they're expensive and cumbersome, thus I won't discuss them further here.

Miscellaneous Accessories

As well as whistles and air horns to signal audibly on the surface if you need help, or to attract the attention of the dive boat, visual safety devices are also available. One is a collapsible plastic tube made of polyethylene, sealed at one end, that's inflated at the surface like a balloon and stands up in the air to attract attention. When inflated, the tube is 6 to 10 feet long and several inches in diameter. These tubes are known as safety tubes or safety sausages. The inflated tube is typically blaze orange or bright red in color in order to maximize visibility and attract attention quickly. When these devices aren't being used, they're rolled up to a very small size and stowed in a BC pocket. The safety sausage is a useful safety item to take along when drift diving, in case you become separated from your boat or dive companions.

F lag Day

- *Always tow a surface float with a dive flag on it when shore diving.*
- *Always tow a surface float when snorkeling in an area that has boat traffic or around a harbor, channel, or pier.*
- *Flags can be rented from a dive shop or often borrowed from the resort where you're staying.*

To use a safety sausage, place your octopus regulator in the open end of the tube and depress the purge button to inflate the tube. Then remove the octopus, twist the end of the tube and hold it shut, and pull the end of the tube you're holding about 6 inches below the water's surface. This will cause the tube to stand upright above the water.

Though the safety sausage is typically used during daylight hours, it can also be used at night. In this case the sausage is inflated and used as described above, with the additional step that the end of the tube is twisted closed over the end of an activated dive light, which lights up the interior of the sausage and makes it visible in the dark.

Another accessory that you may want to take underwater is an identification guide for fish. These guides contain pictures of common fish and their names laminated into a thin waterproof plastic sheet, somewhat like a dive slate. If you're interested in fish, being able to identify them underwater when you see them can add to your diving enjoyment—much more so than trying to remember them all after you return to the surface. These guides are commonly available in dive shops and are quite inexpensive.

If you don't dive with a commercial operation, you'll need a dive flag to display over the dive site to warn boaters that there are divers underwater. Snorkelers in an area with a high volume of boat traffic should also tow a dive flag for safety. Flags are available with various flotation devices and may be towed behind the diver or anchored for display over a dive site. Incidentally, don't tie the flag to yourself or to your equipment. Hold the line in your hand in case you have to release it quickly. Regardless of boating regulations, do not assume that all boaters will respect, or even understand, the meaning of a dive flag.

If you're diving for lobster or fishing underwater, you'll need to check with local authorities for the appropriate seasons, licenses, catch limitations, and other laws that apply to these activities.

Alternate Air Sources

An item that's not essential but is very useful in an emergency is a redundant air source. Every diver has an octopus regulator for emergency use, either by the diver in case of primary regulator failure or by another diver if his or her air supply fails. An alternate source of emergency air is a small additional air tank attached to the side of the main tank. This is called a pony bottle. Pony bottles are available in sizes ranging from 6 to 40 cubic feet of air. Some spare air systems are small enough (less than 3 cubic feet capacity) that they can be strapped to the leg or attached to the diver's BC for fast access in an emergency. Depending on the size

*I*t's All in the Accessories

- Accessories are purchased as you gain experience and needn't all be obtained at once.
- The first accessory should be a good dive watch; this is useful—among other things—for timing safety stops.
- A helpful accessory is a mesh gear bag to carry all your equipment.
- Another important accessory is a dive compass and the knowledge to use it.
- A dive slate lets you make notes to yourself or communicate with your partner.
- Dive lights are often supplied for night diving or may be rented for an occasional dive.
- Light sticks are often supplied for night dives.
- Safety sausages may be required for drift dives, but may be supplied by the boat.
- Guys love dive knives, but they may not be necessary and are hardly ever used.
- Reef gloves are often forbidden and may not be necessary.

and style of the alternate air source, the tank may have an independent regulator and hose, or may have a self-contained regulator built into the bottle. Secondary emergency air supplies don't contain large volumes of additional air, but do allow a diver to breathe the contents for long enough to reach the surface in the event of catastrophic failure of the primary air supply or regulator.

Good dive operators will commonly also hang an emergency second-stage regulator under the boat at a depth of 15 feet, the usual safety-stop depth. This regulator may be used as an emergency air supply by a diver who runs out of air during a safety stop. It should only be used in an emergency, however. With careful planning and attention to air supply, running out of air underwater should never happen.

8

PREDIVE
EQUIPMENT CHECKS

I f the title of this chapter reminds you of astronauts sitting on the launching pad making safety checks for outer space, know that simple equipment checks before diving are not a big deal. Checking equipment on shore or on a boat before a dive can be done in about five minutes and is well worth this small investment of time to avoid potential problem situations during a dive. After some practice, these checks will become second nature to you before you enter the water. Though most of what's discussed in this chapter relates to safety, there are also a few items that relate to good diving practices.

It's important to repeat that scuba diving is a serious sport. To reiterate the golden rule of scuba diving: All divers are solely responsible for their own life and safety. Part of the meaning of this statement is that each diver is responsible for being sure that each piece of equipment that goes underwater is functioning in a correct and safe manner. Therefore, each time you enter the water, it's important to first perform a safety check to be sure all your dive equipment is set up in the correct manner, in the way that you want, and that all aspects of the equipment are correct. Remember also, though, that most diving accidents are due to human error, rather than to equipment failure, which emphasizes the importance of safe diving practices.

When boat diving or at a resort, the dive crew will typically put your BC and regulator onto a fresh tank and set up your equipment for the dive. As conscientious as divemasters are, however, they can still make an error on an occasional setup. It's good diving practice to double-check your equipment

Predive Check at a Glance

This list may not be all-inclusive. There may also be other items that are specific to your individual equipment that should be checked.

Make sure that your:

- BC is at the appropriate height on the tank, not too high or low.
- Tank strap is tight, so that the tank doesn't slip out of the BC underwater.
- Mouthpieces aren't torn.
- Mouthpieces are firmly and correctly attached to the regulators.
- Primary regulator is breathing smoothly and easily.
- Octopus is breathing smoothly and easily.
- Octopus is where you want it to be (for instance, in a holder in the middle of the BC).
- Octopus is firmly and correctly attached to the octopus holder.
- Hose screw fittings are tight.
- Power BC inflator fitting is tight and connected correctly.
- BC inflates and deflates correctly.
- Tank pressure is correct.
- Mechanical depth gauge is reading 0, and maximum depth needle is reset to 0.
- Tank valve is turned off and system depressurized after checks.

setup yourself to make sure that everything is the way you want it. For example, I was on one boat trip where the crew members were excellent, but they made a mistake on the setup of my equipment. When I double-checked before going into the water, I found that the slide connector on my BC inflation hose had been pushed onto the valve fitting on the BC, but not far enough to lock correctly. When I tugged lightly on the hose, the hose slid off the connector. If I had tried to inflate my BC underwater, either the hose would have blown off the fitting or the BC would have failed to inflate. A few minutes spent performing a simple equipment check avoided what could have been a potentially hazardous situation underwater.

To point out the importance of a simple visual gear check, here's another example from real life. I was on a boat with a group of divers for a two-tank dive trip. After the first dive, the divers came back on board and the crew set up their gear for the next dive. While one of the divers was checking her primary regulator and purging it, the mouthpiece fell off. It turned out that the regulator had been serviced just before the trip, and the dive shop that did the maintenance had forgotten to replace the tie strap that should have held the mouthpiece on to the regulator. Her octopus was also missing the strap. Had the mouthpiece on the primary regulator come off underwater during the dive, the regulator would have fallen loose. This diver could then have had serious problems, particularly since the mouthpiece on the octopus also would have fallen off when the octopus was pulled from its holder. My point is that a quick visual check of the regulator would have revealed the missing tie strap before the dive, and the problem could have been corrected before leaving the dock.

Consider also that the dive crew may not know if you have some personal preference for exactly how you want your equipment set up. For example, I had a safety strap on a BC that was supposed to be placed around the tank valve; if the tank were to slip out of the tank band on the BC, this strap around the valve would prevent the tank from slipping down through the band and dragging the regulator out of my mouth. Apparently the crew didn't realize what this strap was for and left it hanging loose. The reason I wanted this strap around the tank valve was that the tank had slipped out underwater once before, and I wanted to prevent any reoccurrence.

Get Ready, Get Set: Gear Setup

- *Always check the tank pressure to be sure you have a full tank.*
- *Make sure the tank strap is tight enough to prevent slippage.*
- *Make sure the inflator hose is attached correctly and securely.*
- *Make sure that your computer is turned on and set for the correct air mixture.*

Mask and Snorkel

Before entering the water, you need to prepare your mask for defogging. This is one of the basic skills learned in training classes. There are several options for preventing fogging. Many divers use one of the commercial defogging solutions that are rubbed onto the inside of the glass to keep it free from fog. Some work well and some don't. Find a brand that works well for you and stick with it. One successful homemade formula mix is a solution of one part of baby shampoo to seven parts of water. Apply and then rinse the mask in water. Do not, however, rinse your mask in one of the tanks reserved for rinsing cameras. Camera owners do not have a sense of humor about this and can become quite vocal about shampoo or defogging agent in the camera rinse tank.

The alternate tried-and-true method is to use saliva. Simply spit onto the dry glass on the inside of the mask, rub the saliva around to thoroughly cover the glass, then gently rinse off the excess in water. Seawater can be used for a rinse, and dipping the mask off the back of the boat is quick and easy. Again, don't rinse off the mask in the barrel of fresh water reserved for underwater camera use. Also don't use a pressure spray to rinse off the glass; this will be strong enough to also wash off the residue of saliva.

For the best results, defogging solution or saliva should be applied before each dive. Whichever defogger you apply, commercial or saliva, you need to do it while the glass of the mask is still dry. Once the glass is wet, neither solution will adhere evenly or securely.

While defogging your mask, make a quick inspection of the mask strap and the rubber skirt to make sure neither is torn or damaged. Be sure the snorkel keeper is attached properly to the mask strap and isn't broken or otherwise damaged. Make sure the snorkel barrel isn't cracked and that all the parts are present, particularly the silicone mouthpiece, which can become easily detached on some models. The snorkel attaches to the strap on the left side when wearing your mask.

Masks and snorkels can be easily damaged if carried in a dive bag along with weights and items with sharp edges. Make sure that the glass on the mask isn't scratched, cracked, or broken. Cracks or scratches on glass, which look like the score marks that a glass shop makes when cutting glass, can break and implode underwater with the added pressure.

One mistake that beginning divers often make is to adjust the head strap of a mask so that it's extremely tight, in an effort to seal out all water leaks. The strap should be snug and hold the mask firmly in place, but it shouldn't be so tight that it causes a red welt around your face after a dive. You should be able to pull your mask about an inch away from your face with relative ease when it's in place; if you can't, the strap is too tight. When diving, the mask should be held to the face by water pressure, not by the tightness of the strap. All masks will leak to some extent underwater and usually will have to be cleared of water during a dive. A very tight mask actually makes it more difficult to clear the mask of water, because more force is required to loosen the mask from your face to purge it.

*L*oosen Up

Most novice divers wear their face mask too tight. A mask should not leave a red ring on your face after diving. To ensure the right fit, you should be able to pull your mask about an inch away from your face.

If your mask seems to leak excessively but doesn't appear to have any cracks or damage around the skirt, then perhaps it simply isn't a good fit for your face. Unfortunately for those with beards and mustaches, hair under the skirt of a mask may cause slight leakage. Likewise be sure to clear any hair from your head that may have become trapped under the skirt of the mask when putting it on, or leakage can occur underwater.

Fins

Fins are very simple to check. Basically, make sure that the straps aren't torn. Be sure that the buckles are firmly secured at the correct adjustment point for your feet and are in the fully closed position. If someone else has used your fins or they've been used with different boots, be sure that they're adjusted correctly again for your feet.

Tanks

Tanks typically have a colored, soft-plastic cap attached to the valve by a cord. This vinyl cap slips over the top of the valve to protect the air outlet from contamination by dirt and sand between uses. This cap is also used to indicate whether the tank is filled and ready for use, or has been used and requires refilling. When a tank is filled, the dive shop will place the plastic cap over the air outlet. After the tank has been used for a dive, this plastic cap isn't replaced over the air outlet and is left hanging by the cord. This indicates that the tank requires refilling.

Another common way to indicate whether a tank has been used or not is by means of a piece of masking tape over the valve outlet. If the tank has been freshly filled, masking tape will be over the valve opening. If there's no tape present, the tank has been used and requires refilling.

Buoyancy Compensator

A quick visual check of the BC and regulator can be made after the equipment is set up with the tank, and should be done before each dive. Look for any tears or damage to the outside of the BC. Be sure the inflator hose is securely attached to the BC's hose fitting.

Check to make sure the BC is at the height on the tank that you prefer so your head doesn't hit the tank valve if you tilt it back while diving. The tank also shouldn't be so low in the BC that it's liable to slip out of the tank band, or that you have difficulty retrieving the regulator hose over your shoulder if the need arises. The top of the tank, where the threads of the valve go in, should be approximately at the level of the top of the BC's backpack.

Be sure the tank strap is tight on the tank and that the buckle is firmly closed and locked onto the strap. Then try to move the BC on the tank. If it moves, the tank band isn't tight enough and must be tightened before diving. I've seen several tanks slip out of their band during a dive and have to be reattached underwater while the divers were in the middle of a dive. Nylon tanks bands often stretch and loosen when wet, and may have to be tightened before a second dive.

If your BC uses a detachable rubber liner inside the tank strap, be sure it's in place under the strap. If you don't have a rubber liner and have trouble with your tank slipping in the band, you can purchase one at your local dive shop.

Regulator and Submersible Pressure Gauge

Look to be sure that the regulator first stage is properly attached to the tank and is in proper alignment with the seat on the tank valve. If the dive staff don't assemble your equipment and you do so yourself, don't overtighten the yoke screw of the regulator on the tank valve. This screw should be only finger tight. The O-ring on the tank and the internal air pressure when the tank valve is open will form the seal to prevent air leakage.

Perform a quick visual inspection of the second stage and octopus to be sure everything is in order. Look for cracks or damage in the regulator housing, particularly if this is plastic. Be sure the regulator and octopus mouthpieces are firmly and correctly seated on the body of the regulator, and that the tie strap is securely in place to hold the mouthpiece to the body of the regulator.

Look at and along each hose to be sure that there are no cracks, cuts, weak spots, or frayed ends. Look particularly at the ends of the hoses for cracking where the hose goes into the first- or second-stage metal fittings. Look for swelling or bubbling along the hose, a condition that indicates it's due for replacement.

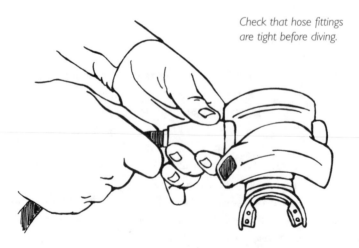

Check that hose fittings are tight before diving.

Check that the metal hose fittings are firmly screwed into the first and second stages. This can be quickly checked with your fingers by trying to lightly turn the hose fitting in its socket. If the hose and its fitting rotate at all, the fitting must be tightened. I found a screw fitting before one dive that had loosened and come partially unscrewed over time, resulting in a regulator that turned loosely on the threads on the end of the hose fitting. To correct this problem was a ten-second job at a dive shop (I tightened the fitting with a wrench), but this looseness could have had serious consequences if the regulator had become completely unscrewed from its hose underwater. Even if it causes no other problems, a loose hose fitting will leak air, resulting in an alarming cloud of bubbles in front of your face and faster depletion of air from the tank.

After visual inspection of the regulator, slowly turn the tank valve partway toward the open position. If there's a loud hissing noise, either the O-ring on the tank is missing or the first stage of the regulator isn't correctly seated on the tank valve. This is why you turn on the valve slowly and only partway: so you can quickly turn it off again if you need to. If you hear leakage, turn the air off again, unscrew the first stage from the tank, and check the regulator, the O-ring, and the tank valve.

If there's a loud popping noise and then a loud hiss when you turn on the tank valve, the O-ring between the tank valve and the first stage of the regulator may have blown out. This is rather alarming the first time it happens, but be reassured that it's not an unusual occurrence. Quickly turn the valve to the closed position again to stop the flow of air. Either replace the tank or replace the O-ring, and try again. A loud pop can also indicate a burst high-pressure hose. This shouldn't happen if the hose has been visually inspected before turning on the tank pressure.

Another alarming occurrence, which luckily is quite rare, can occur if the tank has been sitting in the hot sun for a long period of time at full pressure and the burst disk on the tank ruptures. The burst disk is a thin metal disk used as a safety mechanism. Part of the tank valve, it's intended to rupture and vent air from the tank to relieve excessive pressure before the tank itself blows up, which would be like an exploding shrapnel bomb. However, although this is a safety feature, the situation can still be quite serious because the escaping air may propel the tank along the ground or across a boat deck. Stay clear until the tank has vented itself.

For safety, when turning on the valve, point the face of the submersible pressure gauge away from you, to avoid the unlikely event of an internal failure causing the face of the instrument to blow out. Preferably point the face of the gauge at the ground or the deck of the boat, so that it also isn't point-ing at anyone next to you. SPGs contain a blowout plug as a safety mecha-nism that's intended to relieve the pressure inside the gauge in the event of an internal high-pressure leak.

Listen for air leaks from hoses or fittings, and for any leakage or free flow from the regulator second stages. If there are no hissing sounds that indicate air leaks in the system, turn the tank valve the rest of the way to the full open position, then—just as you were taught in open-water diving classes—close the valve again with a half turn to prevent stress on the valve mechanism.

Look at the pressure gauge in the console. It should read anywhere from about 2,200 to 3,000 PSI, depending on the type of tank you're using and the type of diving you'll be doing. Steel and aluminum tanks in the 80-cubic-foot size can be pressurized to a maximum of 3,000 PSI. Wait a few seconds for the pressure between the tank and the SPG to equalize before turning the gauge around and looking at it. If there's any water evident *inside* the SPG, don't use the equipment; have the gauge serviced.

If the gauge doesn't read the correct amount, there's a problem with either the gauge or the tank. Pressure gauges are very reliable and rarely fail; thus, a low reading probably means the tank was used on a previous dive or wasn't fully filled. Still, be aware that SPGs do have manufacturing tolerances and may not exactly read the true pressure. The dial readings of typical mechanical SPGs are accurate to within about 50 PSI. Note that this is another reason for ending a dive with 300 to 500 PSI in the tank, as you learned during your open-water training. This will account for any tolerances in the dial reading.

If the pressure reading is slightly high, it's usually because the tank has been sitting in the sun and the pressure has risen. When you enter the water to dive, the tank will cool off and the pressure will drop back to a normal read-ing. If in doubt, ask the divemaster what the correct tank pressure reading should be. The pressure in an 80-cubic-foot aluminum or steel tank should not read higher than 3,000 PSI. An 80-cubic-foot steel tank marked with a + symbol may be filled with 10 percent higher pressure, or 3,300 PSI. Tanks in the 80-cubic-foot size with higher pressures than this are unsafe.

If the pressure reading appears to be normal, test the second stage of the regulator for air flow. Depress the purge button to make sure that air is flow-ing through the regulator. Then breathe through the primary regulator a couple of times to make sure it's working correctly and breathes easily. One safety hint when doing this is to bend the side flaps of the mouthpiece out of the way and put only your lips on the air entry in the mouthpiece, rather than putting the mouthpiece in your mouth, as you would underwater. This way the regulator isn't held firmly in your mouth by the mouthpiece if there's any problem with the regulator and excessive pressure comes out when you breathe. This method will allow the mouthpiece to blow itself easily away from your lips. Though extremely unlikely that it would ever happen, high-pressure air coming from a damaged regulator could overinflate and damage your lungs if the mouthpiece is held firmly in your mouth. Test the purge valve and air flow on the octopus in the same manner.

Sometimes the internal valve on a regulator will stick on the first breath if it's been dry for a period of time (which may be as short as a day). This should correct itself after the first breath. If there's continued resistance to breathing or the sound of continuing air leakage through the regulator, the valve seating will need to be adjusted.

Sometimes when a regulator is dry, or soon after it has been serviced, it will make a buzzing sound, like a duck quacking, when you test it or when you breathe with your head out of the water on the surface. This problem will usually correct itself when the regulator is underwater. If you notice a continuing problem with such noises when breathing through the regulator, its valve seating will need to be adjusted.

After the regulator check is completed, press the power inflator button on the BC to be sure that it's working. Partially inflate the jacket to ensure that the valve and BC are functioning correctly. Then press the deflator button to test its operation and deflate the BC.

After all these checks—which after practice should take only a couple of minutes—close the tank valve again and depressurize the regulator system by pushing the purge button on the primary regulator or octopus. Tank valves should always be closed between use for safety reasons in case the tank falls over, and to relieve the air pressure inside the rest of the equipment. Deflate the BC if you don't use it inflated when you enter the water.

One reason for always depressurizing the regulator is that this creates an additional safety check on your air supply before entering the water. When you first put on your equipment to enter the water, your pressure gauge will read zero if you have depressurized the system. Then when your divemaster or dive partner turns on the tank valve, the SPG will rise to display the pressure in the tank again. This offers an additional visual safety check that you've turned on the air in the system. If you don't depressurize the regulator, the system may remain partially pressurized and the pressure gauge may still display the initial tank pressure. In this case you don't know for sure whether the tank valve has been turned on again or the system is still pressurized from previous safety checks.

Mechanical Depth Gauge

If you don't use a mechanical depth gauge, you can skip on to the next section, because this section deals only with mechanical types of depth gauge.

If you have a mechanical depth gauge in your console, look at it to be sure its needle has returned to 0 from the last dive and isn't malfunctioning at some intermediate depth. If you have a console depth gauge that uses a mechanical maximum depth indicator to record the maximum depth reached during a dive, be sure to manually reset it before each dive. Many divers set the maximum depth indicator not at 0, but about 10 feet. This ensures that the variable gauge needle isn't artificially held at zero by the maximum depth indicator.

With the widespread use of dive computers, many divers don't use mechanical console depth gauges, but use their computer to monitor and record their depth during the dive. Still, some divers also carry a mechanical depth gauge as a safety backup in case of computer failure.

Many mechanical depth gauges have a method for finely adjusting the depth indicator needle to bring it to a reading of 0 on the gauge at sea level before diving. One additional safety precaution is to deliberately set the needle to a reading above a 0 before entering the water, in order to give yourself an extra safety factor for the maximum depth reading. In other words, instead of setting the needle to 0 feet on the surface, set the needle to indicate 4 or 5 feet of depth. This way the gauge will always read slightly deeper than you actually dive, thus giving you an extra small margin of safety. If you're using dive tables, use the deepest reading of the gauge during the dive, which will always read deeper than your actual depth because of the initial offset of the depth reading. As a side note, mechanical gauges can have a manufacturing tolerance of several percent in the indicated reading, so this technique also ensures that any depth tolerance of the gauge on the shallow side is accounted for. Most mechanical gauges are accurate only to within 2 or 3 feet.

There is one related equipment tip that's worth mentioning if you travel by airplane with a mechanical depth gauge. If your gauge is adjusted to 0 feet in your hometown, then when it's stored in the hold of an airplane at 35,000 feet during the flight, the lowered air pressure will try to make the needle read less than 0 feet altitude, which will force the indicator needle hard against the lower stop. Though it's unlikely, it is possible for the gauge to be damaged or the needle to be bent when this happens. To avoid it, adjust the gauge so that the indicator needle reads 10 feet or so. Then when the needle goes below what it thinks is the 0 setting at lowered pressure, it will still be able to move and won't be exposed to potential damage. When you reach your dive destination, be sure to remember to reset the gauge to 0 again. If your depth gauge does not have a 0 adjustment, an alternate way to protect it while flying is to pack it in an airtight container so that it won't be subjected to reduced atmospheric pressures.

Mechanical depth gauges are calibrated to read accurately in terms of feet of seawater. Thus, it may be necessary to compensate the readings for diving in fresh water, such as in quarries or high-altitude lakes.

Equipment Problems

Even though well-maintained scuba gear is extremely reliable, at one time or another most divers experience equipment problems of some sort. These can be either minor or major. One dive-related skill is the ability to recognize that there's a problem and determine its importance.

The piece of equipment that's most critical underwater is the regulator. You can lose a fin or a mask, or even drop a weight belt by accident, and still be able to make a safe ascent to the surface. If you suddenly can't breathe at 90 feet because of a regulator failure, however, there may be a very serious outcome. The key to avoiding many regulator problems is to have annual maintenance performed. This usually includes replacement with new parts of all the internal parts that may become clogged, damaged, or worn. This includes items such as the sintered metal screen in the first stage—which may become clogged with salt crystals—the O-rings, and the diaphragm, which could tear after a lengthy period of use.

Problems at the Surface

A predive equipment check before each dive will reduce the likelihood of most major problems. One problem that can be very unnerving when encountered on the surface is when an O-ring on the tank blows. If you're on a commercial dive boat, the crew will have spare O-rings or can give you another tank to use. If you're diving by yourself, you should always carry one or two spare tank O-rings in your emergency repair kit.

Equipment Problems Underwater

Problems with equipment may not become apparent until you're underwater. Good dive practice includes being able to recognize symptoms of problems and to resolve them underwater, if possible.

Regulators

Modern regulators are very reliable pieces of equipment; failures are almost always the result of inadequate care or lack of annual maintenance. Regulators are designed to fail in the free-flow condition, which means that a regulator problem will result in a continuous flow of air rather than the air being shut off, so that air for breathing will always be available. During dive training you should have been taught how to use your octopus, to breathe from a free-flowing regulator, and to buddy-breathe. You should be comfortable with all these techniques, at least to the point of being able to ascend to the surface safely without running out of air.

Small Bubbles

One rather unnerving symptom of possible equipment problems that you may see underwater is a small stream of bubbles coming out of your dive partner's regulator first stage, where it attaches to the tank. Usually this is a symptom of a worn tank O-ring or one that isn't seating properly, thus allowing slight leakage of air. If the stream of bubbles is very small, you can usually complete the dive without a problem. In many cases the bubbles will disappear by themselves as the tank cools in the water or with normal depletion of the air in the tank during the dive.

If you're underwater and the bubbles are tiny, the best procedure is to watch your SPG and make sure the pressure isn't dropping fast. Also watch

Small bubbles coming from an SPG may not be enough to abort a dive, but the problem should be corrected before the next dive.

the leak to make sure that it's only a tiny stream of bubbles, not a huge gush of air. Bubbles coming from the fitting where a hose screws into the first or second stages of the regulator indicate that either the hose isn't screwed tightly into the fitting or the O-ring or fitting gasket is worn and needs replacement.

If the leak is coming from the surface of one of the hoses, or from where the threaded metal fitting attaches to the hose, then there's probably a more serious leak or even a potential for hose rupture; abort the dive and ascend to the surface. Bubbles coming from somewhere along the hose itself indicate a damaged hose. The entire hose should be replaced. If in any doubt at any time as to the safety of a dive or you feel uncomfortable with any air leakage, ascend to the surface and return to the boat or shore to evaluate the problem.

A small stream of bubbles may also be seen coming from around a tank valve when first submerging in the water if the tank has been sitting in the hot sun and the internal pressure has increased. This problem will usually correct itself after a few minutes as the tank cools in the water and the pressure drops again.

A small stream of bubbles may come from around the swivel fitting on a regulator or a pressure gauge in a console. If this is only a small stream, it probably indicates that the tiny O-ring where the hose stem swivels is damaged, has a grain of sand in the fitting, or has inadequate lubrication. The dive can probably be completed in safety, with only a minimal loss of additional air. Watch your SPG for any rapid loss in pressure. If you're in any doubt or you feel uncomfortable seeing bubbles where they shouldn't be, ascend to the surface and have the equipment checked out.

Computer

If a computer should fail or become erratic while underwater, immediately start a safe ascent to the surface. Rate of ascent, with the computer dead, can be roughly judged by ascending at a rate much slower than your slowest bubbles. If you have a depth gauge and a watch, you can use them to judge ascent rate. Make a safety stop at 15 feet for three to five minutes as you normally would. If you have no depth gauge as a backup, you can use a decompression bar, decompression line, or safety regulator as a depth indicator for the safety stop. If none of these is available, use your best judgment as to depth. A safety stop at a depth that isn't quite right is better than no safety stop at all. If you have no watch, estimate the time for the stop by counting slowly.

If you have enough information about previous dives, it's possible to estimate the safety of continuing diving from dive tables. It's preferable, though, to abort any further diving for the day and wait twenty-four hours before resuming diving.

O-Rings

Very rarely, an O-ring may blow while under the water. There will be a loud sound and a cloud of bubbles. If this happens, ascend as fast as possible to the surface, consistent with safe ascent rates, before the tank vents all its air.

Weight Belts

If you're wearing a wet suit, be sure your weight belt is firmly buckled and is tight enough to remain around your waist as you jump into the water and make your initial descent. As you descend deeper into the water, neoprene wet suit material will compress and a loose weight belt could slip down off your hips, resulting in a rapid, uncontrolled ascent to the surface. Particular care should be taken to ensure adequate tightness of weight belts used by children and other individuals whose waist may be the same size as or larger than their hips.

If your weight belt slips off or the buckle accidentally releases, you may find yourself in an uncontrolled-ascent situation. Immediately invert yourself in the water and try to swim strongly downward to retrieve the belt, if the bottom and the belt are close at hand. Obviously, don't swim down deep to retrieve it, as this creates additional safety hazards. If you're successful in retrieving the belt, put it on again. If you aren't successful, swimming downward at least means that you'll ascend to the surface at a reduced speed. If you find yourself in an uncontrolled ascent, try flaring your body by extending your arms and legs in a horizontal position, as taught in scuba training. This will usually reduce the rate of ascent to an acceptable speed.

Save-a-Dive Kit

Some simple repairs can be made to some equipment on the boat or at a dive site and can prevent aborting a dive because of equipment failure. If you don't have common repair items with you, you may have to sit out the dive. This is additionally unfortunate if it's the first of a two-tank dive trip that you've already paid for.

Your repair kit should contain any items that could tear or break and are easily replaceable at the dive site. This includes a spare fin strap, a spare mask strap, a snorkel holder, a spare regulator mouthpiece, and a tie strap to hold the mouthpiece in place. A list of typical repair items is given in appendix B.

9

ENHANCING YOUR DIVE SKILLS

echnical diving skills are taught during dive courses presented by professional dive instructors. Learning to dive under the supervision of a competent professional instructor from an accredited dive organization provides the safest introduction to the world of diving. This classroom work and supervised dive training in open-water conditions lead to dive certification, the C-card, and an understanding of the skills required to dive safely in the underwater environment. This chapter is not intended to replace any of this formal training, but rather to add hints, tips, and advice for safer and more enjoyable diving.

Safety

Before I discuss any diving skills, it's important to repeat a few words about dive safety. The importance of observing safety while diving cannot be overemphasized. As I've noted throughout the text and repeat again here: *Each diver is ultimately responsible for his or her own life and safety.* Nobody else is. To repeat the message from the introduction, if you don't feel comfortable with a dive or dive situation, or if you're not comfortable with your equipment, your dive partner, the weather conditions, the dive site, the current, the water, or any other aspect of the dive, *either don't dive or abort the dive.* There are always other dives, but you only have one life. You are responsible for protecting it!

Safety First

- Never hold your breath while underwater.
- Breathe fully and normally when ascending, in order to prevent lung expansion injury.
- Always dive with a partner and stay close together.
- Plan your dive and follow your plan.
- Abort any dive with which you don't feel comfortable.
- Don't mix alcohol or drugs with diving.
- If you feel chilled, exit the water and warm up.
- Drink plenty of fluids before and after diving to stay hydrated.
- Don't dive below 130 feet.
- Don't push the limits of the dive tables; stay at least one or two dive groups below the maximum limits.
- Ascend at a rate of no faster than 30 feet per minute.
- Make a safety stop on every dive at 15 feet for three to five minutes.
- Don't molest marine life.
- Don't put your hand in a crevice or hole; something may bite it.
- Limit repetitive dives to three per day; reduce diving time and depth during the last day or two of multiday dive trips or take a day off from diving in the middle.
- Plan to consume the air in your tank in thirds: Use one-third on the way out, one-third on the way back, and one-third for completing the dive and performing a safety stop.
- Plan to complete your dive with 300 to 500 PSI remaining in the tank.

There are some simple, but vitally important, rules for safety during recreational scuba diving. These are summarized in the accompanying sidebar.

Just as important as diving safely is knowing when not to dive. This can be summarized in a nutshell by saying you don't dive in conditions or situations in which you don't feel comfortable. Such conditions could include very cold water, very rough water, poor underwater visibility, stormy surface conditions, high winds, strong currents, and approaching darkness. Depending on your individual level of skill, strength, age, comfort in the water, and general fitness, these may all be conditions to avoid, certainly for the novice and probably for the intermediate diver. All divers are responsible for determining whether or not they're able to cope with the conditions they may encounter during the dive.

A further caution is not to rely totally on the judgment of the person you're diving with. An overeager dive buddy may feel that the dive conditions are safe for him or her, while you may not be comfortable. Remember that some divers and divemasters may be younger and more enthusiastic about diving than you are, may have just completed divemaster training and may not be totally experienced in all dive conditions, or may feel that conditions are safe. But you may still not feel that they're right for you. If you feel uncomfortable with the dive, refuse to do it. Most divemasters are extremely safety con-

The Other Safety Factor—Your Buddy

The buddy system is emphasized in scuba training. Some advantages of having a suitable dive partner:

• There's someone to perform mutual safety checks on the surface before diving.
• There's someone to provide immediate help in case of an underwater emergency.
• There's someone to share dive experiences with.
• You have someone to provide psychological support—for example, when you can't see the way back to the boat in 50 feet of murky water.
• There's someone to stay close in case of emergency as you dive deeper, because it's more problematic to dash to the surface from 100 feet than from 30 feet.

If your buddy is mismatched in terms of skill level, underwater interests, or physical conditioning, however, diving will be unpleasant—and can even put one of the divers into a dangerous situation that he or she isn't equipped to handle. So choose a dive buddy you want to dive with and who wants to dive with you, preferably someone you know well.

Factors in choosing a buddy that are just as important are:

• Have the same dive goals and expectations. If one partner wants to descend like a rock and dive a wreck at 120 feet while the other wants to leisurely cruise the coralheads at 50 feet, this is not a good buddy match.
• Have roughly the same level of physical conditioning.
• Have the same type of underwater interests.
• Discuss and practice hand signals together, so that you can communicate quickly and effectively underwater.

scious, but a few may err on the side of letting divers enter the water when conditions may be beyond their ability. Consider poor visibility underwater, strong currents, the risks of scrambling back up the ladder in rough seas, seasickness, and cold conditions when you make your decision.

As a general rule of thumb if you're diving with tables, curtail the dive by one or two surface groups on the tables when it's strenuous or the water is very cold. Computer users shouldn't push the time and depth limits under these conditions.

One important rule for all diving is to always breathe deeply and evenly when underwater. The other part of this rule is to always exhale when ascending to the surface. Sometimes it's easy to forget these rules when you're beginning to dive. When taking a photograph, for example, there's a natural tendency to hold your breath while squeezing the shutter release in order to prevent camera movement. This practice isn't safe underwater, because you may unconsciously drift up or down in depth by a few feet while you're taking the picture. A depth change of only a few feet while holding your breath can result in internal pressure changes in the lungs that can cause injury.

Another safety rule is to try to solve any problems that arise underwater without immediately ascending to the surface, so long as you have an adequate air supply. If a mask or fin falls off or equipment problems arise, try to solve them where you are. Even regulator problems or out-of-air situations can be initially controlled by switching to your octopus or breathing from your partner's octopus. Then when the situation is under control, start a slow ascent to the surface.

If you can still breathe, you generally aren't in immediate danger of drowning. One of the most dangerous situations in scuba diving occurs when a diver panics and starts an uncontrolled ascent to the surface. This often results in lung expansion problems due to rapid ascent. Most fatalities occur at or just under the surface due to drowning.

General Preparations for Diving

It doesn't hurt to repeat the obvious. If you're going on a boat dive, be sure you have all your equipment. It's very frustrating to be twenty minutes from land and find that you've forgotten your mask in your car or hotel room.

For convenience, pack all your equipment into a mesh gear bag to carry and handle between home, car, boat, or shore. Remember to pack the heavy items, such as your weight belt, first and then add delicate items—mask, regulator, gauges—on top, so that the heavy items don't damage the fragile ones. If you're diving at a resort, the dive shop will often supply some sort of dive bag for the duration of the visit and the boat crew will handle your equipment for you.

In hot weather you'll probably want to wait to put on your outer layers, such as dive skin or wet suit, until just before entering the water. If you put on all your exposure gear while on the dock,

We Have Met the Enemy and He Is Us

The most common cause of scuba accidents and deaths is diver error:

- *Forgetting to release a weight belt if problems occur underwater.*
- *Diving in inappropriate water conditions.*
- *Diving in conditions beyond your capabilities.*
- *Failure to recognize hypothermia.*
- *Inappropriate use of drugs and alcohol before and after diving.*
- *Pushing the limits of the dive tables or dive computer.*

you can quickly become overheated while traveling to the dive site. If you're on a boat, you can suit up just before you reach the dive site. After a dive on a boat, you'll probably want to take off your dive skin or wet suit to dry off. Depending on the weather and wind created by the motion of the boat, however, you may find it preferable to continue to wear your dive skin or change to a dry sweatshirt for protection from wind while the boat is in motion.

When you put on your weight belt, be sure to orient it with a right-hand release for the buckle, as taught in dive class. This is to avoid confusing the right-hand release of the weight belt with the left-hand release of the BC in an emergency. Position the weights on the belt so they're distributed evenly around your waist, and check to be sure that one won't be caught under the tank when you put on your BC—this will be uncomfortable.

Some dive classes teach you to put the weight belt on last, after the BC and tank. This is the correct sequence for shore diving. On a dive boat, however, the weight belt goes on *before* the BC and tank. The preferred sequence is that the diver on a charter dive boat dons weight belt and defogged mask, and walks to the stern of the boat with fins in hand. The diver sits on the stern platform and puts on the fins (this sounds like a simple step, but I've actually seen divers forget and jump in without their fins!). The divemaster will then bring the BC with tank to the diver, who puts it on and fastens the straps. The tank valve is turned on, the pressure is checked a final time, the regulator goes in the mouth, and the diver is ready to descend.

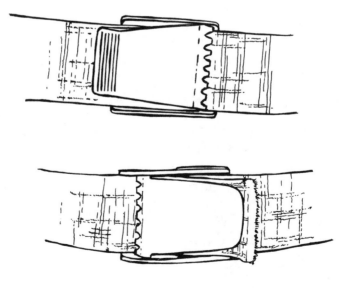

Remember that the weight belt buckle (lower) uses a right-hand release, while the BC buckle (upper) uses a left-hand release.

Other sequences are used by various dive operations. Some dive boats want you to put on your equipment and fins while sitting on the bench, then shuffle to the back of the boat and do a giant-stride entry into the water. If you have any doubts about the entry procedure being used, be sure to ask the divemaster or boat captain for the procedure that he or she expects.

Recheck the tank pressure before descending to ensure that the valve is turned on and fully functional. I once watched an experienced divemaster perform a beautiful giant stride into the ocean from a dive boat and immediately submerge and swim down to join the group he was leading. About fifteen seconds later there was a huge boiling effect at the surface as he shot up out of the water again, spluttering and gasping for breath. He had forgotten to turn on the tank valve and hadn't checked his gauge for adequate pressure. The story speaks for itself. Always check your air pressure one final time just before you jump into the water.

Should your regulator be unexpectedly very hard to breathe through, look at your SPG. If the needle drops with every breath, check to see if the tank valve is fully turned to the on position. Occasionally nervous novice divers open the valve slightly, but not fully. When this occurs, the SPG will read full pressure between inhalations, but the partially open valve won't allow enough air to pass for normal breathing, thus the SPG will drop rapidly to 0 each time you breathe in.

When you put on your mask, be sure that you don't have hair stuck under its skirt. This would allow some water to leak into the mask when you submerge and descend.

Equipment Checks

The most basic of diving skills starts before you ever enter the water. This is the equipment check, discussed in detail in chapter 8. Be sure to perform safety checks on your equipment before leaving the dock on a dive boat. If any items are forgotten or anything is wrong with your gear, you have a chance to correct it before the boat leaves. You may wish to use the checklist in appendix B for a guide.

It's also important to be sure that your equipment is set up correctly and in the way that you expect. Again, it's your responsibility to take care of your own safety, so start by being sure that you're entering the water with safe equipment. Whether you're on a boat dive with experienced dive crew who do all the setup for you, or are diving from the shore with only you and a partner, take the time to be sure everything is assembled correctly and that all items of equipment are working to your satisfaction. If you have any doubts, or some piece of equipment isn't operating correctly, abort the dive.

One reason that I feel so strongly about this is that I've seen equipment set up and divers ready to go into the ocean with items that had been over-looked. These appeared to be small items, but could have had very serious consequences underwater.

Into the Water

During your open-water training, you will have learned the basic techniques for entering the water. To summarize, these include wading in from shore, climbing down stairs or stepladder from a pier, performing a giant stride from a rock when shore diving, or doing a giant stride or backward roll from a dive boat. Larger dive boats usually have a dive platform at the stern from which divers perform a giant stride. Smaller boats, without a platform, require a backward roll over the side. With either method, move away from the boat, dive platform, or entry point as quickly as possible to avoid being hit by a diver entering the water after you.

If you enter the water with a giant stride or a backward roll, place one hand over the mask and regulator in your mouth to prevent them from being dislodged as you jump into the water. Place the other hand across your chest to prevent your octopus from becoming dislodged or your BC strap from accidentally releasing. Some divers prefer to place the other hand over the buckle of their weight belt to prevent it from unexpectedly releasing upon impact with the water.

One of the cardinal rules of diving is to keep your regulator in your mouth whenever you're entering or exiting the water. Older training emphasized changing from your regulator to your snorkel when on the surface to con-serve air, but this teaching isn't commonly used today. Modern thinking is that if you have any problem while in the water, you need a reliable air supply. If you have your snorkel in your mouth and an unexpected wave rolls over you, or you fall backward into the water while climbing the ladder on a dive boat, your snorkel will go underwater, you'll suck in water instead of air, and a potential drowning situation has been created. Of course, if you've run out of air (which you should never do!) on the surface, you'll have to use a snorkel.

Accident statistics generated by the Divers Alert Network (DAN) indi-cate that the majority of problems occur at the surface and that the majority of scuba deaths occur from drowning. Always keep your regula-tor in your mouth when you're in the water to ensure an adequate supply of air.

Occasionally the purge button in an octopus will become stuck and the regulator will free-flow when you first enter the water or start to descend. To stop regulator free flow, momentarily depress the purge button sharply. This normally stops the free-flow condition. If it doesn't, try holding the regulator horizontally, with the mouthpiece downward, and depressing the purge button sharply. This will nearly always stop any free flow. If it doesn't, then there may be damage to the regulator and the dive must be aborted.

When jumping into the water, such as doing a giant stride from a dive platform, don't take your underwater camera or video camera with you. Leave it on the dive platform, enter the water, and have the crew pass it down to you. If you jump into the water with a camera, one of three things may happen. First, the camera may be jarred out of your hand by the impact and sink to the bottom, which isn't good if you're anchored over a deep wall. Second, you may damage the camera internally from the impact. Third, it's common to burst an O-ring on the camera housing during such an entry— which will, of course, flood the delicate inner workings of the camera with rapidly corrosive seawater.

Descending in the Water

In dive training you will have learned to descend, feetfirst, by exhaling and releasing air from your BC. Some divers are comfortable descending like this through open water. Others prefer to use the anchor rope either as a visual reference while descending, or to hold on to for security. The anchor rope or chain may be helpful for stability if an underwater current is present. If you hold on to a chain, be careful not to catch a finger between the links if the chain moves. If you hold on to an anchor rope, watch out for stinging hydroids—feathery fernlike animals, an inch or more tall, that frequently grow on permanent anchor lines. This is a good situation to use reef gloves.

When you start to descend, you may have to tighten your weight belt a little, because very often the belt tends to slide down on the hips when wet. As you go deeper, the material in a neoprene wet suit will compress and the belt may have to be retightened again. If this is a continual problem when diving, weight belts are available with buckles that compensate for depth. These buckles are spring-loaded so that they adjust automatically when descending and ascending, as the need arises. Alternately, a weight harness may be used (see also chapter 7).

Clearing Your Ears

One of the most basic of practical diving skills is clearing your ears to equalize the pressure, and this should have been emphasized during basic diving classes. It's important to start equalizing your ears immediately upon descent and to continue equalizing throughout the dive, as necessary. The greatest volume change for air in body spaces occurs during the initial portion of the descent, or about the first 10 or 15 feet underwater, hence the need to start equalization immediately.

Descending without equalizing the ears or equalizing them inadequately can result in middle ear squeeze and pain. If the pressure inside the air space of the middle ear isn't increased to equal the increasing external pressure created by water pressure as you descend, this unequalized pressure creates pain in the ears and, if not corrected, can result in damage to the delicate mechanism of the inner ears.

As noted, ear squeeze is most common within the first 15 feet of descent, when the external pressure change has the greatest effect on the ears. Pain can start in an unequalized ear, however, at

*L*et's Clear Up a Couple of Things

- Start clearing your ears immediately upon descent.
- Feetfirst descent makes it easier to clear your ears.
- Hold your nose and blow gently to clear your ears; forceful blowing may cause damage.
- If your ears won't clear, ascend a few feet and try again.
- Do not descend if your ears are painful or won't clear; abort the dive.

a depth of as little as 5 feet. Rupture of the eardrum can occur from the pressure created by as little as 11 feet of water. If you feel pain in your ears or can't perform equalization easily, ascend a few feet and try again. The reduction in pressure that results from rising even 3 or 4 feet may make equalization easier. Equalize the ears, then start to descend again.

In class you will have been taught what is called the Valsalva maneuver to equalize your ears. This procedure consists of pinching your nostrils shut, closing your mouth, and then trying to force air into your nose. When you do this, you'll feel and hear a mild pop in your ears as the pressure between the external ear canal and the middle ear space equalizes. What may not have been emphasized in class, however, is that forceful use of this technique can damage your ears. Excessive pressure may be generated, for example, if you're trying to equalize your ears while descending too rapidly. Upon rapid descent, external pressure quickly builds up in your ears and isn't easily equalized. In this case, continued forceful blowing of air into your closed mouth and nose can create enough pressure in your ears to damage the membranes or delicate sensory organs of the inner ear.

The eustachian tubes are the narrow passages connecting the air spaces of the middle ears to the throat. These tubes may become blocked after a head cold or with allergies, due to congestion and swelling in the ears or throat. If the tubes are blocked, air may become trapped in the middle ears. Upon descent, or ascent at the end of a dive, the unequalized pressure can become so great that one of the eardrums ruptures. If this happens, cold water will flood the middle ear, and the rapid drop in temperature of the balance mechanism behind the eardrum will cause an immediate sense of dizziness, technically called vertigo. You may feel that the environment is spinning around or that stationary objects are moving. As the water in the damaged ear warms to the temperature of the other, undamaged ear, this sensation should pass. A normal ascent to the surface should be undertaken as soon as possible, and medical attention sought.

Nasal sprays and decongestants are often used to relieve congestion and swelling in nasal and sinus passages—and while they may produce immediate relief in the obstructed area, they should be used with caution. One problem is that the decongestant effects may wear off while underwater, resulting in a return of congestion during the dive and problems with expansion of trapped air during ascent to the surface. There may also be a rebound phenomenon in which the congestion actually becomes worse when the drug wears off.

The effects of these drugs may vary with ambient pressure, often being amplified by the surrounding water pressures of deep diving. Thus, you should know the effects of a particular drug dosage on you individually before relying on its use and efficacy. Consult a physician for information before using any of these drugs underwater.

As I've mentioned, if you don't equalize your ears as you descend, you'll notice an increasing feeling of pressure in them and, if the increase in depth is large enough, may start to feel pain. Pay attention to your ears, because this can be used as a warning signal. If you're swimming or floating in the water without paying attention to your depth gauge, and you start to feel pain in your ears, this is an indication that you are unintentionally drifting downward. If your ears unexpectedly squeak, caused by pressure reduction in the external ear, you may be unintentionally rising toward the surface.

Unequalized pressure in any hollow, air-filled space can result in a squeeze, and often in pain. Another common type of squeeze results from unequalized pressure in the hollow sinus cavities in the front part of your face, around your eyes and nose. This is called a sinus squeeze. These spaces will normally equalize automatically but if for some reason the ducts to these sinuses become congested or inflamed due to colds, allergy, or other conditions, they won't equalize and pain in these areas may result. A less likely problem, but one that occasionally occurs, is a tooth squeeze, which results from air trapped in a space that contains tooth decay or is under a filling. This trapped air can expand or contract, causing pressure on gum tissue and the nerve in the tooth, with resulting pain.

A condition called mask squeeze or face squeeze can also occur if the air pressure inside the mask isn't equal to the increased external pressure when descending in the water. The lower air pressure inside will create mask tightness and a pulling sensation on your face and eyes. If unrelieved, this negative pressure can result in swollen facial tissue and bloodshot eyes. To avoid this, exhale through your nose into the mask occasionally to equalize the pressure while descending.

*D*ealing with Ear Pain

- *Start equalizing your ears as soon as you start descending.*
- *Descending feetfirst will usually create less pressure on your ears than descending headfirst.*
- *If you experience ear pain upon descent, ascend a few feet and try again to clear your ears.*
- *If ear pain continues, abort the dive.*

Starting the Dive

Once you're in the water, how do you decide which direction to go and how far? Begin with direction: Always swim into the current. This is taught in basic training, but not everyone remembers it. Swimming into the current requires the most energy, of course, which means you want to do it when you're fresh, not on your way back when you may be tired. Also, using more energy for the swim into the current means you're using more air. If you use more air on the outward trip, you'll have an adequate supply of air for the return trip. If you initially swim with the current, instead of into it, for one-third of the initial air supply, more than one-third will probably be consumed coming back, which will reduce either the time you have for a safety stop or will mean that you run out of air before surfacing.

The divemaster on a dive boat will usually recommend starting a dive into the current; still, I've seen divemasters (knowingly or unknowingly) recommend initial directions that were across, or even with, the current. Unless there's some specific or safety reason to do this, ignore the divemaster and swim into the current. Once, in Bonaire, the group of divers I was with followed the divemaster's advice and started with the current. When they returned to the boat, most were almost exhausted due to swimming back into the current. On the other hand, three dive companions and I started into the current, had a very pleasant dive, and swam easily back to the boat with the current at the end.

There are several methods for determining the direction of the current. A boat at anchor will align itself with the surface current, oriented with the bow into the current. Thus, aligning your compass with the bow of the boat from the stern, and swimming toward the bow of the boat when underwater, will ensure that you start your dive into the current.

In order to check the direction of current, very often the dive crew will drop a drift line off the stern. A drift line consists of a rope with a weight attached. The direction and degree away from vertical that the line is pushed when underwater will indicate the current's direction and give some estimate of its strength.

Once you're underwater you'll find other indicators of the underwater current's direction. Be sure to check these signs, since the current underwater may be different from what's at the surface. One way of determining the presence and direction of underwater current is to look at tall sea fans, soft corals, or other flexible underwater plants. If there's a strong current, any flexible vegetation anchored to the bottom will be bent over in its direction. If there's no current or a weak one, they'll generally be vertical, or oscillating gently from side to side.

Also look up in the water and see which way the boat is aligned. As noted, a boat will normally align itself with the bow facing into the current and the stern downcurrent from the anchor.

When you start a dive, align the lubber line (the reference mark or line) of your compass with the forward direction of your body. When you return, simply rotate the compass bezel (the rotating dial that contains the index marks) by 180 degrees—a half turn—and follow this direction back to the boat.

If the underwater current is very strong, it's probably advisable to abort the dive. Most divers can't make much progress when swimming into a current of as little as 1 knot (slightly more than 1 mile per hour). A current of 2 or 3 knots is virtually impossible to swim against for most divers. If you're caught in a strong current while diving with a dive boat, the best advice is to surface, signal to the boat for help, and wait to be picked up. The only type of recreational diving that's advisable for beginning divers in strong currents is drift diving, in which you let yourself be carried along by the current while a dive boat tracks you on the surface and picks you up after the dive is completed. Drift divers should carry a safety sausage and powerful whistle for signaling to the boat in case of emergency. Other techniques for diving in strong currents are beyond the scope of this book and should be learned under local conditions with a competent instructor.

Visibility

Good visibility through the water lets you see where you're going and helps you enjoy the underwater world. Unfortunately, water clarity while diving isn't always as good as hoped. You have to make the decision about the conditions of visibility in which you feel comfortable and can enjoy diving.

Underwater visibility in the ocean can vary from outstanding, perhaps 150 feet or more, through very good, perhaps 60 or 70 feet, to poor, which may be 10 feet or less. Sunlight penetrating the water on a bright day will improve your ability to see underwater, especially when doing deeper dives, as opposed to diving on a cloudy day.

Some of the best visibility for diving in the ocean is found around islands with dry, desertlike land environments, such as the Cayman Islands. The ocean around lush tropical islands like St. Lucia or Fiji tends to have lower visibility. This is because the same rain that keeps an island lush and tropical runs off into the ocean carrying with it silt and plant debris, stirring up the ocean as it enters the water and lowering the visibility. For similar reasons, the visibility in the ocean around an island may be better in winter, when there's less rain, than in summer when there may be more rain and runoff entering the water. Tropical storms, such as the hurricanes and tropical depressions that occur in the Caribbean in the fall months, can also stir up the water and lower the overall visibility.

Similarly, visibility in fresh water can range from very good, perhaps 100 feet or more, to virtually 0. Some of the inland dive sites with the clearest visibility are landlocked quarries with no vegetation, artesian springs and wells, and flooded mines. Rivers and lakes very often have visibility at the low end of the range, due to churned-up mud, silt, dirt, and other debris in the water. Many freshwater lakes feature aquatic plants, animal life, and stirred-up sediment, all reducing visibility.

Visibility in fresh water is affected by many factors, including any flow of water that churns up sediment, boats that stir up the water, suspended plant and animal matter, wave action, the amount of rain occurring over the previous few days, the number of divers present who churn up mud, and any other factors that cause particulate matter to be present in the water. Divers swimming too close to the bottom or banks of a lake can stir mud, silt, or sand and destroy visibility, especially in enclosed areas such as artesian wells or springs. Similarly, divers swimming too close to the bottom in the ocean can stir up sand and cut visibility in areas like a sandy bottom immediately beneath a dive boat.

There are two techniques to prevent stirring up sand or silt on the bottom, or in a cave or cavern. One is to swim sideways. Though it takes some practice, this will reduce the currents of water from the fins onto the bottom that stir up sediment. Or you can swim with one fin vertically over the other, kicking with only the top fin. In this way the bottom fin acts as a baffle to reduce any water currents from the fins that may stir up silt or sand.

Visibility in fresh water is often low in springtime, when lakes and rivers are naturally churned up by runoff from melting snow. Visibility in some land-locked lakes may be as little as 3 to 5 feet, which severely limits what you can see underwater. Diving in these conditions can be very difficult and even hazardous, since it can be difficult to see underwater obstacles and dangers. In conditions of very low visibility, it may be necessary to dive with a buddy line—a short strap or cord that tethers you and your dive partner together so that you don't lose each other underwater. Diving in conditions of extremely limited visibility requires special training, including buddy lines as well as line-attended boat diving techniques, to ensure safety.

Some of the poorest dive conditions I've ever seen were in an inland lake in which a partner and I were practicing rescue diving. We descended holding on to each other's dive tank valves in order to maintain close contact. When underwater, we both released the other's tank, intending to start a practice search pattern. The visibility was so bad that we immediately lost sight of each other, even at a 1-foot distance, and had to abort the rest of the dive. Luckily this was only a practice mission! Diving under such conditions requires special training and a lot of practice. This topic is beyond the scope of this book and won't be discussed further. If you're interested in limited-visibility diving, contact your local dive shop on how to obtain further experience.

Curiously, extremely clear water can also create safety problems. Such clarity tends to remove cues for depth perception and visual distance references. Thus, it's possible to lose depth perspective if you're not closely watching your depth gauge and, consequently, to drift or dive deeper than intended.

Unintentional drifting down in the water can happen in the open ocean when performing what's called blue water diving: diving in clear water in mid-ocean, far from the shore, in an open environment. This might be done, for example, to enjoy the freedom of being in a totally unenclosed environment or may be part of a dive to a group of pinnacles in the open ocean that start at perhaps 80 feet underwater. In these conditions there are no fixed objects, no horizontal references, and no visible bottom to gauge the depth of descent; it's easy to become disoriented and even become confused about which way is up or down, thus descending farther than intended. This disorientation may lead to a sense of falling, even when you're maintaining a constant depth. For safety, this type of diving usually involves a weighted reference line in the water marked with depths at 5- or 10-foot intervals. Divers uncomfortable with this type of diving can be tethered to the line for security.

Mask Clearing

During dive training you will have learned how to clear water that leaks into your mask. Clearing a mask is a very basic skill and must be learned well, because a small amount of water will inevitably enter around the skirt of a mask and will have to be purged as you dive. Even slight adjustment of your mask underwater can cause some water to enter. The solution is not to worry about it and be prepared to clear water out as it occurs. Don't try to keep the mask so tight that it never leaks. A mask will always leak to some degree.

Another technique related to mask clearing is deliberate flooding of the mask to remove fog during a dive.

M ask Etiquette

Don't push your mask up on your forehead while in the water. For one thing, it can easily fall off and get lost. More importantly, this is a signal of distress for some divemasters; they won't be happy rescuing you if you don't need it!

Sometimes, despite your best efforts with defogging solutions, some fogging of a mask lens will occur underwater. The easiest way to resolve this while remaining underwater is to deliberately allow a small amount of water to flood your mask and wash off the fog, then to purge the water out again. This must be done carefully. With your face and mask horizontal in the water, lift the skirt of the mask away from your face *slightly* and allow a *small* amount of water to enter. Keep the front of your mask horizontal so you don't inhale water up your nose. Move your head around a bit to allow the water to swill over the fog on the glass and remove it. Then turn your head upright again and clear the water out as usual. Being able to deliberately flood, then clear, your mask can also be useful on other occasions—say, having an excruciating itch on your nose that can only be scratched by putting a finger under the skirt of your mask.

Air Consumption

A conservative rule for scuba diving is that you should use one-third of your air supply when swimming away from the boat or shore entry point. The second third of your air should be used for swimming back to your starting point. The final third is used for exploring the environment while remaining within visual range of the boat or exit point, and for performing a three- to five-minute safety stop before exiting the water.

Planning to use your air supply in thirds like this provides a safety cushion for returning to the boat or shore entry point before running out of air. If you should use more air than you planned on the outward part of the dive, or use more air than you planned finding the boat or exit point, and you'll still have adequate air remaining to do further exploration close to the exit point.

Regardless of how you plan a dive, you should plan to exit the water with a minimum of 500 PSI remaining in your tank. This ensures a reserve of air in case of unexpected occurrences that cause you to stay underwater longer than planned.

Be aware that fully functional pressure gauges may not be totally accurate. The dial readings of typical mechanical SPGs are accurate only to within about 50 PSI. An SPG with a bent needle can read as much as 300 PSI when the tank is empty. Finally, it's not unusual for an SPG to fail to return completely to a 0 reading with no pressure applied. Thus, an SPG may indicate some pressure in the tank when there is none.

Underwater Communication

One skill that should be mastered as a part of dive safety is communicating effectively underwater. Devices for signaling were discussed in chapter 7. Most of these are intended for attracting your dive partner's attention while under the water. After you have your partner's attention, though, you still need to communicate effectively. Commonly, this is done through slates, also discussed in chapter 7. Hand signals are also popular.

To communicate the amount of air remaining—a crucial message underwater—many divers use a hand signal that signifies 100 PSI for each finger. Holding up two fingers thus represents 200 PSI remaining in the air tank, five fingers represents 500 PSI, and so forth. To indicate more than 500 PSI, either both hands can be used to indicate up to 1,000 PSI, or a single hand may be opened and closed several times to indicate multiples of 500 PSI. Thus if you have 1,800 PSI of air remaining in your tank, you would open and close one hand three times and then hold up three fingers.

For more complex communications, some divers have learned American Sign Language and can sign words to each other underwater. This is useful for those with the patience to learn and practice the sign alphabet or those with prior knowledge of sign language.

It's important to note that hand signals are not universal. One Australian divemaster told me how he had once asked a diver how much air she had remaining. She held up five fingers, a common sign in the United States and Caribbean for "500 PSI." The divemaster didn't understand because he had learned the metric system of air pressure (which uses bars instead of PSI); he had to swim up and look at the diver's air pressure gauge. The moral of the story is to be sure you use hand signals that your dive partner understands.

Depth of Dives

The generally accepted practice is to perform deepest dives first, then dive progressively shallower on subsequent dives. Individual dives should follow the same pattern. Do the deepest part of the dive first, then gradually ascend, looking at underwater features of interest at the shallower depths. Finally, try to end the dive on a shallow part of a reef or wreck, in order to exhale as much nitrogen as possible. Always perform a safety stop before exiting the water.

Recent information suggests that reverse-profile dives—performing the shallower part of a dive before the deeper part (for a depth differential of less than 40 feet)—does not increase the potential for decompression sickness (DCS). What appears to be more important for avoiding DCS is the rate of ascent after a dive. A slow ascent allows more nitrogen to be exhaled through the lungs. Still, spending time at a shallower depth before ending the dive also allows nitrogen to be exhaled, reducing the chances of DCS. Doing the deepest part of a dive first thus remains weighted on the side of safety. Using caution on the limits of the dive tables and making a slow ascent should be mandatory in either case.

The depth limit for safe recreational scuba diving is considered 130 feet. A self-imposed limit for dives of 100 to 110 feet is safer, since this allows some margin for error in case you dive or drift deeper than intended.

While underwater, try to keep a good visual depth reference in sight at all times. Without some frame of reference, it's easy to lose perspective on your depth and drift slowly downward. This is particularly true on wall dives in very clear water. A safety precaution in such cases, especially if you're a novice, is to hold your depth gauge in front of you at all times as you swim so you can continuously monitor your depth. It's very easy to drift downward by mistake and end up deeper than you'd intended. If you're diving on a wall at 100 or 110 feet, there's very little margin for error. Some wall dives may also feature a slight downward current that can push you deeper still, unnoticed. "Listen" to your ears for either pain (unobserved descent) or squeaking noises (unobserved ascent).

When diving on a wall, don't go down tunnels or chutes that start at the top unless you know for certain the depth at which they emerge from the wall. Tunnels can bring you out much deeper than you'd intended—even beyond the limit of safe recreational diving. Instead of starting into a tunnel or chute at the top, descend on the wall on the outside to where the tunnel or chute comes out, then come up through it to shallower water. This way you can be sure of its greatest depth.

Ending the Dive

It's surprising how easy it is to become disoriented when diving from a boat. You can find yourself much farther from the boat than you'd intended, and often in a different direction than you'd thought. It is, however, difficult to become completely lost. If you feel that you're lost or going in the wrong direction, simply come to the surface, make a visual sighting of the boat, and then swim either on the surface or underwater back to the boat. No real harm is done by this. At worst it's inconvenient: Swimming up and down to the surface wastes air and dive time. Still, if you do this too frequently on a single dive, it could become a series of bounce dives—which can have serious implications for decompression sickness. Far better to know where you are and where the boat is.

Many novice divers feel more comfortable underwater if they can see the boat at all times, at least until they gain more confidence in their navigation skills. In very clear water this may be possible, but in most cases you can only do this by remaining directly under the boat.

Sound Bites

On land, sound reaches us via vibrations carried through air; we determine the direction of a sound by slight time differences as sounds reach our ears. Sound travels about four times faster through water than through air. We are unable to correctly interpret these reduced time differences, and it often feels underwater as if sound is coming from all around us. For example, it's difficult to reliably determine the direction of an approaching boat by sound alone; you have to also look around and up to correctly locate it and avoid a potential accident.

Knowing where you are doesn't always mean using a compass. It is possible, and desirable, to also use underwater features to keep track of your position with reference to the dive boat or shore entry point. For example, when diving a wall, the wall itself becomes a navigation feature. If the boat is anchored at the top of a wall, when you descend over the wall and swim along its side you simply have to remember on which side of you the wall is located. When you reach your turnaround point, then, you swim back to the boat with the wall on the opposite side, or swim on top of the wall in the same orientation. The technique can be used with other underwater navigational reference points, such as wrecks or coralheads.

When visibility is limited, it may be possible to use a visual sighting of the dive boat as a reference. Even if you can't see the keel clearly, it's often possible to see the foam and surge of the boat's hull as it breaks the pattern of the open ocean overhead. When returning to the general location of the boat, watch for a large white foamy area at the surface. That's probably the boat riding at anchor. You can also use sightings of the anchor line to find the boat. In murky water the anchor line may be easier to spot than the bottom of the boat. Dive sites with permanent moorings often have a float anchored underwater to keep the mooring line off the bottom. This float may be used as a reference point.

When diving sites that feature some surface current, dive crews usually throw out a recovery line. This is a line with a surface buoy attached that drifts downcurrent from the boat's stern. Divers returning to the boat can then grasp this line to pull themselves back to the stern. The direction that the buoy drifts after being thrown into the water also shows which way the surface current is flowing. Usually a recovery line is only put into the water after the last diver has entered, in order to prevent diver entanglement when jumping in.

Incidentally, when returning to the boat, be sure to come back to the correct boat! There may be multiple dive boats anchored within short swimming distances of each other in a popular dive area. It's not unusual for a diver or two to become disoriented and surface at the wrong boat. No real harm is done, but it means a surface swim back to the correct boat.

Ascending

More important than descent is the rate of ascent after completing a dive. Older recommendations were that the ascent rate to the surface should not exceed 60 feet per minute. Thus, an ascent from 30 feet, for example, at a rate of 60 feet per minute would take thirty seconds. Divers were taught to approximate this rate by ascending no faster than the speed of their slowest bubbles—though this has since been shown to be an unreliable indicator of ascent speed.

Newer recommendations are more conservative and recommend an ascent rate of 30 feet per minute. Remember to breathe slowly and normally while ascending to prevent the lung expansion injuries that can result from holding your breath.

Since the greatest change in air volume occurs in the uppermost 10 to 15 feet of water, the greatest risk of lung damage occurs during the final portion of the ascent. Thus, be sure to breathe evenly when approaching the surface. The volume change for air in the first 10 feet below the surface is about 25 percent; in the subsequent 10 feet it's approximately 15 percent more. Lung expansion injuries can result from rising as little as 4 feet in the water while holding your breath.

Safety Stops

Performing a safety stop for several minutes at the end of each dive, at a shallow depth while still underwater, allows additional time for nitrogen to come out of your tissues and be exhaled through your lungs. This should reduce your chances of DCS. Though recreational divers won't (or shouldn't!) be performing decompression dives and won't need to make decompression stops, it's important to make a safety stop at the end of each dive. Research has shown that performing a safety stop helps reduce the size and number of silent bubbles circulating in the blood, which in turn is theorized to reduce the chances of DCS.

There are several ways to perform a safety stop. The first and most common is to simply stop your ascent, level off under the boat or the surface of the water, and wait there for several minutes. The generally recommended depth for performing a safety stop is 15 feet; the time, three to five minutes. Older diving textbooks recommended performing a safety stop at 10 feet, but this is a difficult depth to maintain consistently and constantly for a period of time. Modern thinking has lowered this depth to between 15 and 20 feet, which is easier to maintain. Stopping any deeper doesn't allow as much nitrogen to be exhaled.

Some dive boats feature underwater devices that help you maintain a consistent depth during a safety stop. Visual indicators may take the form of a weighted rope or a chain with a mark at 15 feet to allow you to stay at the correct depth. Some boats hang a plastic pipe horizontally off the side at 15 feet. Divers may hold on to the pipe while performing their safety stop. This bar, often called a decompression bar or deco bar, can also be used as a visual reference. You don't have to physically hold on to the bar; you may choose to float alongside it, using it as a visual reference to keep a consistent depth.

Be aware that making a safety stop after each dive doesn't guarantee that you won't get DCS. It merely lowers the chances of this happening.

When considering the potential for DCS, remember that dive safety is also related to the discussion in chapter 5 on using dive computers and how particular models calculate allowable remaining bottom time. Some dive computers incorporate aggressive calculations for the uptake and release of nitrogen from different types of tissue, thus recommending longer allowable bottom time than more conservative computers, which assume longer release times for various tissue groups and correspondingly shorter bottom times.

Exiting the Water

Specific methods of returning from the water to a dive boat may vary, depending on the type of boat and the local divemaster's preferences. If there's no current, you can swim to the back of the boat and exit the water up the dive ladder. If a surface current is present, there will probably be a drift line, with a buoy at the end, trailing out behind the boat. You can then hold on to the line and pull yourself back to the boat. Remember to leave the line out in the water for other returning divers.

Divemasters on larger dive boats will have you take off your fins in the water and hand them into the boat, but you keep your tank on your back and your regulator in your mouth while you climb out of the water on a stern ladder. Hold on to the ladder or drift line with one hand while taking off your fins. Stay well clear of divers climbing the ladder until they're in the boat. Folks climbing out could lose their footing or balance and fall backward into the water, and you don't want them to fall on you.

The reason for keeping your regulator in your mouth is to maintain an operating air supply until you're safely up on the boat. If you should slip and fall back into the water as you're climbing the ladder, or if someone falls on top of you, you'll continue to breathe air. Still, there are no absolute rules; some dive operators—typically those using smaller dive boats—will ask you to take off your fins, weight belt, BC, and tank in the water, handing them to the divemaster before climbing back in. In difficult water conditions, such as when large waves are present or the boat is small or inflatable, this technique may provide the safest way to reboard.

If you have a camera, hand it to someone on the boat before you leave the water, thus keeping both hands free. Someone on the boat will place it in a freshwater rinse tank for you.

Exiting the water onto a stern ladder when there's a swell takes some practice. Step onto the ladder or stern step when it's at its lowest point in the water, hold on tight, and climb up rapidly. Use both hands on the ladder and be careful where you place them; you don't want to put fingers or hands in a spot where they could be pinched or crushed, such as between a moving hinged ladder and the hull. After boarding the boat, move yourself and your dive equipment out of the way of other divers coming aboard. Other divers can easily trip on fins or weight belts lying in walkways.

Between Dives

Most diving involves two or three dives on the same day; you'll be spending time on shore or on a boat between dives. In dive training you will have learned how to calculate safe surface intervals before performing second or third dives. This interval is critical for safety. Most modern divers use computers, allowing the computer to calculate and display on the screen the correct profile for the next dive. As you will have learned during dive training, make the first dive of the day the deepest; the second and third should be progressively shallower.

One surface-interval rule of thumb commonly used in the Caribbean is to delay the second dive until your computer indicates that it's safe to perform a 50-foot dive for fifty minutes. Another common rule when performing two-tank first dives to less than 110 feet is to wait at the surface until forty-five minutes have elapsed. Some instructors recommend a minimum surface interval of an hour between dives. Because most second dives in a single day are made to 40- or 50-foot maximum depths, all these recommendations are reasonable. As with all diving, however, be aware of your previous dive profile, ensure that you have an adequate surface interval, and monitor your computer carefully for depth and no-decompression times during the second dive. Allow at least a twelve-hour surface interval between dive days.

Water, Water, Water

Even though you're surrounded by water throughout a dive, it's extremely important to drink plenty of it on a dive trip as well. The effect of breathing dry compressed air during a dive is to deplete the body of large amounts of water, which can lead to dehydration.

Drinking plenty of fluid during the surface interval will help to keep your body hydrated. In general, you should drink plenty of fluids before, between, and after dives, particularly when performing multiple dives on the same day; do so even if you don't feel thirsty. Good hydration is one of the best ways to reduce your chances of decompression sickness.

As a rule of thumb, you should urinate frequently and copiously throughout a dive trip. If you aren't doing this, you need to be drinking more water. Urine produced during a trip should be copious and pale, almost colorless. One sign of not drinking enough water is infrequent, dark yellow urine.

Drinking fluids during the surface interval will also help prevent or wipe away what's descriptively called cotton mouth, a dry, flannel-like taste in the mouth. It often occurs at the surface after finishing a dive and is a result of breathing very dry air under pressure. Drinking water during the surface interval will help alleviate this taste. Drinking a cup of water immediately before diving may also help reduce this condition during the dive. Or you can cut a fresh orange into wedges and suck on the slices during the surface interval. This quickly restores moisture to the mouth and provides a pleasant taste. Slices of other juicy fruits can be used also.

Water that has been stored in a plastic cooler in the sun for a few hours during the boat trip and subsequent dive may develop a strong taste that resembles the cooler, so noncarbonated drinks, such as fruit juice, may be preferable. This will give a much cleaner taste than plain water.

You may like other snacks between dives, such as a candy bar for sugar and renewed energy, or potato chips to help cleanse your taste buds of the dry taste of breathing compressed air and replace salt lost through perspiration.

*J*ust Another Day in Paradise

Here's what a typical day diving from a boat in the Caribbean might involve:

- You'll start with a wall dive or other deep dive of 60 to 100 feet for about thirty to forty minutes.
- This is followed by a surface interval of from forty-five minutes to an hour to allow a reduction of nitrogen in the tissues.
- Then it's time for a second dive of forty to fifty minutes at 30 to 50 feet. Both dives are typically multilevel, so not all your dive time is spent at the deepest depth.
- A third dive is usually offered in the afternoon, after lunch, which gives time for a suitable surface interval. Third dives are usually limited to a shallow reef explorations no deeper than 30 to 40 feet.
- Around dusk there may be a night dive from shore or a boat. Night dives are usually on a shallow reef or wreck, typically at anywhere from 20 to 40 feet deep.

One type of drink to avoid during a surface interval is any type of carbonated drink, such as cola drinks. The bubbles in the carbonation can expand in your stomach during the next dive and cause discomfort, or even create a hazardous condition. Of course, do not drink any type of alcohol during the surface interval. Certainly no alcoholic drink should be consumed until after the last dive of the day, and then only in moderation. If you drink alcohol, also drink plenty of water to offset its diuretic effect.

Natural Functions

Waiting out a surface interval on a boat while drinking water or juice, or halfway through a dive underwater, you may get an uncontrollable urge to urinate. Urinating underwater while diving is a common bodily function, and takes some practice to perform easily. Two effects increase urine production underwater. One is called immersion diuresis, which simply means that if you're immersed in water cooler than the temperature of your skin, you'll produce more urine. Also, the surrounding cold water and changing buoyancy of body fluids underwater will cause fluid to be shunted from your skin and extremities to your torso, where it's detected and excreted through the kidneys as water.

If the dive boat has a head (bathroom), the course of action is obvious. But not all boats have heads. Assuming that the boat is at anchor in tropical waters for the surface interval, the simplest solution to this problem is to jump back into the water, swim around, and take care of what you have to. Another technique, if a dive ladder is present, is to descend into the water on the ladder and use the water. Everyone who dives is aware of the problem, and nobody thinks anything of a person who suddenly has to jump back into the water to "check the paint on the side of the boat," "see what's happening by the propellers," or whatever phrase may be currently popular.

One less pleasant subject is nausea. Vomiting underwater is a tricky practice, and there's probably no good way around it. If this happens to you, there isn't much you can do about it but go ahead and vomit.

There are two generally recommended practices for vomiting underwater, neither of which is totally satisfactory. One school of thought says to always keep your regulator in your mouth when you vomit. This is because vomiting involves a reflex action that causes you to suck in air before expelling vomitus. If your regulator is out of your mouth when this happens, there's a chance that this reflex action will cause you to inhale water as you suck in. If your regulator is in your mouth, you'll suck in air. The other school of thought says that you should not vomit into the regulator, since the contents may clog the regulator and potentially cause malfunction. The use of either technique will compromise safety, and exiting the water as soon as safely possible is a wise precaution.

One other technique that has been recommended is to remove the regulator from your mouth, hold it at the corner of your mouth, and press the purge button to create a free-flow condition. Then vomit. The theory is that if you inhale before vomiting, you'll inhale air instead of water. If you're feeling so nauseated that you vomit, however, you may not be able to perform this procedure safely.

Vomiting while on a boat due to seasickness is luckily the more common situation, and it's a little easier to deal with. Simply vomit over the side of the boat. The one cardinal rule to remember is always to throw up *with* the wind. For obvious reasons, never vomit *into* the wind.

Most boat captains prefer that you throw up overboard, rather than use the head. Otherwise you may clog it up—inconvenient for other passengers and unpleasant for the maintenance crew. You may also find that the closed, confined under-deck atmosphere of the head is conducive to prolonged seasickness. You'll probably feel better outside in the fresh air.

Seasickness results when the brain receives conflicting information from the eyes and the balance organs in the inner ears. Because of this, it may help if you concentrate on watching a steady object while the boat is moving. If you're close to an island, watch the skyline. In the open sea out of sight of land, try watching the horizon. Sitting out in the open to maintain fresh air may help, too. If you suffer from seasickness, try to stay away from the heat and fumes produced by boat engines.

Medications are commonly used for seasickness, although none is free from side effects. The best plan is to avoid them; if you choose to use them, however, be sure you understand their effects on you. Seasickness medication should be taken on the dock before the boat departs. After you're feeling sick is too late to take seasickness pills.

If you need to cough underwater, cough through the regulator but be sure to hold it firmly in your mouth while you cough. If you remove the regulator, you may inhale water while you cough.

After the Dive

Upon completion of your planned dives, disassemble and stow your dive equipment. If you remove the regulator from the tank, be sure to wipe excess moisture from its first stage. Blow any water off the dust cover and replace it over the inlet screen to the first stage of the regulator to prevent the entry of water and debris.

Stow all your equipment back in your dive bag. Be sure to put heavy items such as weights, and rugged items like fins, on the bottom of the bag. Delicate items such as a mask or computer should always go on top of the bag. In many cases it's preferable not to put these fragile items in a dive bag at all, but to carry them separately to prevent any damage.

Diving is typically done in seawater or dirty water or, during initial training dives, chlorinated water in a pool. These will all leave a residue of either salt, dirt, or chlorine on your equipment. Thus, as soon as you reach fresh clean water, such as back at the dock after a boat dive, rinse off all your equipment. One advantage to using a mesh dive bag is that you don't have to remove your equipment: The entire bag can be lowered into a rinse tank and flushed with water.

10

BREATHING GAS
UNDERWATER

reathing compressed air underwater creates a unique situation for land-breathing humans. Some of the effects are described in this short chapter.

Nitrogen Absorption

As you descend in the water, you breathe air under pressure that's higher than the atmospheric pressure at the surface. During this process, nitrogen diffuses into your body tissues due to the pressure differential created underwater between the air and the tissues. Nitrogen is absorbed into different body tissues at different rates. Some types absorb it slowly, others relatively fast. The longer you stay under pressure, the more nitrogen you'll absorb and the higher the concentration of this gas in your tissues. When all your various tissues are fully saturated, no further nitrogen is absorbed.

When you ascend back to the surface, the ambient pressure decreases and the nitrogen starts to diffuse back out of your tissues again. This excess nitrogen gas is exhaled through the lungs. If the ascent is rapid, the nitrogen will come out of the tissues so quickly that it cannot be excreted and exhaled fast enough, and it will form bubbles in your blood. If these bubbles lodge in various sensitive places in the body, such as the joints and the spinal column, their presence can cause a variety of symptoms that are collectively called decompression sickness or the bends. Thus, two factors combine to cause DCS: the concentration of nitrogen in your tissues, which depends on

What You Need to Know about DCS

Decompression sickness is also known as decompression illness (DCI), "the bends," or caisson disease.

General symptoms	• Pain in the back or joints, such as a shoulder, arm, or leg • Weakness • Numbness, tingling, or other strange skin sensations • Itching and rash • Fatigue • Shortness of breath • Paralysis • Dizziness, nausea, vertigo • Difficulty walking • Collapse or unconsciousness
Occurrence of symptoms	Anytime from surfacing up to 48 hours after a dive. However, indications are that symptoms occur in 50% of the cases within 1 hour of completing a dive and in 70% of the cases within 6 hours of completing a dive. The majority of symptoms occur within the first 24 hours.
First aid	• Immediate oxygen administration • Rest • Drink plenty of water
Treatment	The treatment for DCS is a trip to the recompression chamber. Though relief of symptoms may be readily achieved with the first treatment, some cases aren't so easily resolved; repeated treatments and physical therapy may be required. In a few cases treatment may not resolve all symptoms.
Minimizing the risk of DCS	• Dive conservatively; don't push the dive tables or your computer limits. • Allow adequate surface intervals between dives. • Drink plenty of water. • Maintain a personal fitness program throughout the year. • Make a safety stop after each dive (3–5 minutes at 15'). • Avoid rapid ascents (faster than 30'/minute). • Don't drink alcohol before diving. • Though research is incomplete, divers over 40 should dive conservatively.
Recompression chambers	The availability of recompression chambers can vary quite rapidly. New chambers coming on-line, chambers going out of service, chambers down for maintenance, and chambers that are only available to certain groups, such as military divers, make it impossible to provide an accurate current listing of recompression chambers. To find the nearest chamber in an emergency, contact Divers Alert Network (see appendix A) emergency hot line for an up-to-date recommendation.
For help with DCS	For further information and advice, contact Divers Alert Network.
In summary	Dive conservatively. Don't get bent!

the amount of pressure (and is directly related to the depth and length of your dive); and your rate of ascent, which determines how fast nitrogen comes back out of your tissues.

In essence dive tables describe how long you can stay at a certain depth—which determines the concentration of nitrogen in your tissues—and still be able to safely ascend to the surface without dangerous bubbles forming in the blood. This is why you do the deepest part of a dive first, then ascend and complete the dive at a shallow depth. The shallower part of the dive allows some nitrogen to be exhaled before you return to the surface.

Decompression Sickness

The possibility of DCS should be considered by all divers. Be assured, however, that its statistical incidence is very small, particularly among trained, experienced divers who adhere to safe diving practices. Key features of DCS are outlined in the accompanying chart.

To reiterate, DCS results from the release of nitrogen levels built up in your tissues while you breathed compressed air underwater. Different tissues absorb and release nitrogen at different rates. Watery tissues (so-called fast tissues), such as blood, absorb and release nitrogen more quickly than some other body tissues, such as fatty tissue and bone (slow tissues).

DCS is caused by the release of nitrogen from the blood faster than it can be exhaled through the lungs, thus causing the formation of bubbles. If these bubbles grow large enough, they may lodge in the capillaries of your circulatory system, obstructing blood flow and causing DCS. Bubbles can also lodge in the joints, causing pain, or may be trapped in places that cause neurological symptoms—around the spinal cord, for instance. In almost all cases symptoms occur within three hours of a dive. Decompression illness (DCI) is the correct term for a combination of DCS and air embolism. This results when an air embolism due to rapid ascent triggers a case of DCS that would not normally have occurred.

Interestingly, DCS typically isn't the result of equipment failure, such as computer or regulator failure. The most common cause is diver error: pushing dive tables or a computer by diving too deep, staying too long at depth, or not allowing enough surface interval between dives. So, though mechanical failure of equipment is considered rare, improper use of the equipment may be a contributing factor to DCS.

The next most common cause is ascending too rapidly. Keep ascent rates at less than 30 feet per minute. This ascent rate may seem incredibly slow when underwater, but a slow ascent allows some of the nitrogen to come out of your tissues to be exhaled through your lungs. For the same reason, a safety stop of three to five minutes before exiting the water helps reduce problems from excess nitrogen release.

Other factors contributing to DCS are dehydration from not drinking enough nonalcoholic or nondiuretic liquids, fatigue, multiple dives within a single day, multiday diving and very deep dives.

Another situation that can contribute to DCS is multiple ascents to the surface during a deep dive. An example might be coming up to the surface to check location three times during a wreck dive to 90 feet. This is called a bounce dive, because you're bouncing up and down to the surface. Such a dive profile promotes the creation of nitrogen bubbles each time you ascend, yet doesn't allow enough time for the gas to be released through the lungs. A similar hazardous dive profile is created when you perform a normal dive, then make a short, deep return to the bottom—say, to retrieve a lost weight belt or unhook a boat anchor. The best and safest dive profile is to complete the deepest part of the dive first and then dive progressively shallower until you do a safety stop and exit the water.

Common symptoms of DCS, which occur in 90 percent of cases, are pains in the joints, limbs, or back. You may also experience localized itching, numbness, tingling, or other abnormal skin sensations, as well as intense throbbing pain. Fatigue, nausea, and headache may also be present. One important fact to remember if symptoms appear is that DCS will not cure itself. The symptoms will persist and will become worse with time. Seek treatment as rapidly as possible after symptoms start to occur.

Studies have shown that symptoms occur in almost 50 percent of DCS cases while the diver is surfacing at the end of a dive or within an hour of completing a dive; 70 percent of the cases experience symptoms within six hours of completing a dive, and about 90 percent within twenty-four hours. Symptoms occurring forty-eight hours or more after a dive are probably not due to DCS.

Factors other than exceeding a safe time at depth have been linked to increased chances of DCS. Among them are gender, recent illness, and diving in cold water. It's been theorized that women are more susceptible to DCS because they have higher natural levels of body fat than men. The average lean female has 24 percent of body fat, as opposed to the average lean male, who has 17 percent. Experimental proof of this susceptibility is still inconclusive, however, and this hypothesis is probably incorrect.

Susceptibility to DCS does appear to be increased by current or recent illness. This is thought to be related to the compromised circulatory efficiency caused by many illnesses. Diving in cold water has also been linked to DCS, because cold impairs the circulation, particularly in the extremities, thus slowing down the elimination of nitrogen from the tissues.

Even after conservative diving within no-decompression limits and including a safety stop before exiting the water, there is evidence that minor bubbles form in the bloodstream. These are often called silent bubbles, because they aren't felt or heard. They don't appear to be harmful and eventually dissipate after a long enough surface interval. Still, problems can occur if these bubbles grow in size and block capillaries or cause other circulatory problems.

The formation of small bubbles in the blood and tissues can also lead to a form of bone degeneration called dysbaric osteonecrosis. This disorder is usually found only in older divers, typically commercial divers who have made many deep dives with long bottom times over a lifetime. The condition is thought to be due to nitrogen bubbles that occur within the marrow and small arteries of long bones, blocking the small blood vessels that supply the bone. This problem usually isn't of concern to casual recreational scuba divers who dive to depths of less than 130 feet. There is one situation to be aware of, however: It is thought that this bubble formation can cause future problems in very young divers whose bones are still developing. Thus, it's advisable for preteen divers to limit their dives to 60 feet to reduce any chances of problems.

Even though as yet unproven, two situations are theorized to increase possible problems with nitrogen bubbles after diving. The first is taking a very hot, prolonged shower immediately following a deep dive. Application of hot water to the skin will cause dilation of the capillaries and increase the rate of blood circulation. Raising the temperature also decreases the solubility of gases; thus heat can cause dissolved nitrogen to be released more rapidly from blood and tissue, enlarg-

*T*he One-Tank Bends

A common myth says that it isn't possible to get the bends when diving with only one tank of air. This isn't true. On some deep dives your air supply can last longer than what's a safe time at that depth. Always use a computer or calculate a dive profile with the dive tables.

ing existing bubbles. Similar heating effects of the skin are produced by soaking in a hot tub immediately after a dive. Until this theory is proven or disproven, it's wise to avoid very hot showers and baths immediately after diving.

The second potentially hazardous situation is drinking alcohol immediately following a dive. Alcohol causes rapid dilation of the capillaries and increased blood flow in the extremities, both of which can lead to the increased formation of bubbles due to additional nitrogen release from the tissues. Drinking before a dive or between dives is also thought to increase the possibility of absorbing excess nitrogen in the tissues during the subsequent dive. Excessive use of alcohol, or diving with a hangover after an evening of heavy celebrating, has been linked to increased chances of contracting decompression sickness. The mechanism that causes this problem is probably linked to dehydration, which results in a reduced blood flow in the capillaries. Alcohol should thus be drunk only in moderation during a dive trip and never before a dive.

One factor that is known to decrease the chances of contracting DCS is drinking plenty of noncarbonated, nondiuretic fluids before, between, and after diving. Diuretic drinks such as tea or coffee can reduce the volume of body fluids through diuresis. Alcohol also has a diuretic effect and will lead to dehydration.

Nitrogen Narcosis

Inert gases, when breathed at several atmospheres of pressure, have a narcotic effect. Thus, as well as the potential for DCS, the other important effect of breathing nitrogen under pressure is the induction of nitrogen narcosis— the so-called rapture of the deep. This is a state of euphoria induced by breathing nitrogen under pressure. The effect generally doesn't occur at depths of less than 100 feet. Below about 100 feet, however, most divers will start to feel some degree of light-headedness, stimulation of the senses, general euphoria, and overconfidence, all of which can impair judgment. These effects are magnified with increasing cold, so divers without adequate thermal insulation may be even more susceptible. Below 150 feet you can experience disorientation, delayed responses, a loss of concentration, and even unconsciousness. Symptoms disappear rapidly when you ascend to less than 100 feet. Nitrogen narcosis does not produce any lasting effects.

Susceptibility to nitrogen narcosis varies with individuals. Some can dive very deep without symptoms; others are affected at shallower depths. Novice divers appear to be more susceptible to narcosis, an effect probably increased by a feeling of anxiety at depth.

Drugs and Diving

Though the subjects may not seem at first to be related, drugs and diving are also linked to breathing gas underwater. The reason for this is that the effects of some drugs can be amplified when you're subjected to increased air pressure underwater.

The use of drugs while diving and their relationship to diver safety is problematic and certainly controversial. The term *drugs* covers several different categories of ingested chemicals, including prescription drugs to treat an illness or ailment, self-prescribed over-the-counter (OTC) drugs, and mood-altering drugs ingested recreationally.

Alcohol is commonly used as a recreational drug. Before a dive or during a surface interval it has two effects. One is to promote dehydration, because alcohol is a diuretic. Dehydration is a major factor in DCS. The second effect is that even one drink of an alcoholic beverage will impair judgment and degrade your performance, neither of which is desirable. Studies have shown that divers who consumed alcohol displayed decreased coordination and increased reaction times. Most commercial dive operations insist that alcohol only be ingested following the last dive of the day.

Various OTC and prescription drugs are used for a variety of ailments, including seasickness, traveler's diarrhea, headaches, and nasal congestion. Individuals may react differently to many of these drugs. The use of any medication should be discussed with a physician knowledgeable in diving medicine. Also, before using any medication, it's your responsibility to understand how it affects you personally and to be sure that there are no deleterious effects underwater, such as drowsiness.

Decompression Dives

The short story on decompression diving for recreational divers is—don't. Ever. It's too dangerous. End of story.

Flying After Diving

Ascent in an airplane after diving results in a reduction of the ambient air pressure you experience. Therefore, gas retained in your blood and tissues under pressure at sea level—which is typically nitrogen absorbed under pressure during a dive trip—will also effectively be under reduced pressure. The gas may try to escape your blood or tissues rapidly, which can result in the formation of bubbles—and DCS.

To reduce the chances of this happening, a certain period of time must elapse after diving and before flying. General safety rules, adhered to by most island resorts, are that no diving is allowed on the day of arrival or of departure. For those leaving on a morning flight, typically no diving is allowed after the morning dives on the day prior to departure. Beyond these general rules, the picture becomes a little cloudier, mostly because it has been difficult to carry out research on this topic on human subjects, for obvious reasons.

Older recommendations were that a diver should have a long enough surface interval to desaturate to a Group D diver in the navy tables. Testing of this concept has shown it to be unreliable.

Current thinking is for a diver to wait before flying for a minimum surface interval of twelve hours after a single dive. After multiple dives you should wait at least eighteen hours. Other recommendations specify that divers with less than two hours of no-decompression diving should wait twelve hours before flying, while divers who've done multiday diving should wait eighteen to twenty-four hours before flying.

Modern dive computers also include an algorithm that calculates the time for nitrogen in the tissues to decrease to a safe level before flying. The computer will typically display a do-not-fly symbol on the screen while making desaturation calculations based on the record of the previous dives.

Nitrox

Nitrox, more correctly named enriched air nitrogen (EAN), is a blend of oxygen and nitrogen in different proportions than those in compressed air. Nitrox has been used in diving for more than fifty years. Employed by military, scientific, and commercial divers, it allows longer bottom times than does compressed air.

Nitrox is composed of a higher percentage of oxygen and a correspondingly lower percentage of nitrogen than compressed air. Typical nitrox mixes use either 32 or 36 percent of oxygen, also called Nitrox I and Nitrox II, respectively. The standard method of specifying enriched air mixes is to use the shorthand term EANxx, with the xx being percentage of oxygen in the mix. Thus EAN32 is an enriched air nitrogen mixture with an oxygen percentage of 32 percent. Nitrox tanks are always clearly marked, usually in bright yellow and green, to distinguish them from compressed air tanks.

Because of the lowered percentage of nitrogen in the mixture, breathing EAN means decreasing the amount of nitrogen that accumulates in your body tissues. You can thus stay underwater longer than when breathing compressed air, assuming the same risk of decompression sickness. Because of this potential for longer dives, the use of nitrox is becoming more common among recreational divers. Many divers also report feeling less postdive fatigue after diving with EAN.

The logical extension of this thinking is to breathe as much oxygen as possible and as little nitrogen as possible. As you will have learned in dive classes, however, pure oxygen becomes toxic at very shallow depths, typically between 30 and 35 feet. Thus, the maximum depth at which EAN may be safely used is dependent on the percentage of oxygen in the mix: The higher this percentage, the shallower the deepest part of the dive will have to be to ensure safety. EAN32 is considered safe to 130 feet, or the limit of safe recreational diving.

It's important to receive the correct training before using enriched air mixtures. Classes on the use of nitrox for recreational diving teach the theory of diving with gas mixtures other than compressed air and provide instruction in associated techniques, such as measurement of gas mixtures. The level of detail required is beyond the scope of this book, and the interested diver is referred to specialized dive training classes at a local dive shop.

Some computers are specifically designed to display the modified dive profiles used for diving with nitrox. For accuracy, nitrox computers allow you to enter the percentage of oxygen in the mix you're using.

It's also possible to dive using nitrox with a computer that calculates dive times for compressed air. Some authorities believe that this will result in an increased safety factor for decompression sickness. Some divers, particularly older divers, routinely dive with nitrox mixtures using air computers to obtain this extra safety margin, compensating for the unknown increase in risk for decompression sickness that may be present with advancing age and performing multiple dives during a single week's dive trip.

Diving with nitrox may require modification to other dive equipment. Because gas mixtures with high oxygen content can react with some equipment components and the lubricants used during service, special O-rings and lubricants may have to be used to reduce the potential for equipment problems. Most regulators intended for compressed air can be used with EAN32. Richer oxygen mixtures generally require special regulators. Follow the recommendations of the manufacturers of your specific equipment.

11

HAZARDOUS
MARINE LIFE

Viewing and understanding the life-forms underwater is a fascinating and enjoyable part of diving. Of concern to many divers is the potential for danger in the ocean, so this chapter will concentrate on potentially hazardous marine life. Most of the poisonous creatures that occur in the sea are found in the waters of the Indian and Pacific Oceans. These include the lionfish, venomous sea snakes, the Australian blue-ringed octopus, and the Pacific sea wasp. Marine creature of the Caribbean are mostly harmless unless molested or provoked.

Most marine life is nonaggressive and will attempt to escape when disturbed. Almost all sea creatures will swim rapidly away when they see divers. Very few ocean creatures are naturally aggressive, and even potentially dangerous underwater animals can be observed safely from a prudent distance. Still, most will turn aggressive if startled or provoked, a situation that can result in a nasty, or even lethal, encounter. For example, stingrays tend to bury themselves in the sand. An unsuspecting diver who descends, intending to stand on a sandy bottom, without watching below can end up on top of a ray by mistake. The jagged barb in the tail of a stingray provoked in this manner can inflict a nasty wound in the foot or leg.

The accompanying sidebars outline some safety rules for observing marine life. In general, do not touch or pick up anything unless you know exactly what it is.

Fish-Watching Safety

- Don't molest marine life. In most cases creatures can be observed without danger, but certain species may become aggressive or even dangerous if molested or provoked.
- Resist the impulse to pet, stroke, fondle, or pick up any marine life. In most cases touching marine life, such as coral or fish, will injure it.
- Avoid waters known to be frequented by dangerous sharks. Leave the water if an unidentified shark appears.
- Leave the water if you have a bleeding wound. This may attract undesired creatures.
- Don't dangle hands and feet in the water from boats. Something may bite them.
- Avoid carrying shiny objects, because these seem to attract the curiosity of sharks and barracudas.
- Consider all marine life to be poisonous until you know for sure what it is.
- Do not put your hand in a crevice or hole. Something may bite it or sting it.

Bristle Worms

Also known as fire worms, bristle worms are small green or orange, fuzzy, segmented marine worms, about 1 to 2 inches long, that crawl freely along the bottom or on eel-grass, feeding on smaller animals or sea fans. They're covered with sharp translucent bristles that look like fine glass spines. These fine bristles can easily penetrate the skin, where they detach or break, causing pain, swelling, and tenderness that can last for weeks.

Cone Shells

Cone shells, found primarily in the Indian and Pacific Oceans, harpoon snails and small fish with their long stinging tongues. The tongue looks and acts like a sharp dart and is used injects venom into the victim. There are approximately 400 species of cone shell, and all are venomous. The degree of toxicity depends on the size of the animal, and the size and type of food that the particular species feeds on.

Divers who handle these shells carelessly can also be stung. Stingers can easily penetrate gloves and neoprene wet suits. These wounds produce numbness or paralysis, and can prove fatal. Some venomous cone shells are also found off the Florida coast and in the Caribbean.

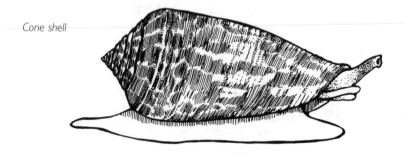

Cone shell

Eels

Moray eels are long, thin, snakelike creatures that hide in holes and crevices in coral reefs and around wrecks, with only their heads protruding. Occasionally they're seen out of their dens, free-swimming in the water or slithering around coralheads. Moray eels look particularly frightening because they breathe with their mouths open to ventilate their gills, giving them an aggressive appearance. Green moray eels average 5 to 6 feet long; spotted morays typically grow up to 4 feet. The green moray is actually blue in color, but a heavy coat of yellow mucus makes the skin appear green underwater.

Dealing with Stings

No matter how careful they are, at one time or another almost all divers have a brush with some sort of stinging marine creature. The most common nuisance stings result from encounters with jellyfish or parts of jellyfish, brushing against fire coral, or handling sea anemones and sponges. These animals have stinging cells, called nematocysts, that discharge upon contact and inject a mild poison into the skin. Far more serious, but luckily quite rare, are encounters with the Portuguese man-of-war, the box jellyfish, or cone shells, all of which are found primarily in Indo-Pacific waters.

The degree of reaction to the sting depends on the type of jellyfish or coral, your own health, and your individual reaction to the toxin. Typical mild symptoms are a skin eruption at the site of the sting, redness, welts, a stinging or burning sensation, swelling, blistering, and itching. In rare cases or very severe stings, allergic individuals can exhibit respiratory distress and even cardiac arrest. There doesn't appear to be cross-sensitivity to jellyfish stings for individuals allergic to bee and insect stings.

Immediate first aid consists of flushing the skin at the site of the sting with copious amounts of household vinegar (5 percent acetic acid). This helps inactivate the remaining nematocysts. Fresh water or alcohol should not be used for this purpose; either can cause nematocysts remaining on the skin to fire and worsen the sting. Also, rubbing the skin while flushing will cause remaining nematocysts to fire and isn't recommended. Applying ice to the site of the sting may help relieve symptoms; hydrocortisone cream will relieve the itch.

Countermeasures for sting prevention consist of wearing a nylon, Lycra, or neoprene exposure suit, because nematocysts can't penetrate this protective layer. A dive hood may be useful at night, because it's difficult to see jellyfish when you're surfacing in the dark.

Morays can be aggressive if molested or cornered. Their powerful jaws and sharp teeth can leave a nasty, jagged wound that's highly prone to infection. Never, ever stick your hand into a dark hole underwater; this is inviting a bite from anything living in there. Once an eel inside a hole has bitten down on something, it may not release its hold while it's alive, and divers are reported to have drowned while being held underwater in this manner.

Garden eels are interesting small, nonaggressive eels. About the size and length of a common lead pencil, these eels group in large colonies on sandy bottoms. They stick up out of small holes in the sand, looking like stalks of grass waving in the current. When approached, they slide back down into their holes until they eventually disappear. After any perceived danger has passed, they will slowly emerge again.

Jellyfish

Most jellyfish are relatively harmless, but some can produce a painful sting (especially to the face) or leave a painful welt if contacted by bare skin. Jellyfish, which are not fish at all, primarily drift helplessly with wave action and the tide, though the rhythmic contractions of their bodies can give them a slow method of movement. They're often found near the surface.

Jellyfish and some corals, such as fire coral, contain microscopic stinging cells called nematocysts, that act like tiny harpoons and inject venom into the skin of an unfortunate diver when triggered, typically by brushing against them. Stinging cells may remain active even in apparently dead jellyfish washed up on the beach.

You can avoid or at least minimize stinging problems by wearing lightweight protective material, such as a dive skin. Remember, however, that your face, neck, and hands are still exposed. Many stinging jellyfish rise to the sur-

Jellyfish

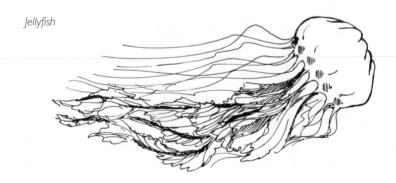

face at night; they're often encountered when divers are coming out of the water after a night dive. Use your dive light to check above and around you as you surface to avoid being stung on the face.

One extremely dangerous jellyfish is the box jellyfish, or Pacific sea wasp, found around the northern and northeast coasts of Australia and in the Philippines. This is a square-shaped jellyfish, up to 7 inches across, with attached trailing tentacles that can be up to 6 or 7 feet long at each corner of the box. These dangerous jellyfish contain a lethal venom. Death typically occurs from heart failure or respiratory arrest within minutes of being stung.

Box jellyfish

The generic Australian name for dangerous jellyfish occurring in the coastal waters is stinger. This terminology includes jellyfish such as the fire jelly, the bluebottle, the blubber, and the quaintly named snottie. The most common is the *Chironex*, or box jellyfish.

Australian beaches on the north and northeast coasts are generally closed to swimming from October to May, when juvenile jellyfish are feeding and growing. To provide some measure of protection, mesh nets are put into the sea, but there's no guarantee that a jellyfish still won't drift somehow into the supposedly protected area. Swimming from June to September should only be done with care.

The recommended treatment for jellyfish stings is the application of household vinegar, which neutralizes the nematocysts. In problem locations, such as the Queensland coast in Australia, bottles of vinegar are strategically located on the beaches, along with instructions for first aid.

Lionfish

Similar to the scorpionfish is the lionfish, also sometimes called the zebra fish, cobra fish, or turkey fish; it's found only in Indo-Pacific waters, usually near reefs. The lionfish is a colorful fish, typically about 12 inches long. They may be seen free-swimming above a reef or, more commonly, down on the reef itself. The dorsal spines contain a potentially lethal venom. Typically when they're observed, the poisonous dorsal fins will already be raised toward the diver, whom the fish perceives to be a threatening object.

Lionfish

Octopi

The octopus has a small hooked beak used for crushing shellfish for food. These creatures rarely bite, preferring to hide instead; if trapped, however, they can inflict a painful wound that's susceptible to infection. In addition to the bite, a mild venom produced by the salivary glands can enter a wound and cause irritation.

The only dangerous octopus for humans is the Australian blue-ringed octopus, whose bite contains a venom that is frequently fatal. When this octopus is disturbed, rings on its body turn a bright iridescent blue color.

Marine Injury First-Aid Items

You may consider adding a few additional items to your travel first-aid kit in case of an unpleasant encounter with a marine animal.

- **Household vinegar (5 percent acetic acid).** *Use this to flush the skin after encounters with stinging creatures. Many dive boats carry this routinely. If you bring your own, be sure the bottle seals well to prevent leaks.*
- **Hydrocortisone cream.** *This may be used to reduce inflammation and rash due to stings. If a rash is not improved within forty-eight hours, consult a physician.*
- **Antibiotic ointment.** *Use this on superficial cuts and scrapes to prevent infection due to contact with seawater and animal debris.*
- **Allergy medication.** *Individuals who have a known history of severe allergic reactions may wish to add an epinephrine injector, which is a prescription item available under brand names such as EpiPen or Ana-Kit. Oral medications to reduce swelling include Benadryl. Discuss this with your physician.*

Portuguese Man-of-Wars

A dangerous creature that looks like a jellyfish, but isn't, is the Portuguese man-of-war. This actually consists of a large colony of stinging animals attached to a purplish gas-filled bladder, 3 to 12 inches across, that floats on the surface. Movement of the creature is primarily via the wind and prevailing ocean currents. The colony has trailing tentacles up to 40 feet long for the Atlantic version or 90 feet for the Pacific type. Tentacles often drift, unseen by the diver, for up to 50 feet behind the bladder. These tentacles contain a dangerous toxin. Severe pain and welts result from contact with these whiplike tentacles, and the effects produced range from burning pain to respiratory arrest. Even contact with the tentacles of dead creatures that have washed up on shore can produce the same effects.

Portuguese man-of-war

Scorpionfish

Scorpionfish are highly poisonous, but usually nonaggressive, fish. The spotted scorpionfish, also known as the sculpin in the ocean off the California coast, is found along both coasts of the United States and in the Caribbean. These fish can grow to 12 to 18 inches long, with venomous glands at the base of their dorsal spines. Contact with the spines forces poison into the resulting puncture wounds, causing great pain and usually infection. These fish have no swim bladders and spend most of their time lying on the ocean floor, where they may look like rocks on the seabed. Their skin has a rough appearance and mottled color, often with algae and bits of debris draped over it, allowing them to camouflage themselves among shells and rocks on the bottom. Be cautious about standing on or descending to the bottom if scorpionfish are known to be in the area, because it's easy to accidentally step on one without seeing it, unless you look very closely at the bottom before standing on anything.

Sea Snakes

Sea snakes are venomous ocean creatures typically found only in Indo-Pacific waters and not in the Atlantic Ocean. Still, some freshwater habitats also contain poisonous snakes, such as the cottonmouth moccasin found in the southern United States. Like other reptiles, sea snakes breathe air, but they can swim underwater for long periods of time.

Pacific sea snakes can grow to 3 to 9 feet long. Most are closely related to the cobra, and all have a venomous bite. Generally they're shy, not aggressive, and won't bite unless handled or provoked. Many times they exhibit the alarming habit of coming up and rubbing against a diver's leg, somewhat in the manner of a domestic cat. If left alone, the snake will swim away after apparently satisfying its curiosity.

Free-swimming snakes in clear water are generally not thought to be aggressive, except perhaps during their mating season, which occurs in winter. Danger from bites appears to be highest in murky water, especially around river mouths, if you accidentally come into contact with a snake or step on one. Sea snakes don't have the long fangs of their land-dwelling relatives for injecting venom, and their relatively short teeth generally can't penetrate a wet suit. Therefore not all sea snake bites are fatal. In any case of snakebite, however, medical attention should be sought and the bite treated immediately.

Sea Stars

Most sea stars (which used to be called starfish, but aren't fish) are harmless. An exception is the crown-of-thorns starfish of the Pacific, which is covered with highly poisonous spines and shouldn't be handled.

Sea Urchins

Long-spined sea urchins, as their name suggests, have long, rigid, pointed spines. These creatures look like a mass of black knitting needles, wedged in holes in coral reefs.

The brittle spines are sharp enough to penetrate gloves, exposure suits, and dive boots. If accidentally stepped on, they'll break off under the skin and cause localized swelling and pain.

Sea urchins may be a problem when diving close to the shore at night. Use a flashlight to avoid stepping on one by mistake.

Long-spined sea urchin

Stinging Corals

Also called fire coral, these are tan, orange, or brownish colonies of stinging animals that look somewhat like the hard corals, and are in fact distantly related to them. Just the lightest touch of this coral on the bare skin can leave

Understanding Coral

Coral reef exploration is one of the underwater activities that divers enjoy most; indeed, it's been estimated that almost 80 percent of all diving is on reefs. Once thought to be plants, corals are animals, part of a scientific family that includes jellyfish and anemones.

Some corals are hard, rocky structures that live in colonies that create massive reef configurations. Reef-building corals consist of a limestone skeleton with a thin layer of living coral polyps on the outside. As the animals grow, a coral reef grows larger over time, though at a very slow rate. In contrast, some species are soft, such as sea fans, and look more like plants than rocks.

Corals have a symbiotic relationship with the algae, called zooxanthellae, that live in the inner layer of the coral polyp and give a coral its characteristic natural tint of green, yellow, or gray. Reef-building corals require sunlight to survive and grow, and are found primarily in clear, shallow ocean waters where temperatures are between 75 and 85 degrees Fahrenheit. If the water temperature rises above this, photosynthesis stops, the algae are expelled, and the coral turns white—a process called coral bleaching. This phenomenon is on the increase worldwide and is thought to be due to a 2- to 4-degree rise in water temperature that has occurred as a result of global warming.

Touching a coral reef while diving will injure or kill the animals. Good buoyancy control is therefore essential to avoid damaging a living reef. The use of reef gloves is also discouraged or prohibited in most coral areas.

an intense burning sensation that turns into slow-healing red welts. A dive skin or exposure suit is sufficient to prevent skin contact. Some species of sponge can also affect the skin with toxic compounds, causing burning, itching, and painful inflammation.

Stingrays

Stingrays are flat with long whiplike tails. They can grow to 5 feet in length. Rays are not aggressive and are generally harmless, except when stepped on or otherwise disturbed.

The southern stingray is a common sight in Atlantic and Caribbean waters. Gray on top and white underneath, these rays are often seen gliding across sandy bottoms in search of food. When they sense a buried clam or other bivalve, they'll stop and snuffle in the sand, digging their mouths in deeper until they find what they're looking for. Then they grind the shells with their strong teeth.

Stingrays have a sharp, venom-laden spine on the side of the tail. If molested or provoked, a ray will lash its tail sideways or up over its back, and can drive its spine deep into wood or bone. The spine is 2 to 6 inches long, depending on the size of the ray, covered by a sheath that often detaches and remains in the wound. The usual outcome of such an encounter is swelling and pain. A stingray wound can be fatal if the spine is driven deep into the chest or stomach.

Stingrays partially bury themselves in the sand to rest, thus they may be unobserved by someone walking in a lagoon or a diver descending underwater to stand on the bottom in a sandy place. Rays will rise out of the sand and move away if they know you're coming close, hence the common recommendation is to shuffle your feet if walking over sandy areas in the water.

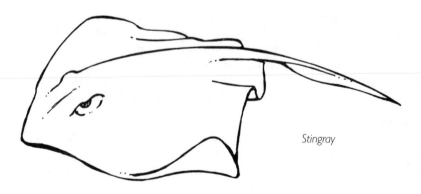

Stingray

Jaws: Sharks and Barracudas

There are approximately 350 species of shark in the world—but only about 10 of them have been known to attack humans. Sharks range in size and temperament from the dangerous great white sharks found off the coast of Australia, where they are known as "the White Death," to relatively docile nurse sharks. Scuba divers are more likely to encounter nurse sharks, which are often found sleeping under ledges of coral reefs. They're generally nonaggressive but will attack if molested or provoked by a diver.

The International Shark Attack File at the University of Florida reported eighty-four confirmed shark attacks worldwide during 2000, with a total of twelve fatalities. In 2001 attacks numbered seventy-six; there were five deaths. Most of the attacks appear to be in water that has been baited for sharks or in locations where sharks regularly feed. Sharks generally don't pose a serious threat to divers, but common sense will go a long way toward preventing any problems. Obviously, do not deliberately provoke a shark, put yourself in a dangerous position regarding a shark, or dive in an area known to be inhabited by dangerous sharks.

Barracudas are long, silvery fish, shaped like a slim torpedo, that grow to be up to 6 feet long. Nicknamed the "Tigers of the Sea," barracudas are commonly seen in the ocean, often hanging motionless in the water underneath a dive boat. Divers returning to a dive boat for the first time and seeing a large barracuda hanging there can receive quite a shock. Barracudas are unlikely to attack an object the size of a human for food; still, they've been known to attack humans in murky water, possibly mistaking them for prey.

Not as common as the southern stingray is the spotted eagle ray, which may be seen gliding effortlessly out in the open water by wall divers, and occasionally feeds in sandy shallows. The yellow stingray is smaller, about the size and shape of a small kitchen frying pan. Yellow stingrays can grow to be 15 inches in diameter and can inflict a nasty wound if accidentally stepped on. The largest of the rays, the manta ray, can be up to 20 feet across. These animals are nonaggressive and have no venomous spine, but their sheer size could make an encounter dangerous. The torpedo ray, found on the west coast of the United States, generates enough biological electricity that the resulting shock can stun a diver.

Stonefish

Related to the scorpionfish is the stonefish, one of the most venomous of all fish. It's found in the Pacific and Indian Oceans. A wound from the spines of

First Aid for Marine Injuries

First aid should be limited to immediate care at the scene of the injury, primarily to stabilize the victim, deactivate stinging cells, control bleeding and provide CPR. First aid should not take the place of or delay proper medical care.

General

All wounds acquired while diving will be contaminated by bacteria and other organisms that are present in fresh or ocean water, as well as sand, venom and other organic debris. To reduce the possibility of infection, all visible debris should be removed and the wound should be cleansed well with soap and water. A dilute disinfectant, such as 5 percent hydrogen peroxide solution, may assist in killing bacteria.

Antiseptic cream or antibiotic ointment may be applied to superficial cuts. Large wounds should receive medical attention and evaluation for a course of antibiotics. Be aware of any signs of infection, such as redness, swelling, pain, discharge, fever, or a red streaking of the skin. Should any of these occur, seek immediate medical attention. In all cases of injury, seek immediate medical attention if other symptoms occur, such as severe pain, swelling, paralysis, shock, shortness of breath, or difficulty in breathing.

In the case of jellyfish or similar stings, if vinegar is not available to deactivate the remaining stinging cells, flush the sting with sea water, not fresh water, since fresh water (or rubbing alcohol for some stings) will cause remaining nematocysts to fire, thus worsening the sting. Also, do not rub the sting while flushing or further nematocysts may discharge.

Divers Alert Network (DAN) can advise victims or physicians on the appropriate and immediate care of marine injuries.

Marine Species	Injury Mechanism	First Aid
Australian blue-ringed octopus	Bite contains lethal venom	Seek immediate medical attention.
Box jellyfish (Pacific sea wasp)	Highly poisonous stings	Seek immediate medical attention. Flush liberally with vinegar to discharge remaining stinging cells. Perform CPR as required. Ice may be used over stings for pain. Antivenin in available.
Bristle worm (Fire worm)	Fine bristles (spines) irritate the skin	Flushing liberally with vinegar may speed healing.
Cone shell	Poisonous dart (sting)	Seek immediate medical attention. Perform CPR as required. No antivenin is available.
Coral cut and scrapes	Laceration/scrapes and irritation from stinging cells	Flush liberally with vinegar to discharge remaining stinging cells, remove any remaining foreign material and cleanse laceration well. Cuts are often slow to heal and may leave a scar.

Marine Species	Injury Mechanism	First Aid
Crown-of-thorns sea star	Poisonous spines	Remove residual fragments of spines in the wound. Soak wound in very hot water (110–115° F) for 30 to 90 minutes to deactivate the poison in the spines.
Jellyfish	Stings	Flush liberally with vinegar to discharge remaining stinging cells, then wash well with soap and water. Hydrocortisone may reduce skin irritation.
Lionfish (zebra fish, turkey fish)	Poisonous spines	Seek immediate medical attention. Soak wound in very hot water (110–115° F) for 30 to 90 minutes to deactivate the poison in the spines.
Moray eel	Bites (jagged lacerations that are highly susceptible to infection)	Clean wound well and control bleeding. Sutures and antibiotic treatment may be required for extensive lacerations.
Octopus	Bites (which may also contain mild venom)	Cleanse wound well to reduce possibility of infection.
Portuguese man-of-war	Highly poisonous stinging cells	Flush liberally with vinegar to discharge remaining stinging cells. Seek immediate medical attention. Ice may be used over stings for pain. Perform CPR as required.
Scorpionfish	Poisonous spines	Soak wound in very hot water (110–115° F) for 30 to 90 minutes to deactivate the poison in the spines. Seek immediate medical attention.
Sea cucumber	Slime on surface on animal irritates skin	Wash slime away well with soap and hot water. Hydrocortisone may reduce skin irritation.
Sea snake	Poisonous bites	Bites are rare. In case of a bite, keep victim immobile and seek immediate medical attention. Perform CPR as required. Antivenin is available.
Sea urchin	Puncture wound; spines break off in wound	Carefully remove residual fragments of spines in the wound with tweezers. Soak wound in very hot water (110–115° F) for 30 to 90 minutes to deactivate the poison in the spines. Seek medical attention to remove pieces of spine trapped in the wound.
Stinging coral	Stinging cells	Flush liberally with vinegar to discharge remaining stinging cells, then wash well with soap and water. Hydrocortisone may reduce skin irritation.
Stingray	Poisonous barb on tail; laceration	Remove sheath of barb or other debris left in wound, and cleanse well. Soak wound in very hot water (110–115° F) for 30 to 90 minutes to deactivate the poison. Seek medical attention for laceration.
Stonefish	Poisonous spines	Soak in very hot water (110–115° F) for 30 to 90 minutes to deactivate the poison in the spines. Seek immediate medical attention.

Stonefish

this fish leads to excruciating pain, sometimes accompanied by paralysis of an affected limb. Heart failure and respiratory arrest have resulted from stonefish venom. The names *scorpionfish* and *stonefish* are often used interchangeably for these two species in different parts of the world, even though they may not be technically accurate.

12

CARE OF DIVE EQUIPMENT

ince the correct operation of dive equipment is crucial for safety underwater, all scuba gear must receive periodic inspection and maintenance. Care and maintenance of scuba diving equipment falls into three categories:

1. Immediate cleanup that should be given to equipment after completing each dive.
2. More thorough cleanup and care that should be given to equipment after a dive trip.
3. Technical maintenance that should be performed at annual intervals on equipment such as regulators, and every two years on BCs.

Cleanup Between Dives

Minor cleanup should always be performed on scuba equipment immediately following completion of diving for the day. Cleanup starts with removing the regulator and BC from the tank and stowing gear away in your dive bag. You will have learned in scuba classes that immediately after the first stage of the regulator is removed from the tank, you should blow compressed air on the rubber dust cap to dry it before placing it on the regulator. The inlet screen to the regulator first stage consists of a sintered-metal mesh filter that plugs very easily, particularly with salt crystals that remain from the evaporation of salt water. Drying the cap is accomplished by opening the valve on the tank slightly and allowing a stream of air to blow off any remaining moisture. After the cap is dry, it should be replaced over the inlet screen to prevent water and dirt from entering the first stage of the regulator. Don't screw the yoke down tightly on the dust cap; tighten it only enough to create a good seal, preventing the entry of moisture and dirt.

The next step in the immediate care and cleanup is to rinse off the equipment with fresh water. Diving in the ocean leaves a residue of salt water, which will evaporate and leave salt crystals on regulators and BCs if the equipment isn't rinsed. Similarly, diving in fresh water often deposits silt or mud from streams, rivers, and quarries. Therefore, rinse equipment thoroughly in fresh water as soon as possible after each use or each day's diving.

Cleanup: The Short Term

- *Always rinse equipment as soon as possible to remove salt and dirt.*
- *To prevent water entry, don't press the purge button when rinsing a regulator's second stage.*
- *Don't allow water to enter the filter on the first stage; blow the dust cap dry with the tank air.*
- *Soak and then rinse everything well at the end of a dive trip.*

Obviously this isn't always practical, depending on the facilities at the dive site, but rinsing should be performed as soon as possible after returning to shore, hotel, or home. Typically divers use a rinse tank on a dive dock, an outdoor shower at a dive site, or an indoor shower in a hotel bathroom to accomplish this.

The second stage of the regulator and the octopus should be rinsed thoroughly and carefully. Run a stream of water into the mouthpiece and through the holes in the air exhaust manifold in the sides or front of the regulator. When rinsing the second stage of a regulator or the octopus, remember not to depress the purge valve; otherwise water will enter the regulator and hoses and can cause subsequent malfunction.

Other dive items, such as BCs, fins, and masks, don't require such thorough cleaning, but can be dunked in a rinse tank to remove dirt, debris, and salt water. Drain out any water that has accumulated in the bladder of a BC during the dive by turning it upside down and depressing the low-pressure deflator valve, as taught in your certification course.

When diving on multiple days, a simple rinse and dry between dives is adequate to keep equipment clean.

Post-Trip Maintenance

After completing a dive trip, perform a thorough equipment cleaning and postdive checks before storing your scuba gear until the next trip.

The first step is to soak everything well in fresh water. A daylong or overnight soak works nicely. Prolonged soaking in warm, clean water helps dissolve encrusted salt and grime as well as any debris that has worked its way into holes and crevices in the equipment that are not easily inspected. An easy way to soak equipment at home is to fill up the bathtub with warm water and leave all your equipment in it overnight.

After the equipment has soaked, it should be rinsed off well with warm water and allowed to dry thoroughly before being stored. Rinsing can be conveniently performed with a shower spray attachment in the tub.

After the equipment is completely dry, it should be stored in a cool, dry place away from sunlight and sources of flame, heat, or chemical fumes. Chemical fumes will cause the neoprene rubber in fins, masks, hoses, regulators, and wet suits to deteriorate. Heat will cause the rubber in these same items to dry, crack, and eventually break down. Equipment should be located away from solvent, paint, oil, and gasoline fumes; thus the garage isn't a good choice. Delicate equipment, such as computers, regulators, and masks, should be stored in the original box, if possible, to prevent mechanical damage.

Following the cleanup of equipment, in preparation for storage, is a good time to inspect all equipment for obvious problems that require repair. It's easier to have equipment repaired at this time than to find out that something's broken while packing for your next trip. Some simple checks on individual pieces of equipment are outlined below.

Regulators

Before storing a regulator, perform a visual inspection for any obvious external damage. First, inspect the sintered-metal filter in the first stage. This is the regulator air inlet filter attached to the tank outlet; it's located directly underneath the dust cap. This filter should have a dull, rough, silvery metallic appearance. If it shows signs of corrosion, which may look like black or white particles adhering to the filter screen, the regulator should be serviced. If the filter is covered by reddish brown particles, the probable cause is rust originating inside a steel scuba tank. Salt water entering the first stage of the regulator may deposit a greenish or white residue on the filter. Any particles present on the inlet filter will clog the filter and make breathing difficult. This contamination can even work its way through the filter and either cause further damage or be inhaled when you breathe through the regulator.

Inspect the second stage of the regulator and the octopus for cracks or breaks in the housings, cuts or tears in the mouthpiece or exhaust ports, or any other type of obvious damage that might have occurred during a dive or

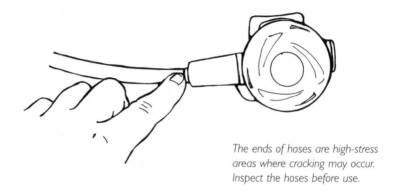

The ends of hoses are high-stress areas where cracking may occur. Inspect the hoses before use.

transport back home. Look carefully at hoses for cuts, tears, nicks, or worn sections that could compromise their integrity. The braided inner lining of hoses should not be visible through cuts, cracks, or worn sections. This may occur toward both ends of hoses, where they bend and are stressed during use or storage. Black neoprene rubber mouthpieces should be replaced with translucent silicone mouthpieces. Silicone rubber will last longer and does not have the distinctive taste and smell of neoprene rubber.

Look closely at the ends of the hoses where they enter the metal hose connections. These are hose stress points and are the places most likely to show wear. Look for cracks across or around the hoses, a situation caused by back-and-forth motion of the hose at either the first- or second-stage fittings. Hoses with bubbles or swelling along the body should be replaced.

Stress on the ends of hoses can be reduced by using hose protectors, which are flexible rubber or plastic tubes assembled over the ends of the hoses at the metal fittings of the primary and secondary stages. These devices relieve the stress points at the ends of hoses next to the threaded metal connectors. Hose protectors are used on both ends. Many regulators have hose protectors already installed when you purchase them. Some have hose protectors only on one end. I recommend installing one at the other end as well.

Neoprene rubber hose protectors are more flexible than the vinyl plastic kind, but also tend to deteriorate more rapidly. Neoprene models are usually

*R*egulator Storage

- Inspect the sintered metal filter (at the first stage air inlet for corrosion before storing.
- Don't store a regulator tightly coiled or hung by the hoses; this will damage the hoses.
- Store regulators flat with the hoses coiled loosely.
- Store all dive gear in a cool, dry place.

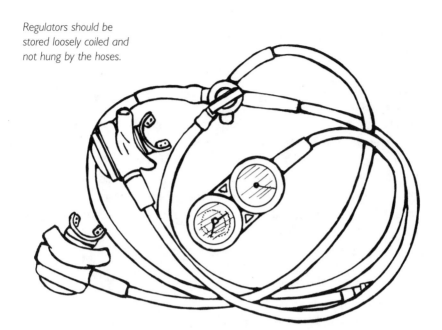

Regulators should be stored loosely coiled and not hung by the hoses.

easier to stretch and install over metal hose fittings than the plastic type, which are stiffer and often harder to assemble. For installation, plastic protectors are soaked in very hot water to soften them and make them flexible. This allows them to stretch and slip easily over the hose fittings. If you don't feel completely confident in unscrewing the ends of the hoses and installing hose protectors yourself, this work can be performed by a dive shop.

After cleaning and drying, it's important to store your regulator and other dive gear in a suitable environment if it'll remain there for any long period of time. The best spot is a cool, dry place, away from any chemical fumes that may cause rubber hoses or other delicate parts to deteriorate. As I've noted, garages make inappropriate storage areas: The fumes from oil, gasoline, and paint thinners may cause rubber parts to harden, crack, or otherwise deteriorate.

Regulators should be stored flat, preferably in a box in a cool, dry place. There are two methods to avoid. Don't store a regulator with the hoses coiled tightly—for example, in the zippered regulator carrying pouches used for transport on airplanes. This configuration will cause undue strain on the ends of the hoses and hose fittings, and can cause premature failure at these points. Storing the hoses tightly coiled can also cause the hoses to exhibit permanent bends and kinks. Instead, leave the hoses coiled loosely so that there is no stress or pressure on the hoses or hose fittings.

The second way *not* to store a regulator is hanging from a peg or hook on the wall for an extended period. This places stress on the hoses and hose fittings from the weight of the second stage and octopus. It may also create a sharp stress bend where the hoses hang over the hook. Dive shops often use this method of storing regulators, but these regulators are being constantly used, taken off and put back on the hooks. Such constant use prevents the buildup of stress in one place in the hoses, which is what happens when hoses are stored this way for a long time.

To prevent hose and fitting stress, regulators should be stored flat, preferably in a closed box for protection, with the hoses coiled loosely inside. Before storing, make sure there are no sharp bends or kinks in the hoses. When storing a regulator, some manufacturers recommend attaching a special device to the second stage to depress the purge button and thus relieve pressure on the valve seat during storage.

Buoyancy Compensator

Care of BCs consists primarily of rinsing the jacket and inner bladder thoroughly after use and ensuring that any water is drained from the bladder. The power inflator valve should be flushed and rinsed with water. Check the valve operation for freedom of movement and ease of operation. Don't attempt to lubricate any part of the valve mechanism, because this will cause dirt to accumulate and result in malfunction of the valve mechanism.

A surprising amount of water can accumulate in the bladder of a BC due to inflating and deflating it underwater. If left inside, seawater will evaporate and precipitate out salt crystals, leaving them on the inner surface of the plastic bladder. The bladder of a BC is made from thin plastic film, similar to a heavy-duty freezer bag. If salt crystals remain inside, they can abrade the inner surface and produce worn spots, or even poke a hole in the bladder material. Thus, rinse the inside of the BC bladder thoroughly with fresh water to ensure that all the salt water is removed, and that any residue remaining inside is thoroughly diluted.

Dive classes usually recommend cleaning the inside of a BC by running water backward into the bladder through the oral inflator valve until it's one-quarter to one-third full of water. Then move the water around to thoroughly rinse the inside of the bladder, turn the BC upside down, and drain the water back out from the inside again through the valve. This method works, but it's slow and often doesn't result in large amounts of rinse water flushing in and out of the valve.

For those more mechanically inclined, there may be easier ways to run rinse water in and out of the BC bladder, depending on the particular jacket design. On some BCs, the low-pressure inflator hose and valve are designed to be unscrewed with the fingers (without tools!) from the body of the jacket. This allows rinse water easier access to the body of the bladder through the fitting. On other jackets, the dump valve or relief valve is designed to be unscrewed, which allows faster and more complete rinsing. It should be emphasized, however, that if you don't feel comfortable taking things apart, or don't understand the design of your particular BC, it's better not to unscrew anything without understanding what it is and how the pieces go back together again. In this case, use the method of rinsing the bladder through the inflator valve.

Before storing a BC, all its functions should be carefully checked. These include the power inflator, the oral inflator, the overpressure valve, and the emergency dump valve. If you use a power inflator with a CO_2 cylinder, this mechanism should also be periodically checked and the jacket inflated.

To test the integrity of the bladder in a BC, fully inflate the jacket and leave it for five to ten minutes. After this time, recheck the BC to make sure it's still firm and fully inflated. If the BC has lost its firmness, there's a leak somewhere in the system. This could be a leak in the inflator valve, in the overpressure valve, or in the emergency dump valve. An air leak could also be caused by a small tear or pinhole leak in the body of the BC bladder. If this is the case, the BC should be returned to your dive shop or to the factory for repair. A pinhole leak can be repaired. In the case of a large tear or split in the internal bladder, it's often possible to have the bladder replaced without replacing the entire BC.

Periodically you should also test that the emergency dump valve is operating correctly. Do this by inflating the BC and then activating the dump valve to ensure that the BC deflates quickly. I once saw a brand-new BC whose dump valve was assembled incorrectly. When the dump valve cord was pulled during a safety check, nothing happened. Upon disassembly, it could be seen that the valve spring had not been assembled in the valve in the correct sequence, apparently at the factory. It was a simple matter to reassemble the valve in the correct manner, and it functioned from then on. The point is that if this feature hadn't been checked prior to diving and the diver needed to rapidly dump the air out of the BC in an uncontrolled ascent, he or she could have been in trouble.

When storing a BC, inflate it slightly to prevent the interior surfaces from sticking together.

Masks, Fins, and Snorkels

Maintenance of masks, fins, and snorkels involves rinsing them well in clean water after use and drying them before storage. Also before storing, inspect the straps of fins and masks for wear and any tears or cracking in the strap material. It's easier to replace these items before storage than it is to look for a fin strap the night before a trip. Make sure there's no sand or dirt in the snorkel drain valve or mask purge valve, so that the valve seals well during use and doesn't leak water back in.

Inspect black neoprene rubber parts for signs of cracking and splitting, or a gummy feel to the surface. These are indicators of advanced age and the need to replace the equipment. Neoprene rubber has a strong rubbery smell and taste that some people object to.

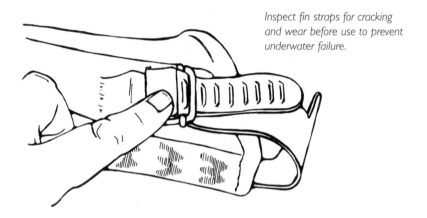

Inspect fin straps for cracking and wear before use to prevent underwater failure.

Computers and Compasses

Wrist-worn dive computers and compasses should be rinsed and dried thoroughly, then stored in a cool, dry place where they won't be damaged. When rinsing compasses, either the wrist- or console-mounted type, rotate the bezel back and forth several times while rinsing under running water to flush out any sand or dirt that may interfere with the rotation.

Dive computers require periodic battery changes over their lifetime, the specific change intervals depending on the brand of computer and the number of dives performed. Usually a low-battery indication of some sort will appear on the display when it's time for replacement. It may also be wise for you to note when the battery was last replaced and replace it again at intervals recommended by the computer manufacturer. The batteries in some computers will perform satisfactorily for up to ten years. Some can be replaced by the user; others require that the computer be returned to a dive shop or the manufacturer.

Wet Suits

Wet suits should be soaked in a tub after use, then rinsed well in clean water and dried thoroughly before storage. Damp items can mildew very quickly.

Wet suits should be stored flat in a cool, dry place away from any exposure to chemical fumes. Don't fold a suit; this will create stress creases at the folds and may result in permanent thin spots in the material at these places. Also, don't stuff a wet suit into a bag for storage. If you store your suit on a hanger, be sure it's one of the wide hangers intended for wet suits, to prevent creases and stress at the shoulders and arms. The use of a hanger for long periods of time tends to stretch and deform the rubber in the shoulders.

Inspect the wet suit for any nicks or tears in the material. Neoprene can be repaired with special wet suit cement, available from dive shops. Before storing, lubricate the zipper lightly with silicone grease.

After several days of continuous diving, dive skins and suits tend to generate unpleasant smells. Most can be washed in a washing machine during or after a dive trip. If the smell becomes very bad and a washing machine isn't available during a trip, try washing the skin in a sink or bathtub with hair shampoo. This can reduce the smell level to tolerable for the remainder of the dive trip.

Wet suit zippers should be occasionally lubricated with silicone grease in order to ensure continued smooth and easy opening and closing. Alternately, you can rub a wax candle along the zipper to lubricate it. Zippers may be cleaned with soap and water applied with a nylon fingernail brush or a toothbrush. Rinse after scrubbing and reapply silicone lubricant. Note, however, that dry suit zippers normally aren't lubricated with silicone, which can cause them to leak. Use the lubricant recommended by the dry suit manufacturer.

Tanks

If you've purchased your own tank, it needs periodic maintenance. Tanks require an annual internal visual inspection for corrosion and cracks. If you use the tank frequently or fill it often around salt air, it should be inspected more often, perhaps every six months.

During inspection, the tank valve will be removed and the inspector will use a special light and mirror or a flexible, fiber-optic borescope to inspect the interior. Tanks aren't legally required to undergo an internal visual inspection, but most facilities won't fill one unless it has a recent visual inspection sticker.

Tanks are required by law to be hydrostatically pressure tested at no more than five-year intervals. During this test, the tank will be specially pressurized to determine if it's still safe for use. If the tank passes the test, the test date will be stamped on the neck as proof of testing. If the tank fails, it will be condemned. Only a small fraction of a percent of tanks fail the hydrostatic test.

Tanks should never be completely drained of air. A few hundred PSI of residual air will prevent contamination of the tank interior due to moisture entering from the outside and will reduce the formation of corrosion of the interior surface.

Tanks transported by airlines are required to have all the air drained out and the tank valve either fully opened or removed. These conditions are not appropriate for good tank care. Instead of taking a tank, rent a tank at your destination.

Dive Lights

Maintenance of underwater dive lights begins with a thorough soaking and rinsing in warm water after each dive. If possible, soak the light in water for an hour or so to dissolve any salt crystals or debris that may have crusted on it. Rinse the light and dry it thoroughly. If the light is to be stored for any length of time, remove the batteries. Batteries, especially those that are discharged, can leak and will then corrode the inside of the light during storage.

Before each dive, or minimally before each dive trip, several maintenance procedures should be performed. First, test the light to make sure it works correctly and doesn't have a burned-out bulb. If the glass of the bulb is starting to discolor or darken, this is a sign that it's reaching the end of its useful life. It's wise to replace it before diving in case it fails during the dive. When replacing the bulb or disassembling a light to replace the batteries, don't touch the silver-colored light reflector. The oils and acids present on the skin of your fingers can etch a permanent replica of your fingerprint in the metallic coating.

If your light uses rechargeable batteries, be sure they're fully charged; you don't want them to go dead halfway through the dive. If your light uses disposable batteries, replace the batteries before each night dive, even if they aren't completely exhausted. The cost of replacing the batteries is minimal compared to the aggravation and inconvenience of dead batteries during a dive. Use alkaline cells in a nonrechargeable light to obtain the best performance. Alkaline cells cost a little more than standard or heavy-duty cells but will provide a whiter, brighter light for a longer period of time. If the flash-light is intermittent, try cleaning the metal battery and bulb contacts by rub-bing them with a pencil eraser or fine steel wool.

It's advisable to carry a spare bulb and set of batteries with you on a dive trip. This ensures that you'll be able to replace them quickly and easily when needed. This is particularly important if your light uses a nonstandard bulb or batteries. It's very frustrating to spend time looking around a remote island for a replacement bulb if you need one and don't have a spare with you.

It's important to periodically clean and regrease the rubber O-ring in the light (or O-rings, if your light uses more than one). To do this, disassemble the light and remove the rubber O-ring. Usually the ring just pops off or out of the groove that holds it. Clean the ring well with facial tissue or a paper towel. Be sure to remove all the residual dirt and pieces of tissue, because even a small speck of dirt or lint can cause the integrity of an O-ring seal to fail underwater. Also, clean out the groove that the O-ring fits into. This can be done with facial tissue or with a cotton-tipped applicator. It's important to remove all grains of sand and any other debris that may be in or around the groove. Then place a little dab of silicone grease onto your fingers and work it thoroughly onto the O-ring. Use only a light coating of silicone, then re-assemble the light. Silicone grease is available in small tubes from dive stores.

Don't use petroleum jelly (Vaseline) or other oil-based lubricants, because they will cause neoprene rubber O-rings to deteriorate. Silicone grease won't. Also, don't use excessive amounts of grease, which can cause the seal to fail underwater.

Dive Knives

After each dive, your dive knife should be rinsed off well in warm water and both the knife and its sheath dried completely. Storing a damp knife in a wet sheath will promote the formation of rust spots. Any small spots of rust on a carbon-steel knife can be removed by rubbing the discolored area lightly with steel wool. Then the knife blade should be coated lightly with silicone grease or silicone spray to protect the blade from further rust marks.

Annual Service

The third major category of scuba equipment maintenance is technical service. Annual service by a competent professional is essential for regulators, where routine maintenance forms a part of the warranty. The parts inside a regulator are typically warranted to the original owner for the lifetime of the equipment, provided that annual maintenance is performed by an authorized dealer.

There are several reasons for this requirement. First, you want your equipment to work flawlessly when underwater. Swimming with 80 feet of water over your head is not a place to try to save on costs by omitting maintenance. Second, regulators require periodic maintenance checks in order to provide maximum reliability, even if they aren't used frequently in the water.

*C*leanup: The Long Term

- Always have regulators serviced annually, even if you don't use them.
- Inspect equipment for problems well before leaving on a trip.
- Equipment must be maintained in top-notch condition for ultimate safety.

For example, the seating of the valves in a regulator may change due to constant pressure on the working parts and may cause the regulator not to work at its peak performance level if it's stored without use for long periods of time. As another example, there will be some saltwater residue left on metal surfaces even if the equipment is rinsed well after each dive. Salt residue can very quickly corrode and block up the inlet screen of a regulator. Typically the inlet screen, rubber diaphragms, O-rings, valve seats, and other sensitive working parts inside the regulator are routinely replaced under the original warranty during annual service, whether they appear to need replacing or not. Since the warranty covers replacement of these parts, it's foolish not to take advantage of the opportunity to maintain a regulator at peak performance.

If you own your own scuba tank, an annual visual inspection for internal corrosion, cracks, and problems that cannot be seen from the outside is required. A pressure test and recertification are required for scuba tanks every five years. Some dive shops recommend a maintenance check on other equipment, such as BCs, every one or two years, to reduce the possibility of problems during use.

Equipment Repair

Repair or modification of scuba equipment by an individual diver is not recommended. Since regulators and BCs are life-supporting equipment, any repairs or modifications should be performed only by trained equipment technicians. Again, remember the golden rule: You are responsible for your own life. Thus, you want all your equipment to be in top-notch condition and working flawlessly when underwater.

Those divers who are mechanically inclined and inquisitive about the inner workings of their equipment may be interested in taking an equipment specialty training course at their local dive shop. The point of this training is not to teach you how to repair equipment but to give you a better appreciation of its inner workings. This helps you understand various mechanical aspects of complex dive equipment, such as regulators, and explains how to provide care and repair for noncritical items like wet suits and underwater flashlights.

A more complete understanding of the subtleties and inner workings of scuba equipment also prepares you to better recognize equipment problems or potential problems before they occur. This extra knowledge will help you be more aware of, and on the lookout for, potential equipment problems, such as worn hoses or loosened connections.

Having said this, it *is* possible for divers to perform minor repairs to equipment; this is, however, strictly under your own initiative and responsibility. For example, equipment manufacturers generally don't recommend that a diver attach a second-stage regulator or octopus to the first stage of the regulator because of the potential danger of cross-threading the fittings and either damaging them or causing an air leak. This risk certainly exists, but individuals who feel mechanically competent and are willing to assume the responsibility for working on their own equipment will find these small tasks relatively simple to perform. Similarly, minor maintenance of noncritical items, such as dive lights and wet suits, can be safely and easily performed. More complex procedures, such as annual maintenance of regulators, adjustment of flow rates, or replacement of internal parts like regulator diaphragms, should obviously be left to competent repair professionals.

13

EXPANDING DIVING OPPORTUNITIES

nce you've mastered basic dive skills, there are many opportunities to dive in specialized situations that may interest you. The following are brief descriptions of some of the possibilities. Even more possibilities (not discussed here) include hunting for underwater game, underwater modeling, reef exploration, fish-watching and identification, river running (similar to shallow drift diving, but using only mask, snorkel, and fins), treasure hunting and bottle collection, and volunteer educational activities in schools.

Medical and Rescue Skills

An invaluable skill for both divers and nondivers is first aid. Formal classes in first aid and cardiopulmonary resuscitation (CPR) are held locally by organizations such as the American Red Cross and by most dive shops as an associated part of training for rescue diver certification.

First aid not only relates to diving, but can also be useful on shore during a trip and in everyday life. Anytime you travel to remote dive locations, it's wise to create a small first-aid kit to treat minor cuts, scrapes, stings, and other minor problems, such as headaches (see also appendix B). Preassembled first-aid kits are available from many local drugstores and camping supply outfitters. Such kits should also contain any prescription medications that you commonly use.

Advanced Diving Skills

Basic open-water diving classes teach the novice to dive to approximately 60 feet under conditions of calm, clear water with an experienced dive partner. This produces obvious limitations on diving experiences. For those wishing to gain further diving skills and experience different dive situations under the supervision of an instructor, an advanced diving course may be desirable. Skills taught in an advanced diving course usually include introductory exposure to deep diving, further navigation skills, some light salvage, and some diving in limited-visibility conditions, including diving at night when visibility is restricted by lack of light, rather than by suspended matter in the water.

Rescue Diving

After you've mastered the skills taught in an advanced diving course, a rescue diving course may be the next step on your road toward expanded diving skills. The knowledge gained during the course work and practical training in the water will enhance your diving abilities and better prepare you for safe diving. Many rescue courses also emphasize the prevention of problems before they occur. So as well as learning to help others in difficult situations, you'll learn to be a more responsible diver.

Stress and subsequent panic are the most common factors behind diving accidents, and emphasis is given in this training to recognizing, understanding, and dealing with both physiological and psychological stresses before they cause a serious problem. General first aid and the basics of CPR are included, along with a brief introduction to emergency oxygen administration, which is the first treatment of choice for most diving accidents involving possible cases of decompression sickness. Training also covers basic search techniques and techniques for in-water and out-of-water rescue situations.

Instructor Ratings

Beyond rescue diving, further training often splits into two pathways. One path is a noninstructional expansion of diving, which involves specialty diving courses that increase the skills and experiences of individual divers. This pathway is used by individuals who enjoy diving for themselves, but don't wish to teach others.

The other pathway is toward instructor ratings. These include earning divemaster and instructor credentials, and eventually lead to an instructor rating for teaching specialty courses and for training instructors. Individuals interested in a career in diving, who enjoy teaching others, or who'd like to use their diving skills to earn money may wish to explore instructor ratings.

Night Diving

One of the first diving options that appeals to the novice diver, and probably the second most popular diving activity after reef exploration, is diving at night. Diving on a reef at night is different from diving the same reef during the day. By dive light, as opposed to sunlight, a reef takes on a completely new appearance. Many different marine creatures are active at night, as opposed to those seen during the day.

Though the night environment may seem, at first, to be the home of underwater spooks and goblins, the reality is that diving at night can reveal a new world of beauty and serenity. It's preferable to perform initial night dives on a site that you've also visited during the day. This will help dispel a fear of the unknown that may occur when diving an unfamiliar site for the first time at night.

Night diving requires a different dive etiquette than day diving. For example, it's thoughtless to shine your light in another diver's face. Don't do this even to attract attention, because it quickly destroys the other diver's night vision. A commonly accepted method for attracting attention underwater is to shine your beam in the same place as your partner's light, and then move your light beam rapidly back and forth across his or hers. Hand signals can also be used if you light them with the beam of the dive light. Before diving, discuss underwater communication with your partner and agree on a common signal to attract attention.

Wreck Diving

For those who enjoy machinery and large equipment, wreck diving can be a fascinating pastime. Part of the enjoyment comes from researching information about wrecks and from photographing them in their current condition.

Diving to observe sunken shipwrecks and swim around them on the outside doesn't require any special background. Penetration and exploration of the interior, however, does require training in specialized dive techniques. The interiors of wrecks are often full of twisted metal and sharp objects that can cut you or your air hose. Silt kicked up by divers can almost instantly change the inside of a wreck into a zero-visibility environment and create a hazardous situation for swimming and exiting the wreck. Wreck divers must understand preparations for potential emergencies that would normally require ascent to the surface—which is impossible in an environment that's enclosed overhead.

Some wrecks that have been deliberately sunk have large holes cut in the sides for diver safety and for ease of entry and exit. In most cases, though, lighting inside a wreck is limited. Because of this, visibility may be poor, and lifelines are required to safely navigate and find your way back out again. Safety problems may be increased if silt is kicked up by divers in the interior.

Underwater Photography

Underwater photography is an ideal way to bring back memories of diving and dive companions. It has been estimated that more than half of all certified scuba divers are involved in some form of underwater photography. This can be as complex or as simple as you wish. Still cameras for use underwater range from simple point-and-shoot styles, with fixed focus and aperture, to very complex cameras with multiple adjustments. Another popular activity is shooting underwater video to record moving images, instead of still pictures. Given the wealth of details involved in serious underwater photography, it's useful and informative to seek professional instruction.

Underwater photography obviously differs from photography on land because of the underwater environment. A sealed camera or a watertight, sealed housing mechanism for an unsealed camera is required to exclude water and prevent damage to delicate camera parts. For photography during snorkeling it's possible to use one of the inexpensive, disposable plastic cameras intended for underwater use to depths of about 10 feet. The housings of these simple cameras will leak water if used at greater depths.

> # Care and Feeding of the Dive Camera
>
> *Underwater still photography and video equipment is fragile and expensive; treat it with care:*
> - *Most commercial dive boats have a padded camera table for camera storage while the boat is in motion.*
> - *Most boats also have a tank used for rinsing cameras. Do not clean masks or equipment in this.*
> - *Cameras should be placed in the rinse tank immediately after a dive to remove dirt, debris, and salt crystals.*

Deep Diving

Another specialty that's often pursued soon after open-water qualification is deep diving. Open-water diving certification is considered to qualify a novice to dive repetitively to depths of less than 60 feet. Deep diving is considered a no-decompression dive that de-scends anywhere from 60 feet to the recommended safe limit of recre-ational scuba diving.

The reasons for doing deep dives are several and varied. Some marine life-forms, such as black coral and giant sponge formations, only grow at deeper depths. Many of the best shipwrecks are located at deeper depths. Some natural features, such as the stalactites at the Great Blue Hole in Belize, only appear at the limits of recreational scuba diving. These are all legitimate reasons to pursue deep diving. Still, you needn't always dive deep for these pursuits; those interested in marine life will

L ights, Camera, Action!

• *The deeper you go in the water, the less light penetrates, thus requiring additional forms of lighting.*
• *Photographs taken without supplementary lighting in only 10 feet of water will appear very blue.*
• *The deeper in the water that a photograph is made, the more the remaining sunlight will shift toward the blue end of the color spectrum.*
• *The easiest solution to the color shift problem is to use a supplementary form of lighting, such as a strobe flash or an external lights for video.*

find that the majority of fish, coral, and other reef animals live within 60 feet of the surface, where the sunlight is the strongest.

Some individuals like to go deep because it's perceived to be a macho way to dive. This is not a good reason for deep diving. All deep dives should have a purpose and a sensible dive plan—and divers must adhere to that plan.

As well the obvious fact that there's more water overhead when doing a deep dive, human physiology dictates some other considerations. Diving to depths greater than 100 feet may induce nitrogen narcosis, as described in chapter 10. Nitrogen narcosis is often unpredictable, and while you may feel fine and be coherent on one dive to 120 feet, the next dive to 90 feet may result in narcosis. If nitrogen narcosis is suspected, immediately ascend to a shallower depth. The narcosis should resolve by itself without lasting effects.

When discussing deep dives, it's also important to mention reasons *not* to dive deep. It uses up air quicker, so deep dives will be shorter than shal-low dives. Deep diving also results in more nitrogen being absorbed by the tissues. Both factors mean that the allowable bottom time for the dive becomes much shorter. As you will recall from diver training, the allowable no-decompression bottom time limit in the dive tables is 130 feet for 10 minutes. Any error in judgment, such as staying at the limit for a few more minutes than planned, can make the difference between diving safely and a serious DCS situation developing. Safety is extremely important when diving deeper than about 60 feet, and dive partners should stay within an arm's length on deep dives in case of air failure or any other underwater problems.

Underwater Navigation

Navigation with a compass is mentioned briefly during beginning open-water training, and is discussed more extensively in advanced diving courses. The techniques of underwater navigation should be among the first skills a new diver learns. More than simply learning to navigate with a compass, however—which is relatively easy—these skills should be broadened to encompass the whole subject of knowing where you are underwater in relation to where you started out and where you want to complete the dive.

In an enclosed body of water with good visibility, such as a small lake or quarry, it's relatively difficult to become lost. Even in a lake, though, it's better to exit the water where you want to be, rather than having to make an additional surface swim or face a long walk along the shore back to your starting point.

Drift Diving

Orientation with a compass doesn't apply to drift diving. On a drift dive the boat keeps track of you, instead of you keeping track of the boat. This is sometimes called live boating. The boat captain watches for your bubbles as they break the surface, and follows the bubbles with the current until you surface. If the ocean surface is rough, the divemaster may tow a surface buoy to indicate the group's position to the boat crew.

Drift diving involves very little exertion. You simply allow the current to carry you along, while looking in the direction you're going. For obvious safety reasons, it's important to stay close to the folks with whom you're diving if the current is strong, so that nobody drifts off into an unsafe situation. Currents can carry divers for several miles on a drift dive, so it's important that the boat be able to locate you easily at the end of the dive, or in case of any unforeseen emergency. It's a good idea to have a safety sausage and a whistle to signal to the boat, in case you're separated from the rest of the divers.

Drift diving can be very relaxing as you drift along and watch the world go by underneath and alongside you. The disadvantage is that it's more difficult to stop and observe a fish, coralhead, or other item of interest in more detail, since the current tends to pull you along whether you want to go or not. Often the current is very strong and you move along very fast.

Cavern Diving

Cavern diving is defined as "diving within the natural light zone provided by entrance of an underwater cave or overhang." To qualify as cavern diving, the natural light illuminating the entrance must be visible at all times. *Cave diving* means "penetration of the underground environment beyond the natural light zone." Cavern diving consists of minimal penetration into a cave, but still requires an understanding of diving in this specialized environment, including training in the use of reels and safety lines, navigation in limited visibility, good buoyancy control, and emergency procedures. Most commercial cavern sites require cavern diver certification before divers are allowed to penetrate the cavern zone.

Cave Diving

Training in cave diving techniques is more complex, because cave diving involves a completely closed overhead environment with no direct access to the surface, and because this is an environment with no natural light. Other hazards include poor or no visibility due to silt and debris in the water, and underwater currents. To offset these dangers, specialized training is required in the appropriate cave techniques, such as the use of redundant air supplies and other equipment, safety lines, lighting, disorientation, silting, and emergency procedures in closed environments with no surface access. Note that a cavern dive at night is considered a cave dive.

Numerous cave drownings were reported during the early days of the sport. In most cases divers drowned because they didn't have training before entering caves, and because they violated the basic safety rules of cave diving. The three major causes of death were becoming lost because of not running proper guide lines from the entrance, running out of air because of disregarding basic safety rules of cave diving, and diving too deep in the cave. Extensive training,

Blue Prints

As you descend deeper into seawater, the apparent color of the remaining light changes. Red colors disappear first, being absorbed by about 30 feet below the surface. Yellow light is all absorbed by about 85 feet, leaving the remaining light to appear greenish blue. The human eye adapts easily to changes in color and intensity of light, so these color balance shifts may not be apparent to our eyes. On camera film, however, there appears to be a definite shift toward blue in deeper water.

practice dives with a qualified instructor, meticulous planning, and the use of redundant dive equipment have made cave diving a safe sport.

No matter how much open-water experience you have, you should never enter a cave beyond the light zone without special training in cave diving techniques. Water can silt up almost instantly, safety lines can break, lights can fail, and underwater currents in the cave can change. Special training is required to be able to safely overcome all these situations.

High-Altitude Diving

High-altitude diving is defined as "diving at any elevation over 1,000 feet (approximately 300 meters) above sea level." It requires special training to understand the effects of reduced pressure on equipment and on divers. For example, mechanical depth gauge readings will be inaccurate unless the gauges are equipped with adjustments for altitude, because they're calibrated to indicate depth in seawater when starting at sea level.

Arriving at a high-altitude dive site from a lower altitude is the equivalent to the body of surfacing from a dive. At the lower atmospheric pressure of a high-altitude location, you'll be releasing nitrogen from your tissues and will have to wait at least twelve hours to eliminate this excess nitrogen before diving.

Because of the lower atmospheric pressure at high altitude, pressure increases with depth much faster than at sea level. At 10,000 feet, a dive to 60 feet is equivalent to a sea-level dive to 87 feet. Thus, allowable bottom times need to be correspondingly shortened. Many computers are available that automatically compensate for diving at high altitudes; if you dive at high altitude, be sure your computer contains the correct algorithm to compensate for the effects of reduced pressure at different elevations. Even if it adjusts for altitude variations, remember that the computer assumes that the gases in your body have reached equilibrium at altitude before diving. Therefore, be sure to wait an appropriate interval before diving.

When diving at high altitude, equalization needs change and ascent rates are slowed to correspond to the surface elevation of the water. Safety stops are made at a shallower depth. Dive tables that compensate for high altitudes are available, but they're based on theoretical calculations, and very little field research has been performed to confirm them. Other factors involved in high-altitude diving include cold water temperatures, because many high-altitude lakes are formed from melting snow, and added levels of exertion due to exercise at high altitude. Caution must be taken to dive conservatively under these conditions, and a reasonable safety factor should be added to stay well below the appropriate no-decompression dive limits.

As well as the actual diving experience, the "high-altitude" part of a dive trip can also include high elevations encountered while driving to and from

Diving in high-altitude lakes can be fun but requires special attention to dive tables.

a dive site. Typically this occurs after diving in the mountain West. For example, a diver traveling north to Denver, Colorado, after diving at the Blue Hole in Santa Rosa, New Mexico, will have to cross 7,800-foot Raton Pass. In diving terms, this is the equivalent of flying after diving. Therefore, you must allow a sufficient surface interval after diving before you cross the pass.

Ice Diving

The term *ice diving* conjures up visions of clear water, ethereal light bathing the underside of the ice, unlimited underwater visibility, and floes of ice extending downward for hundreds of feet. Unless you're lucky enough to be able to experience the polar environment, however, the reality of ice diving in a local lake is more likely to be a dark, murky environment with very poor visibility, limited light filtering in through the snow covering the ice above, and a feeling of extreme cold from the water. For those dedicated to extending their diving skills to the limits, though, ice diving can offer a new and incredibly exciting diving experience.

Like cave diving, ice diving involves a closed overhead environment with no immediate access to the surface; thus special safety techniques must be used. Safety harnesses are worn for immediate retrieval in case of problems, underwater dive times are calculated for extreme cold-water environments

Continuing Education

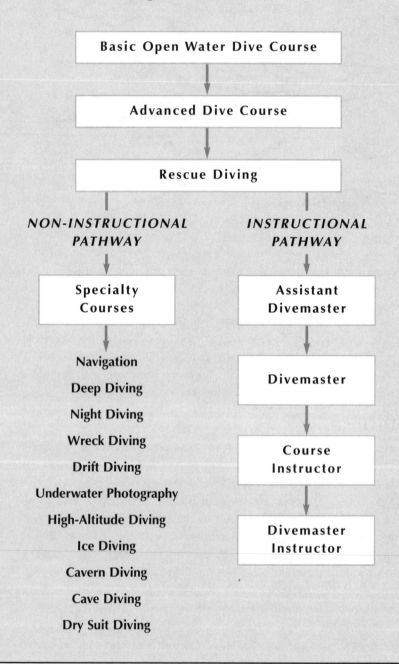

Basic Open Water Dive Course

Advanced Dive Course

Rescue Diving

NON-INSTRUCTIONAL PATHWAY

Specialty Courses

Navigation

Deep Diving

Night Diving

Wreck Diving

Drift Diving

Underwater Photography

High-Altitude Diving

Ice Diving

Cavern Diving

Cave Diving

Dry Suit Diving

INSTRUCTIONAL PATHWAY

Assistant Divemaster

Divemaster

Course Instructor

Divemaster Instructor

and for high stress and exertion levels in very cold dark water, and safety divers are suited up and ready to plunge under the ice in case of an emergency. In addition, scuba equipment requires special preparation. Regulators for warm-water diving can literally freeze in the environment of ice diving, so special lubricants are used to ensure correct operation and reliable delivery of air.

If this sounds scary and intimidating, it's meant to. Ice diving has inherent dangers. With the proper training, supervision, and a prepared dive crew, however, it's also extremely safe and provides a fantastic opportunity to explore a bold new environment that few divers are privileged to see and experience.

Dry Suit Diving

In extremely cold conditions—such as when ice diving—a dry suit may be used. Before you do so, however, you must obtain training in dry suit techniques, including how to get in and out of the suit, buoyancy control in a dry suit, and emergency escape techniques in case of inflation valve freeze-up or failure.

The techniques of dry suit diving learned during ice diving are also useful for other types of diving. Anyone who dives frequently in cold water, particularly for extended periods of time, may find a dry suit to be much warmer and more comfortable than a wet suit. You'll pay much more initially for a dry suit than a wet suit, but if you dive frequently in cool or cold water, this investment will pay off in additional diving comfort. High-altitude lakes, in particular, may not thaw out until late in spring and may stay near freezing all summer long.

Equipment Specialist

This type of training course is intended to familiarize you with the operation and maintenance of dive equipment. It's not intended to teach you to repair your own equipment. The training offers the opportunity to better understand dive equipment and how to perform minor repairs and maintenance on dive equipment that isn't life supporting. It'll help you spot potential equipment malfunctions before they become a problem, and to be aware of the problems that malfunctions can cause.

Snorkeling

Even though the emphasis in this book has been primarily on scuba diving, snorkeling is a related skill that should not be overlooked. Many divers assume that they'll no longer snorkel once they're certified for scuba diving. In reality, snorkeling should be viewed as an integral part of the total diving experience. Resorts, beaches, and islands often have protected lagoons enclosed by reefs right in front of them, and snorkeling is a relaxing way to float on the surface and view fish around colorful coralheads. Shallow inland lakes can provide interesting snorkeling experiences.

Snorkeling is a pleasant way to extend your enjoyment of the ocean after you've finished diving for the day due to nitrogen loading. You may also encounter situations where scuba is not allowed. The manatees in Florida's Crystal River, for example, can only be viewed via snorkeling.

APPENDIX A: RESOURCES FOR DIVERS

Centers for Disease Control

Medical information for travelers to international destinations can be obtained from:

Centers for Disease Control and Prevention (CDC)
1600 Clifton Road NE
Atlanta, GA 33033
(404) 639–3311
Traveler's information hot line: (877) 394–8749
www.cdc.gov/travel

Divers Alert Network

The premier organization dedicated to the medical aspects of dive safety is the Divers Alert Network (DAN). This is a nonprofit organization dedicated to providing expert up-to-date medical information and advice for divers and the physicians treating them. Every diver should be aware of DAN, its mission, and its medical resources. Ideally, every diver should be a member. The DAN emergency phone number is used to place you or your health-care provider in contact with an on-call physician specializing in diving-related medical problems. The nonemergency number is used for routine nonemergency questions.

Divers Alert Network
6 West Colony Place
Durham, NC 27705
Emergency hot line: (919) 684–4236
Nonemergency phone: (919) 684–2948 or (800) 446–2671
www.diversalertnetwork.org

Passport Information

For information on passport requirements, call the National Passport Information Center at (900) 225–5674 or (888) 362–8668. Fees are charged for the use of both telephone numbers. Alternately, see the U.S. State Department Web site at www.travel.state.gov.

U.S. Department of State

Warning bulletins for countries and other information can be found on the Internet at http://travel.state.gov/travel_warnings.html. Bulletins posted here also recommend vaccinations that may be required for particular countries or areas of the world.

APPENDIX B:
DIVE CHECKLISTS

A Traveler's First-Aid Checklist

First Aid

- ❏ Assortment of adhesive bandages
- ❏ Small sterile gauze pads
- ❏ Adhesive tape
- ❏ Antibiotic ointment for small scrapes and cuts

Miscellaneous

- ❏ Personal or prescription medication
- ❏ Eye drops
- ❏ Sunscreen
- ❏ Insect repellent
- ❏ Scissors
- ❏ Nail file
- ❏ Tweezers
- ❏ Birth control/feminine products

OTC Remedies for the Following

- ❏ Headache
- ❏ Seasickness
- ❏ Upset stomach
- ❏ Traveler's diarrhea
- ❏ Colds
- ❏ Aches and pains
- ❏ Nasal congestion
- ❏ Sunburn
- ❏ Insect bites

A Tropical Checklist

From Clothes to Everything Else

Most tropical destinations are quite casual, and shorts and T-shirts are widely accepted. Excess exposure of the body generally isn't appropriate, however, and most resorts and towns don't like people to walk around in swimsuits in public areas (except swimming pools). Wear clothes or some sort of cover-up.

Clothes

❏ Tennis shoes
❏ Sandals
❏ T-shirts/regular shirts
❏ Shorts
❏ Jeans
❏ Casual pants/skirts
❏ Underwear
❏ Socks
❏ Two or more swimsuits—wear one while the other is drying
❏ Sweater—for cool evenings
❏ Light nylon shell for cold/rain protection
❏ Hat—for protection from the sun
❏ Sweatshirt—for warmth or on the dive boat
❏ Towel—for beach or swimming, though most hotels provide pool towels
❏ Rain jacket or umbrella—for tropical showers

Other Useful Items

❏ Pen and paper
❏ Travel clock with alarm
❏ Scout knife with scissors
❏ Small day pack or fanny pack
❏ Water bottle
❏ Books to read—though many hotels have a take-one/leave-one library
❏ Small field glasses

Optional

❏ Heavy travel jacket—for travel to the airport in cold climates in winter, but you may wish to leave it in the car at the airport, along with a warm hat and gloves

A Carry-On Checklist

❑ Prescription medicines
❑ Prescription eyeglasses
❑ Sunglasses
❑ Airline ticket
❑ Passport
❑ C-card
❑ DAN (or other) dive insurance card
❑ Current driver's license—for identification and for renting a car
❑ Credit cards—but only those you'll need on the trip; leave the others at home
❑ Traveler's checks, if used—store check receipt separately in case of loss or theft
❑ Hotel reservation confirmation, and other similar travel documents
❑ Telephone credit card
❑ Camera
❑ Camera film—since X-rays of checked baggage going overseas may fog camera film
❑ House keys and car keys
❑ Pen—for filling out immigration and customs forms on the plane
❑ Any valuables, such as money or jewelry—preferably take only the money you need and don't take valuable jewelry or jewelry with sentimental value
❑ Book(s)—to read on the plane
❑ Swimsuit—in case luggage is delayed
❑ T-shirt and shorts—in case luggage is delayed
❑ Mask—or pack this, well protected, in your checked luggage
❑ Dive computer—if a separate wrist-worn unit
❑ Regulator and gauges—padded regulator carrying bags are available
❑ Cash for international airport departure fees—if needed

A Dive Equipment Checklist

Basic Equipment

❑ Mask
❑ Snorkel—and snorkel keeper, if it
   detaches
❑ Fins
❑ Dive boots—if you wear them
❑ Wet suit
❑ Hood and gloves—if required for
   water conditions
❑ Buoyancy compensator (BC)
❑ Computer—if wrist-worn and not
   mounted in a dive console
❑ Regulator and gauges
❑ Weight belt—and weights, if diving
   locally
❑ Dive gear bag
❑ Towels—for drying
❑ Plastic tarp or trash bags—for
   equipment that stays on the ground
   during shore dives
❑ Tank—filled, if you're diving locally

Accessories

❑ Dive knife
❑ Dive light
❑ Secondary light—if night diving
❑ Light sticks—if used for night diving
❑ Spare batteries and bulb for flash-
   light or dive light
❑ Dive watch—if you use one
❑ Reef gloves—for snorkeling
❑ Underwater slate with attached
   lead pencil
❑ Spare parts/tool kit—if you use one
   (see the Gear Repair Checklist that
   follows)
❑ Plastic trash bags—for wet stuff,
   gear, or clothing
❑ Dive flag—if you're diving on your
   own
❑ Safety sausage—if used

Documents

❑ C-card—can't dive without it!
❑ DAN (or other) dive insurance card
❑ Dive logbook
❑ Dive tables—as a safety backup

Gear Repair Checklist

These items can all be kept in a small plastic box. Plastic kitchen food storage boxes are ideal.

Small Items

❑ Spare snorkel keeper
❑ Spare mask strap
❑ Spare fin strap for your fins
❑ Spare regulator mouthpiece, with 6-inch attachment tie strap
❑ Spare tank O-ring—perhaps several if you dive on your own
❑ Selection of O-rings for your particular gear—if you feel competent to replace them; even if you don't, it may be helpful to have your own in case a remote dive shop is out of the size you need

Small Tools

Tools should all be chrome-plated to prevent rust or corrosion from seawater.

❑ Set of small screwdrivers
❑ Slip-joint pliers—the 6-inch size works well for most jobs
❑ Fixed ⁹⁄₁₆-inch wrench—or whatever commonly fits your equipment and hose fittings
❑ Adjustable 6-inch crescent wrench
❑ Probe for O-ring extraction
❑ Allen wrenches in sizes that may be required for your equipment

Miscellaneous

❑ Spare pencil stub(s)—for dive slate
❑ Small tube or can of silicone grease or spray lubricant
❑ Cotton-tipped applicators
❑ Facial tissues
❑ Spare batteries for your underwater light
❑ Spare bulb for your underwater light
❑ Wet suit cement for minor repairs
❑ Duct tape—one of those items that everybody recommends, but nobody can remember exactly what it's used for!

INDEX

ABOUT
THE AUTHOR

Jeremy Agnew is a master scuba diver with more than eighteen years of active diving experience in the United States and overseas. He has written outdoor articles for *Empire Magazine* and is the author of two previous books. He lives in Colorado Springs, Colorado.